For Jo

Whose masterful
introduction has really
caught the essence of my
heart, and my love.

In appreciation -

Helen K. Cratiner

July 14, 1997

Many of the chapters in this book have appeared in Saddle & Bridle Magazine as columns of Helen Crabtree's and have been adapted for use with their permission.

Copyright 1997 by Saddle & Bridle, Inc.

All rights reserved including the right of reproduction in whole or in part in any form.

Saddle & Bridle, Inc.
375 Jackson Avenue
St. Louis, MO 63130

ISBN 0-9655501-1-7

Library of Congress catalog card Number: 96-71962

Manufactured in the United States of America

10 9 8 7 6 5 4 3 2 1

Contents

Chapter

Forward 5
Dedication 6
Introduction 8

1. How Times Have Changed 11
2. Judging After Move to Simpsonville 43
3. Achievements 71
4. Girls at Dayton Show 75
5. Beginning of Reunion 79
6. Perfect Attire? Don't Be Too Sure! 87
7. Caretakers 91
8. The 10th Anniversary 93
9. Here's to the Boys! 97
10. Red Faces in the Show Ring 100
11. Doing It Right: Victory at Louisville 103
12. A Great Win - A Great Loss 107
13. A Giant of the Industry 111
14. Garland Bradshaw 117
15. William P. Harsh 121
16. George Gwinn 125
17. Mrs. Sinclair 130
18. "Big Mama" and Laurie 133
19. The Little Goat Who Thought He Was a Dog 137
20. "Butch" Phi Beta Kitty 145
21. The Bull Rings Of Kentucky 157
22. R.C. Flannery 163
23. Hang in There 166
24. Judging Memories 169
25. Mothers and Motivation 172
26. The Humor of Texas 176
27. Dual In Houston, Texas 179
28. Colonel Boyle and Art Simmons 187

Contents

Chapter		
29	Logan McDaniels	191
30	Getting a Start	195
31	The Horse Dealer	198
32	The Secret	201
33	The Wayward Falsie	204
34	Storm Cloud	207
35	Glenview's Warlock	213
36	Legal Tender - Born To show	227
37	Carlyn and Glad Tidings	251
38	A Wild and Wonderful Mare - Flamenco	259
39	LaLa Success	267
40	The Elusive Mare and the Available Stallion - Glenview Radiance	271
41	Saturday Knight - Champion Pony and Horse	277
42	How I Got Home From New York	281
43	The Big Broadcast	289
44	Jimmy Joe - The Best of Two Breeds	293
45	Captivation - A Wild and Beautiful Champion	299
46	A Horse Worth Waiting For	302
47	Seeds Of Compassion	307
48	Wild Party	312
49	Fancy Stonewall - A Very Bright Horse	315
50	The Happy Hour	319
51	Rick Rack	323
52	My Last Show	329
53	Friendly Advice	333
	In Closing	337

Helen Crabtree

Charlie Crabtree

Redd Crabtree

The Crabtree Family

Foreword

There are four people without whose talent I could never have written this book.

First, let me thank my husband, Charlie Crabtree for putting up with me for 53 years.

Then comes our son, Redd Crabtree, who eventually took on my "graduates" and made them a big part of American Saddlebred history.

Without their taking over my duties when judging and clinics called me away from Kentucky, I would never have had the exciting and hilarious experiences that make up a great part of this book.

Kim Crabtree read back to me every word of "Hold Your Horses", as did Debbie Wathen. Not only my eyes, they corrected each other's spelling!

Dedication

This book is dedicated with love and gratitude to
my assistant trainers

Ruth Kaufman (Palmer)

Mary Bateman (Angel)

Frankie Bird (Purdy)

Jennifer Turner (Joiner)

Lisa Rosenberger (Heres)

Debbie Basham (Wathen)

Ruth Kaufman (Palmer).

Mary Bateman (Angel)

Lisa Rosenberger (Heres).

Jennifer Turner (Joiner).

Frankie Bird (Purdy).

Photo by Morris

Debbie Basham (Wathen).

Introduction
by Joe Pfeffer

"Camarado, this is no book. Who touches this book, touches a man."
—Walt Whitman

The words Whitman wrote many years ago could, with slight alteration, apply to the book you hold in your hands. It is a book, all right, but to read it is to touch the unique and awesomely varied life of Helen K. Crabtree. The reader enters a world known to few who have not spent a lifetime at the center of the Saddle Horse world, and encounters Helen Crabtree as friend, boon companion, colleague, teacher, and born storyteller.

Many people, by no means all of them in the Saddle Horse business, "know" Helen Crabtree already in various ways. They know the doyenne of saddle seat equitation, the winner of countless awards for lifetime achievement and contributions to horsemanship, the discerning judge, the female head of the famous Crabtree family of trainers, perhaps above all the author of *Saddle Seat Equitation*, still the authoritative work in the field after more than 15 years.

Now, the average reader can "know" Helen Crabtree the person. Reading this book is like sitting in front of the tack room at Madison Square Garden while a two-hour jumper class runs its course, listening to Helen talk about some uproarious snafu that took place while getting the horses into New York City. It puts you in the middle of a group of trainers while Helen swaps stories of Garland and Frank Bradshaw, Lee Roby and Art Simmons, as well as lesser known but no less colorful characters like Bill Hill and her own beloved teacher, Logan McDaniels. It's like riding home with Helen, Charlie, and a bunch of weary kids on the way back from a county fair horse show while Mrs. Crabtree dissects the classes she has just seen. It's like being in the Crabtrees' living room in Simpsonville, when the day is done and it's not yet time for sleep, hearing Helen reminisce about long ago and far away days in Illinois, Missouri, Arkansas, and Tennessee — the days before Helen pioneered what came to be called, not always affectionately, the "Kentucky Style" of saddle seat horsemanship.

This is a book to be taken up, put down, come back to, savored, treasured. The stories and anecdotes are so varied in style and subject matter that each reader will likely have particular favorites, ones he or she will want to return to again and again. My personal favorites are the stories of Dandy Jim the goat and Butch the cat. In these stories, Helen Crabtree's extraordinary sixth sense of empathy with animals, what she calls her "close and sympathetic understanding of what would now be termed animal psychology," is fully on display. Her observations of the interplay among the Crabtrees two dogs, their goat, and their cat makes her a virtual Mozart of animal psychology.

Others will no doubt be surprised to find Helen Crabtree, of all people, literally descending into the subterranean world of X-rated movies in, of all places, Switzerland. They may be even more surprised to find her unexpectedly caught up in a hilarious game of "Who did that"with an old Irish horse trainer back in Missouri. Still others will find themselves hopelessly caught up, grabbed by the throat as it were, by the book's climactic sections on Storm Cloud, Glenview Warlock, and Legal Tender, long sections that have the momentum and drama of a great championship stake at Louisville. As in Mrs. Crabtree's life, there is something here to delight and surprise everyone.

Years ago, I wrote an article in Saddle & Bridle in which I referred to Helen Crabtree as "Dorothy Parker in jodhpurs." The image still seems to fit: the unfailingly sharp and at times witheringly acerbic woman standing tall and erect with riding whip in hand, never at a loss to find the perfect phrase to tell a rider what she's doing right or wrong, the quip to cut down to size an exhibitor complaining about her judging, or the narrative gift to make one of the legendary "old timers" come alive with a perfectly crafted anecdote that manages to capture the person's essence. Helen Crabtree's extraordinary ability to communicate verbally, her wide-ranging literacy in the sense of being a truly well-read, genuinely cultured person, is one of her great contributions to the Saddle Horse world.

This book is autobiographical without being an autobiography. It is not written as linear history or as a story of how a person developed psychologically, and it does not try to present any philosophy or theory of life or even of working with horses. Yet an overarching philosophy does come through. I think of Whitman again, one of whose greatest poems is the "I think I could turn and live with animals" section of *Song of Myself*, when I read Helen Crabtree on Shauna Schoonmaker and Warlock, "Shauna thought like a horse and Warlock thought like a person." Or when she talks about thinking 20 steps ahead of Storm Cloud. Or when she writes of Legal Tender's caretaker Johnnie Washington, the "master of animal psychology" who had "a voice that would calm a hungry cobra, hands that were like satin, and an understanding of a horse's brain that very few people have," even to his knowing that "Cash" needed a chicken rather than a goat for a companion because "he'd be jealous of a goat and would kill him." This concept of "animal psychology," of "thinking like a horse," of somehow entering the animal's brain and becoming one with him, seems the driving force and ultimate meaning of this book and the life it celebrates. It is very different from, and so much richer, more subtle and humane than the standard idea of man gaining dominance over beasts. It is what gives Helen Crabtree's book the quality of lived experience that it takes on at its best. And it is what separates the truly great horse trainers and riders from the very good ones, right down to Michele Macfarlane's near miraculous transformation of an extravagantly gifted but wildly erratic three-gaited horse into perhaps the greatest performing five-gaited horse in Saddlebred history, described in this very book as "the supreme communication of horse and rider." To absorb this lesson is to be somehow transformed , to have one's consciousness raised to a level of understanding and empathy one had not known before.

In the end, though, there is nothing to do with this book but enjoy it, savor it, read it at those odd times when you want to do nothing more than "settle down with a good book," perhaps on a rainy night in November. Like some ideal friend, it will always be there when you want it, always entertain, enlighten, and dazzle you with its wit and humor. Welcome to the wonderful life of Helen K. Crabtree.

1
How Times Have Changed
(S & B March, 1994)

I spent my first ten years of my life on a farm on the outskirts of Jacksonville, Illinois. Those years from 1915 to 1925 were a constant delight to me and I had an opportunity to be near the farm animals and to study animal behavior and to get a very close and sympathetic understanding of what would now be termed animal psychology.

It was December 14, 1915 and Edna Kitner had just had a child. "Mrs. Kitner," crooned the doctor, "you have a lovely little girl." "Is he healthy and strong?" my mother asked, "Yes healthy and strong, but it is not a boy, you have another girl."

Family lore does not reveal my mother's reaction, but I feel sure that she was getting ready to give the news to my father that he had three girls and no son.

Perhaps this is the right moment to give credit to Edna and Harry Kitner for the lifetime of love that was the wonderful heritage of Marjorie, Martha, and now Helen, the three daughters. My first name came easily, "Helen" was about as close to "Harry" as one could get and the middle name was Elmore like my father's, thus making me as close to a junior as a girl could get.

When friends inevitably asked if there were horse trainers in my family background, the answer is, "No-not a one in the lot," but I did the next best thing and became my father's shadow on the farm, as he would have wanted a boy to be, interested in every living creature. The fact that my father raised draft mules, not horses made no difference to this child who developed a complete love for any equine, a trait that grows ever stronger through the years.

On our farm my father did not have any horses - only mules. My very earliest memory is finding myself in a corral where I had toddled away from my mother. I looked up and saw a lot of big ears and shining eyes. I was surrounded by some young mare mules and my mother was frightened to death. My father calmly went to

Harry and
Edna Kitner, 1919.

Helen and her
hobby horse.

Helen at age two on farm
mule Jack, 1917.

The picture that
changed my life.

the barn and brought out a bucket of shelled corn and the mules went over to him, allowing my terrified mother to open the gate and carry me out. I heard that story so many times in my lifetime that I do not really know whether that was my first interest in "horses" or not. However, by the time I was two years old, I was obsessed with the desire to ride. I would wait at the lane for my father to come back with the mule team so that I could ride "Old Jack" back down to bring the cows up from their pasture. I can definitely remember the thrill of being up on that mule's back and taking the overcheck rein in my hands and pretending that I was riding a spirited stallion. That dear mule would have gone for the cows with a sack of wheat on his back, but I felt that I was really controlling him. I am sure that was not an uncommon thing to do. What was uncommon was that I never deviated from that first love of riding to have it grow with the years and become the fulfillment of my childhood dreams ... to be a lady horse trainer when there were none for me to follow.

Home was a lovely 80 acre farm in the lush prairie land of mid-state Illinois near the small college town of Jacksonville. In the present day, an 80 acre farm is a very small farm. But in the early 1900s when farming power was equine and men slaved over many field implements which they held in place by sinewy hands and arms, farming was brutal. How vivid are my memories of my father holding the plow in the rich loam, harness lines draped over the right shoulder. His commands of "gee" and "haw" were literally the first words I ever said-not mother and father.

At the age of 17 my father had been forced to leave the Whipple Academy for Boys in Jacksonville to take over the entire operation of the family farm upon his father's death. The family consisted of two sisters, and his widowed mother, Anne Francis Massey Kitner.

His mother, "Aunt Frank" as she was known, apparently had delusions of grandeur. She ensconced herself in the eight bedroom farm house and became the "grand dame" of what she considered her "Massey Farm" empire.

Never having known my grandfather, I can only surmise that he was a wonderful, kind man to have produced the marvelous, caring and loving man, who was my father. Grandma was a snob and remained an imperious old lady for her entire life - no billowing aprons and a peppermint candy in every pocket type lady was grandma.

No one in my background had any particular interest in horses. It is still a mystery to me why I had such a compulsion to ride and to make training and teaching a profession, because there were no riding academies or women even considered as trainers. I would blaze a trail for other girls and young women to follow.

Once, when someone asked my grandmother why Helen had become a horse trainer, she replied grandly that Robert E. Lee, HIMSELF had wanted to buy her father's prize horse! Proudly she added that the offer was refused. This is not the explanation of my fascination with horses that I am proud of or even believe, but it is as close to an explanation as one can come.

My mother, Edna Shields, was a beautiful woman in every way. A true "Irish Blonde" with raven hair, kindly blue eyes that always sparkled with the joy of living and the rosy cheeks and brilliant smile of a woman who lived a full life based on love and the "Golden Rule."

In the ten years from 1915 to 1926, my life on the farm was a series of adventures. My wonderful parents recognized the drama and excitement of farm life. They made every happening an adventure and shared the phenomena that made for wonderful memories.

Mid-state Illinois may have been flat and uninteresting to many, but I recall the times when my mother would waken me in the middle of the night to share the enchantment of viewing the northern lights that danced and glowed with heavenly colors, the midnight treks to the kitchen to see the wonder of a night blooming cereus and the heart-stopping touch on the shoulder with the news that a tornado had just twisted the top of the windmill and sent it crashing into the center of the large kitchen. In the bone-chilling winter nights the very best memories are those of a fairyland of lights, moonlight breaking through freezing mists that transformed every ice-laden tree branch into diamond wands.

Sex education on the farm was supposed to be automatic, but nothing much went on with the mules. Cows were serviced at the neighbors' cattle farm. The sows also made conjugal visits, so my understanding of sex and procreation fell to my observing chickens! I spent ten years thinking that a rooster perched atop a hen was merely taking a ride. To be honest, I still do not understand what is going on!

Of all the farm memories, the one I cherish the most is of my father bringing little newborn piglets in from the bitterly cold winter nights to be brought back to life, swaddled in gray flannel on the open oven door of the large iron cook stove. Milk was heated and spooned into the waiting jaws of the little beasts. I still can hear the little clicking sound of the tiny piglets chomping down on the thin silver teaspoon.

One of my favorite pastimes, of course, was playing horse. Marjorie, my oldest sister, was all girl and reluctantly joined Martha and me in our wild gallops. Martha was always Black Beauty, but that was too tame for me - I was Wildfire!! My two sisters really took advantage of sending me on every kind of errand and urging me on faster and faster with the exhortation, "Run, Wildfire Run." When Marjorie had enough of the roughhousing, she would lure me up an apple tree, then leave me.

We children always referred to our father as "Pop." He and Mother had worked out a wonderful plan for raising three girls. We learned morality and responsibility by observing our parents. We did not fear them but they had our complete respect. Our family lived by the Golden Rule and we girls seldom earned spankings - but when we did, our mother, not Pop had to deliver the punishment. It was bare bottom spanking while draped over mother's knees that made "right" so much preferable to wrong. Mother would weep when she spanked us. I always hurled myself into her arms and hugged and kissed her to quiet her sobs. She was either the world's best actress or generations ahead of child psychologists.

Many people today do not believe in punishing a child for wrong doing, but swift and honest correction not only teaches a child what is right and wrong, but establishes in their mind the fact that the parent really cares what the child is doing.

I had one temper tantrum in my life. As all farmers did, we went to town every Saturday. One day Mother and I were touring the dime store and I spied the most beautiful silver cap pistol in a real leather holster. I was five years old and I had never wanted anything so badly in my life and Mother explained that we could not afford the toy because it costs 75 cents, whereupon I proceeded to crouch down, stomping my feet and shrieking bloody murder. The first shriek was barely out when my mother grabbed my arm, jerked me upright, told me to hush immediately and that I would receive a spanking when we got home. That had to be one of the longest days of my life. When we got home, it was almost an anticlimax, swift and quick, but I had learned a lesson that stayed with me all my life.

When I was nine my father bought a little pleasure mare with the inspired name of Lady. I rode her every moment I could get and shared her with my sister Martha. But Lady was too tame for me and I taught her to kick-up when I swung the whip over her hips. This was a lot of fun until my father discovered what I was doing.

In that era photographs were very precious, therefore there was a limited number of pictures. So when my mother took a picture of me astride the mare; I could hardly wait for the return of the picture. When I saw it, I was horrified and heartbroken. I looked absolutely awful. Probably at that moment my philosophy of riding and training was born. Never again would I be ugly on a horse or permit any of my riders to be anything but beautiful; because beauty is balance and balance is control.

When my father sold the farm and moved to Jacksonville, there was a barn behind our house that served as a garage as many did in those days. In addition to Lady, my father brought a milk cow. The barn-garage fascinated me because I discovered some remnants of harness hanging on the wall. What a treasure trove! I combined those pieces of harness with a cotton rope lariat and managed to hitch the mare to our sled. On the sled I mounted a wooden box in which a quart of fresh milk would sit then I would get on the sled and start down Lafayette Avenue, the brick street fronting our house, to make a two block trip to deliver the milk. This may not sound too ridiculous, but consider the fact that this was in the middle of summer and I was driving a sled. Our poor neighbors must have thought the "Beverly Hillbillies" had just moved in. This performance lasted only that first summer because the depression was deepening cruelly and we had to sell the mare and the cow. My riding was reduced to sharing rides with my childhood sweetheart, A. Wadsworth Applebee, who read the encomiums when I was awarded an honorary doctorate many years later.

My destiny was shaped by the fact that our home was near the fairgrounds, and a wonderful black man, Logan McDaniels, was training saddle horses there. It was there that I had the privilege of riding the young horses and actually learned to show a horse by helping to gait the colts. Soon the novel news that there was a young girl who could ride became known. I was thrilled to be asked to ride horses through the weekly horse sales so they could be announced as "kid broke". My father was so proud of me that he saw no danger in what I was doing. When he gleefully told my mother that he had overheard one man say to another, "That must be a broke horse" only to have his friend say, "You'd better be careful of those horses that that little girl rides!" My mother was horrified and that was the end of my sales rides. However, I was being asked to show ponies at the local county fair. What a pest I must have been - barely existing from one fair season to the next in hopes of getting to show.

One day, a man came up to me during the fair and asked me if I would show his five-gaited mare in the ladies class. I shall never forget his name - Dink Rainwater. Of course I accepted the offer immediately. He said, "Little lady, how much would you charge me to show the mare? I am sure that was a purely rhetorical question and he did not really mean it. But that was the moment, at the age of 12, that I became a professional. I told him that I would charge him a dollar to ride and another dollar if I won anything. I could hardly run home fast enough to tell my mother so that she could make a riding coat for me. (I had already talked her into making some jodhpurs.)

The next night I was at the stalls waiting for the thrill of getting to show a "real show horse". Finally the time came for me to get on the mare and start for the ring which was in front of the grandstand. As I started toward the ring, Mr. Rainwater said, "Little lady, this is a ladies class and the judge will ask you to back the mare up in the lineup. When he does, pretend that you do not hear him." Well, I had ridden enough foolish horses that I knew he was doing everything but telling me that the mare would rear up and fall backwards. This was merely a challenge to a kid who thought that she was the best rider in the world. I do not remember the class or what ribbon I got, but I did manage to get the mare's feet tangled up and we backed for the judge. When I rode back to the stalls, the owner was all smiles and handed me some money. I discovered a mistake and told him that he had given me three dollars instead of the two that I charged. He said "Little lady, keep the money. That is the first time that mare ever backed up." So, you see, I became a professional, being paid two dollars for going forward and a dollar for going backward!

Grammar school was uneventful for me. Merely the time between weekends when I could go the fairgrounds to ride colts under the tutelage of Logan McDaniels who would figure prominently in our lives. The horse activity was the most important thing in my life.

"Northa"

My first training horse was a Standardbred Pacer named Northa Light. The mare had been ruled off the race tracks by the state ruling body of county fairs because of her dangerous habit of running out of the driver's control. The owner, a local man, had finally given up any hopes of curing this very dangerous habit. In apparent desperation, he had decided to forget racing and to put the mare under saddle to sell her as a pleasure riding horse.

Since I had no horse of my own to ride, I was delighted when the owner asked me to train the mare. I realize now that my best advantage was the low training charge which was feed and bedding costs plus one dollar a day. This was in 1927 and The Great Depression had almost finished the public training of Saddle Horses.

Since my father was a retired farmer with nothing to do, he was delighted to care for the mare, groom her and clean the stall. So, my one dollar per day was clear profit!

My father had sold our 80 acre farm for a record price of $400.00 per acre and $32,000 dollars was a great amount of money at the time. But my father had three daughters to educate and even at that time it would be expensive to give us a college education, as he was forced to give up his formal education at Whipple Academy for Boys when, at 17 years of age, Pop took over the farm when his father died. That academy later became Illinois College, my alma mater.

So there I was, actually earning money for doing what I best loved. The terrible financial straits forced many grown men into the bread lines when a dollar a day could have kept them going.

My delight at having a training horse paled the first day. Not only did the mare try to throw me (never having been broken to saddle), but when she stopped bucking she proceeded to run off with me. If she had galloped it would not have been so bad, but she was a pacer and anyone who has ridden a Saddle Horse inclined to pace can imagine what I had to ride at runaway speed. It has entered my mind that whoever patented the "mixmaster" years later must have gotten the inspiration from riding a pacer!

But I was being paid to train this creature! Shoeing was expensive, so I had only the "simple" task of breaking the mare of the runaway habit. I could not afford to try to shoe the mare to break up her lateral gait, nor could the owner. After several days of the mare calling the shots, it became evident that I had to do something drastic.

The next Saturday my father had an appointment, so I tacked the mare. I got myself ready with a good sized "whip" from the neighbor's wild cherry tree. I got in the saddle and very carefully walked "Northa" to a wide smooth road that stretched at least two miles westward. My plan was to pretend that I could not hold the mare, which would start her on the runaway dash. Off she took and at the end of the road my mount was willing to slow down and head back home in control. I had a different idea.

I began to apply the switch every time she wanted to slow down. In a short time, we were back home and I stopped the mare and dismounted. At that very moment my father drove into the circular drive. He jumped from the car, shouting, "Helen, what in God's name have you done?" His use of profanity startled me as much as his question. "I think I have broken her from running off."

Only then did I look at Northa Light. She stood spraddle-legged, her head hung down with the mouth opened. Rivers of sweat cascaded down her sides.

"Jerk the saddle off her, and start walking," my father said. "Don't even stop to halter her." Then he rushed into the house to get a large sponge and a bucket of cool water. He put the sponge between her ears, securing it with the crown of the bridle, then he dipped more water on the sponge.

There was a large flower bed in the middle of the cinder driveway and it was around this circular bed that I walked the mare for more than two hours, hesitating only briefly when my father applied more ice water to the sponge atop the tortured mare's head.

Perhaps it is a tribute to the Standardbred horse that the mare did not founder. Surely my father's wise council which reflected a farmer's knowledge of how to care for his horses and mules resulted in averting what could have been complete disaster.

That was a lesson that I have used many many times over the past seven decades. Namely, that extreme measures are seldom justified and that every phase of horse training must be rooted in logic and compassion.

Oh, I was successful in breaking the mare of her bad habit. Never again did she attempt to run off, but only because of my father's wise council was I able to salvage a dubious cure from what could have been a fatal idea.

Mine was a rather lonely existence during high school days. No longer was I a child "playing horse" with real live Saddlebreds because I found myself a majority of one where riding and showing were concerned. How different were those times from today when equitation and show riding are overwhelmingly female also. Jacksonville was a town divided. Those who lived east of the public square were considered by those west of the business district as socially inferior. This came as a great shock and disappointment to me, a child who had no idea of prejudice and one who did not tolerate it.

Being a "west sider" made it almost impossible for me to join the local group of girls who could only be defined as snobs. Consequently, I immersed myself in a great number of school activities. Oh, I was a real eager beaver, interested in everything and president of most of them. This does not denote popularity on my part, only a willingness to dig in and do a good job.

I liked boys, they seemed more honest and it was this perspective that led me to choose the co-educational Illinois College, over Illinois Women's College where my sisters had studied.

Sports were, and still are, a vital part of my life, but I was insulating myself from the girls and felt truly justified in my opinion that women were "catty," "snooty," and neither to be admired nor trusted.

This worried me when I prepared to enter college. I told my mother that I did not like girls and their snobbish ways. I thought all girls were like my neighbors. Right then my mother gave me the most precious gift any young rebel could receive. She said, "Helen, sit down. This may come as as a shock to you, but you are not God!" That statement opened my narrow mind in a flash. "There is something good in everyone and it is up to you to find it. You have been raised by the Golden Rule and it is time you practiced it!" At that moment I fell in love with the human race.

College was wonderful and I continued on my path of gulping

down every educational opportunity. I even took a semester of football, and continued my hard-working ethos.

What I did not know was that my interest in collegiate tennis and basketball, the riding class, writing for the college newspaper and editorship of the Rig Veda, our class of '39 yearbook, were preparing me for a wonderful and productive lifetime in the horse business. I do not intend to preach, but any young person hoping for a career in our business should take advantage of every opportunity to learn, to teach anything and to develop a vocabulary that makes one's ideas understandable. And learn to lighten up and enjoy life. A sense of humor saw me through many tough decisions and is a saving grace in involuntary retirement.

In 1987 I was truly surprised to learn that I was to be inducted into the Illinois College Sports Hall of Fame. When I arrived, there was one survivor of my era in attendance. The rest of the members looked like children to me. There were three inductees. The first was a football player long since deceased. Then they came to me and I had the feeling that I was a relic of the past, one step after deceased. When it was apparent that I was expected to respond to the kind identification and introduction, I stood up and made the beginning of the dullest "thank you" speech. It was boring all of the young members to the point of the fixed smiles and glazed eyes.

Fortunately for all, I saw what was happening, and said, "But of all the things I learned at Illinois College the most important was - never play Ping-Pong with a cross-eyed opponent."

I sat down to grateful applause.

I continued to get horses to train, and I was getting more and more calls to ride horses in the shows. In the 30's, classes were quite varied in the Illinois shows. For me the most exciting of all were the Ladies and Gentleman pair classes. Louis Robinson, who would later gain fame as the J.L. Younghusband Stable trainer, had a public stable at the Illinois State Fairgrounds in Springfield. I would be the lady rider in both the three and five-gaited events. Robinson was a rather rough trainer and showing his horses involved as much training as it did riding. Many a time I came out of the ring with knuckles bleeding from a valiant effort to hide the fact that the ladies part of the pair was not exactly a ladie's horse.

At Robinson's stable was a black three-gaited mare. She and Louis did not get along, they were a bad combination. He was

Illinois College
Tennis Team, 1936.

Clay model
by Helen, 1937.

Vanity Dare.

MacMurray College
Riding Team.

nervous and of short disposition. The mare was excitable, fractious, and hard to control. It was obvious that the combination was doomed from the start. I reasoned that the only way to get this mare trained was not through subjecting her to the trainer's will, but rather, to use extreme patience to allay the mare's nervousness to the point where one could be quiet and reward her when she did right. While I never joined the "FLICKA School of Horseman-ship" I did realize the value of channeling the horses' behavior not demanding it.

Louis was glad to accept my offer of $500 to get rid of the uncooperative mare. When I took her home I found that the mare was so nervous that she took an uneven stride at the walk, a full stride with the right front foot and a half stride with the left. So I put the mare on the end of a lead shank to walk in small circles with the short stride on the outside. The ploy worked and I was on my way to having a very fine three-gaited mare. It was also reasonable to assume that the mare would be more fractious in training at home where she had no distractions than in the show ring. Therefore I put up with some of her foolishness at home not wanting to force her behavior. I named the mare Vanity Dare and seldom suffered defeat at the Illinois shows. Charlie recalls Robinson coming to him practically in tears of frustration to ask that I stop my father from gleefully rubbing it in every time I won. I suppose this was justifiable fatherly pride, but to be perfectly candid my success with the mare came about because I could devote an unlimited amount of time to her each day, a luxury not possible for the time-budgeted schedule practiced in large training stables.

I showed Vanity Dare throughout my college years and my first two years at MacMurray College, where I headed the riding department. The program there was very successful, sending riding teams into tri-state riding competition without defeat. I loved teaching, but the opportunity to operate a large training facility in St. Louis lured me away from the college.

Charlie and I had been married for less than a year when he was called in the service of WWII. Thus began almost three years of training, teaching, and operating Missouri Stables, a huge facility. When Charlie returned at the end of the war, he briefly took over as manager and trainer of the stables and I continued my training and teaching. This was not a happy arrangement as the new owner was not entirely an honest person. So we were very fortunate to lease the beautiful Riding and Hunt Club Stables which adjoined Missouri Stables.

Consuela

Some of the old classes we had many years ago were very interesting and had a lot of variety. There was a very famous exhibitor of Hackney horses named Cuneo of the Cuneo Press in Chicago, who had the fancy Phaeton of old with a liveried footman sitting in the rear very erect, arms folded, eyes forward, very formal, and quite elegant. The big high-trotting Hackney horses driven around the ring with their jingling harness driven by a lady, Consuela Cuneo. Memorable was the marvelous pair of Hackneys and always as it seemed to me to win all of the classes and deservedly so.

One night at the big St. Louis Horse Show there was a fireman's demonstration where they had a big platform high in the arena, and the firemen were to leap out of that and demonstrate how to land into a safety net. One fellow hung around the stables, because people always needed extra help. One night prior to the show this fellow saw the platform and started to climb up. Everyone yelled for him not to go up knowing he was well lubricated with whiskey, fearing what he might do and knowing he was a free spirit, to say the least. Well, sure enough he climbed up the platform and leaped off shouting, "I don't need a net!" He hit the tanbark. It would have killed a sober person. He simply crumpled up, then got up, brushed himself off, and walked out of the arena. He was the talk of the horse show.

The Phaeton class came in the ring and here was Consuela beautifully attired in a long dress and it was the style to wear a big broad brimmed, elegant flowered hat, the height of elegance. Seated behind her in the groom's seat was Dugan, this same fellow who had jumped off the fire platform. Dugan was wearing the required formal livery. He was sitting up just as properly as can be and then you heard the audience start to giggle a little bit. I looked up and here was Dugan. Every time Consuela would come to the end and make a turn, he would lean perilously out the side and then he would lean back, and then he would lean to the other side. After Consuela had made a few passes around the ring, her face was scarlet. She had no reason to believe that people were not laughing at her. It had to be one of the funniest things I have ever seen. The trainer yelled at Dugan and asked him to stop, and told Consuela to continue and she did go on to win the class. It was not always sixes and sevens at horse shows, sometimes hilarious things did happen.

The Hackney horses were very prominent at that time. Wonderful trainers abounded and some of the big wealthy stables were the main ones who had the Hackneys. There was one exception. Bob Mannix was one of the first really good equitation teachers, and he loved Hackneys. He had a pair of old Hackneys. He found some used harness somewhere and put it together and got a Phaeton. One night at the Indiana State Fair he said to me, "Helen would you drive my Hackneys?" I thought the class was so elegant I said, "I would love to."

Just before I went in the ring Bob said to me, "One of these horses does not want to go as much as the other one. You may have to get after him." What he did not say was one of these horses really took hold and the other one did not. I got in the ring and we had not gone half way around when I thought this one horse on the off side was going to pull my arm out of the socket and I hung in as valiantly as I could. I was in high heel shoes and I was trying to look like an elegant lady out for a pleasure drive. Let me tell you, this was no pleasure! Judging the class here again was my nemesis, the lady from New York, who had seen me struggle with the ponies Fame and Fortune. I do not know whether Mrs. Cox had a misplaced sense of humor, whether she did not like Saddle Horse people invading the Hackney territory, or whether she had a puckish sense of humor, but that class lasted forever. Just at the very last when it appeared that the horses were going to get rid of me, the call came to line up. My experience with that beautiful class was one of despair and hilarity.

It was here that our names became known in the horse business. Our riders were tops in equitation and performance classes and we had a few nice stake horses to show. In 1949 Charlie decided to listen to his brother, who was an automotive parts manufacturer in St. Louis. Hugh thought that Charlie was wasting himself in the horse business and "gave" us the state of Arkansas as his traveling territory, in the used generator business. Sometimes one can look back to see that there is more than coincidence in the direction life takes.

Surely this was the reason we went to Arkansas. Not to be in the automotive parts business, not to operate a small public stable, but to meet a wonderful young boy who was to change our life forever. It was here that we met an 11-year-old who would become our son and be an integral part of us for the rest of our lives.

The youngster chose the name Charles Edward Crabtree, Jr. otherwise known in our profession as Redd Crabtree. After two positions, the second being Graystone Manor Farm where Redd developed his first World Grand Champion, Chief of Graystone, he returned to Simpsonville, Kentucky to become a third partner in Crabtree Farms. This enterprise soon became the largest training stable of American Saddlebreds and continues to this date to hold the record for the most winners of World Championships in a single year. This was at a time when multiple divisions were not common and many times we would have five or six stablemates competing in the same class. On that record year we entered and showed 58 head of horses, a record that still stands. I am not sure that these mind-boggling numbers indicate anything but willingness to work our fingers to the bone.

By this time we had purchased the two adjoining farms and Crabtree Farms was a literal reality. Those years must have been the most productive and rewarding years of our lives. Perhaps this is the place to recognize the many wonderful owners that made for a successful business. Those blessed people were the greatest owners anyone could wish to have, and several of those original owners are still with our grandson, Casey Crabtree at Crabtree Stables.

After Charlie's return to the horse business in Little Rock came the Gregnon years in Collierville, Tennessee. After four delightful years the tax advantage was about up and we wisely agreed to come to Louisville, Kentucky to become managers and trainers of the famous Rock Creek Riding Club. We spent four very fruitful years at Rock Creek from 1954 to 1958. In 1956, Charlie, sensing the important trend towards Shelby County purchased a 43 acre farm that was to become the original Crabtree Farms. Work immediately started on stable construction. We had anticipated moving to Simpsonville in ten years. However, fortune smiled upon us and our careers prospered to bring us to a more rapid move to the country.

Randi Stuart Coming To Crabtrees

When we first moved to Simpsonville from Rock Creek we did have some riders come from out of town to stay and have instruction. They brought their own horses and yet we had one or two nice horses there that were for sale. It was a smart thing to do to let incoming good riders use these horses with the permission of the owners, because in that way we got a lot of horses sold. One day, shortly before Easter, the phone rang and it was a lady with a rather high pitched chirpy little voice who introduced herself as Mrs. Harold Stuart from Tulsa, Oklahoma. She said that her daughter, Randi, wanted to know if during the upcoming Easter holiday, she could come and take instruction. She further explained they were good friends of the McGees of Kerr-McGee Oil Co. in Oklahoma who had come to us when we were at Rock Creek.

Thus began a long line of Oklahoma oil people. At one time the place was completely filled with Oklahomans and we had no local owners. This may seem a little strange, but I liked it that way because I was never very interested in a lesson program where every Wednesday you knew little LouLou was going to come for her lesson at 4:30 and somebody else was coming at 5:00 whether you felt inspired or not. The good thing about having out of town customers is that the only time they could come was on national holidays or the summer holidays.

Mrs. Stuart came and with her was this tall, shy quiet girl named Randi. I had gotten a horse in to sell and I had arranged for Randi to use this horse. They stayed at the hotel and the mother would studiously bring the daughter out to ride twice a day. At first she was just another long legged, shy, inexperienced rider. But as time went by and before they left, I could see this was an extremely intelligent child and anything you told her she would do. There was never any equivocation; at all, she did it. By the time they went home, Mrs. Stuart was delighted Randi had developed a keen interest, because her mentality had been challenged as well as her physical ability. In later years when we all came to know Randi, we realized what an extremely intelligent and level-headed person she was and that such an approach was the right thing to do with her. It was the only approach I knew to use with anyone but it particularly applied to Randi.

Then came other calls and someone else from an oil company called and they wanted their daughter to come to Simpsonville. By this time we had a little difficulty with where we were going to put these students because they were staying in our guest room in our house and the cottage on the farm fitted out with bunk beds.

One day Mrs. Stuart called and she said, "Helen there is a lady here named Mrs. Gallagher and you know I think she would spend ten thousand dollars for a horse." Mrs. Gallagher, upon her husband's death, remarried and became Mrs. Sinclair, so Mrs. Stuart's evaluation of what Katherine would do for the horse business was somewhat underrated, to say the least. Mrs. Sinclair, her daughter, MaryLou Doudican, Randi and her daughter, Kate, are still with the Crabtree organization.

Two years ago Randi introduced me at a clinic and said I was her idol, her mentor, and most of all she was proud of the fact I was her matron of honor at her wedding 25 years earlier. Randi was here several years before she married, so you can see that many of the people at Crabtree's have been here not just a few years, but many have been here an ordinary lifetime.

All these good people who come in to ride, and are well-received, given their money's worth, and are encouraged to learn and challenge their mentality as well as their physical prowess — those people will stay. Not only in our organization but all around the country you see people who have been in this business for years and years. They would not be here if they had been ill-treated, so there is so much to be said for this business. The main thing is that the people who do the best job, are the ones who look upon their riders as being important as people first, and as riders second. I know I did. It was important to me that these riders grew up into fine people and that riding was not only something they liked to do, but something that developed their mental skills, the ability to anticipate a problem, and to deal with it, which applies to every part of life.

In the mid 1980s after many wonderful years as Crabtree Farms Incorporated, Charlie and I built our "dream stable" on the eastern half of the original farm. Redd became the proprietor of the remaining 60 acres. We sold the Whittenberg Stables, which we had purchased several years before. Located across the highway from the present farm, it now comprises a Thoroughbred training facility and Premier Stables owned by Rob and Sarah Byers. The original training farm was sold to Edward Gaylord.

We continue to be active in this sport that has been our life blood for over 65 years. Although technically retired from active training, Charles and I lease our stable to Mike and Nancy Spencer of neighboring Gold Leaf Farm and keep a young show prospect in training each year, however the main business of our Charles and Helen Crabtree Stables is concerned with the development and marketing of the material encompassed in the book to be known as *Hold Your Horses*, the monthly articles to the prestigious *Saddle & Bridle Magazine*, the continuation to oversee an equitation video tape by Video Horse World, and the National Bridle Shop's handling of the Crabtree adjustable stirrup bar show saddle. The book *Saddle Seat Equitation*, first published in 1970, then revised in 1982 continues after 25 years to be used not only by trainers and teachers involved with the American Saddlebred horse, but by all other exponents of flat saddle riding.

Recently, I discovered 40 hours of lesson tape that had been set aside for future editing. These are actual lessons most of which dealt with my guest rider program involving two hours of instruction per day, one hour of which was individual and one with the two students who came to the farm for the program. While there were many American Saddlebreds involved in this program, Morgan and Arabian horses comprised the majority. It was interesting for me to discover that in listening to the tapes that the approach to the various breeds, be they pleasure, show or equitation horses, was practically the same underlining — my life long belief that one approaches horsemanship from a logical, mental standpoint, tempered only by the varying conformations of the different breeds.

Clinics and speaking to the riders of various local stable camp groups, plus a very strong interest in the development of an American Saddlebred division of the Equine Science program at Midway College are keeping my interest alive and well.

Only the growing loss of sight keeps me from actively riding and showing, but I have learned to accept the inevitable by redoubling my literary efforts and maintaining my life-long interest in teaching riders to ride and train horses. Charles manages the selection of our breeding stock and their training.

Our home adjoining the new stable is a busy place. The close proximity to Redd and Nancy Crabtree's Farm Incorporated, plus

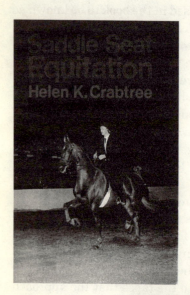

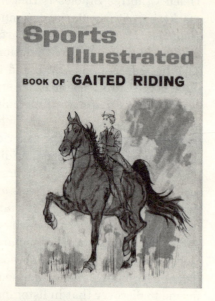

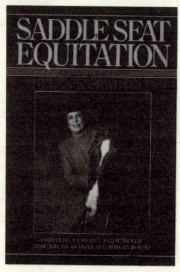

the added joy of being next door neighbors to our grandson Casey Crabtree and his multi-talented wife Kim, who is the long suffering editor of this work, bring us much joy and make it possible for Charles and Helen Crabtree Stable to continue to be a viable force in our industry.

When we moved to Simpsonville it was a tiny hamlet of 220 people and we were the first public training stable to come to Shelby County. Almost 40 years later, we now find that tiny little Simpsonville is the Saddle Horse capital of the world. Perhaps our ad in a Shelbyville Horse Show program best expresses our deep feeling for our Kentucky roots. The ad simply stated, "The First To Come, The Happiest To Be Here."

I had long been a reader of *Saddle & Bridle Magazine.* One day I called the publishers and asked if I might write a column on equitation. This was a time of great change and transition and I wanted to get it documented and to help educate people. I did not ask for any money, I just thought it was kind of them to let me write this and of course seeing a good thing for nothing, they agreed.

I called this column LINE-UP PLEASE. I had written it for three years when I received a call from Alice Higgins a good friend and former student. She had gone to New York to undertake the position of horse editor for *Time-Life magazine.* Then, when *Sport's Illustrated* came into being, Alice began to write a horse show column for them. *Sport's Illustrated* had started a series of instructional books on how to ride a horse, how to play golf, how to swim, etc. anything that pertained to sports. Alice, always a very smart, heads-up person said, "Helen, I believe if I talk to these people that we can get them to accept a book on five-gaited riding." I said, that would be wonderful to get this in book form, a nationally recognized source. It would be beneficial to the industry. *Sport's Illustrated* accepted her idea. She had to tell them she was writing this book in conjunction with me in order to get it published. It is credited to Alice Higgins assisted by Helen K. Crabtree.

Actually Alice was so busy doing other things and being an old student, she had the feeling that maybe she ought to let the teacher write this whole thing rather than the pupil.

Sport's Illustrated Book of Gaited Riding, was produced by Lippincott Press in 1962. A beautiful little volume, very well illustrated by Frank Mullen. The subject of all the pictures was Mary

Ann O'Callahan Cronan, riding her five-gaited mare Scarlet Ribbons. Mary Ann is the mother of Sarah Cronan, who is a top equitation rider today as her mother had been at that time.

We had our foot in the door to start getting the Saddle Horses, and how we rode them, nationally recognized. When I received a telephone call from one of the staff at Doubleday Publishers, who at that time was the largest book publisher in the world, asking me to write a book for them, I nearly dropped dead. I kept the confirmation letter and framed it. I was amazed! I did not know if I would ever write the book, but just being asked was excitement enough.

Then they started sending me what books they had about riding and horses in the Doubleday library. I was shocked because these were not the kind of books I wanted to write. They were elementary. For instance, this is a horse, this is a saddle, this is a rein, this is a riding habit, etc. In fact, if you owned a good Funk and Wagnalls, you could have written the books.

I held the advance royalty check. Every year when I went to New York I would take the check with me and call to try to give it back. They would say "No, just keep it and surely you will write the book. Finally, Bill Steinkraus, who was on the Doubleday board of editors said, "I think you are scaring Helen off. She is writing articles for *Saddle & Bridle Magazine* and I think that is what she would like in her book." The publisher agreed. That is the way the format of *Saddle Seat Equitation* came about in its first form, a rather small book that came out in 1970, with a great deal of help from my assistant at that time, Debbie Basham.

Then I wrote the revised edition which is the book we now know and that came out in 1981. The manuscript had been turned in and I was in New York with horses and riders when Doubleday contacted me and said we would like to get a color picture for the cover of this revised edition. We had Warlock at the show and who was more handsome than he? I asked if we could shoot the picture between sessions at the Garden?

They came with all this sophisticated paraphernalia, reflectors, umbrellas, and 15 different cameras. Out I rode on Warlock. If anybody has a copy of that first revised edition, they will notice the rings on the end of the curb bit are going sideways and the reins are going in the same direction. So I must explain. Warlock was a wonderful horse always alert and looking around. However, by the time the camera crew had gotten set up, the horse was bored to death and so was I. They took picture after picture, even suggesting I get off and stand there and hold the bits and look lovingly at his head like some six-year-old with her first pony.

I said, "No, I am sorry I just will not do that, let us get a seated picture. We will try even harder to get the horse's attention and I will try to look like I am alive." They suggested I take all of the reins over the horse's head and then put them on the left side. "Hold these in your left hand, lean over to the side and pat the horse on the neck with your right hand." That way they could get a full face picture of the horse and me. I was so tired I did not know what I was doing so I did what they said and all of a sudden I thought, "I am falling off!" Sure enough here stood the horse absolutely still. I had my body tilted to the left, both arms on the left side of that horse's neck and I was about to hit the ground. Fortunately my reflexes were quick enough and I grabbed the horse around the neck and landed on my feet. I looked over to see Woody Henry just about to die laughing. It must have been a ridiculous sight. It was the savior of what we were trying to do because it was so ridiculous. The horse woke up, I think even he thought it was funny. I got back on and could not stop laughing. The photographers must have taken 20 excellent pictures. Of all the pictures I have ever had taken, it is the best. That is where the cover of the revised edition of *Saddle Seat Equitation* came from.

The present cover is of Ruth Anne Lewis. The publisher felt that they needed an action picture to create more interest in the book. I did not have one in color, so I asked if I could substitute a student. The one I picked was my last equitation student and a wonderful rider, Ruth Anne Lewis.

In the early years after 1958, Simpsonville was a tiny hamlet and the post office was in part of a grocery store. It was manned by Mr. and Mrs. Buckman, who have to be two of the nicest people in the world. They were so cheerful and they made everyone feel welcome and happy to be in this little town.

AHSA Horsewoman of the Year, 1964. Helen and Eddie Arcaro.

St. Louis National Hall of Fame, 1979. Joe Allhoff, Charles Crabtree, "Gussie" Busch and Mrs. Otis Brown, Sr.

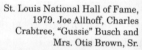

A. Wadsworth Applebee, Helen Crabtree and President John J. Wittich.

Marjorie, Helen and Martha.

One day I went in and there was a letter from the American Horse Shows Association and I thought, "what are they writing to me about?" This was in 1964. I opened the letter right there and discovered to my total amazement that I had been named by the AHSA as the Horsewoman Of The Year. I just let out a big yell and scared the Buckmans to death. I said, "No, I am happy, this is a wonderful honor." The association had been dominated by the hunter and jumper people and they were finally recognizing someone from the Saddle Horse industry. The thing that excited me the most and I suppose this sounds pretty cheap of me, but Charlie and I had been to the West Coast and had visited with the great team of trainers Jimmy and Mousey Williams. The two of them had won this same award and I had seen the trophy and it was simply beautiful. It was the prettiest thing I had ever seen. While I was exuberant about this honor, I was actually more excited at the fact I was going to get one of those magnificent trophies.

When the appointed time came, I went to New York for the convention. I had not been in the hotel an hour before getting a call from a professional photographer who wanted to come over to take my picture. I was in such a state of excitement over the honor. I thought that this is what they do, sending over a photographer to take your picture. I had also been told by someone that the *New York Times* had mentioned I was going to receive this award. My head was in the clouds and evidently not working very well when the photographer came. After he had taken my picture, he told me they would rush to have the pictures ready in two days and he handed me a bill.

Then I came down to earth and realized this was just some smart photographer who had read about this honor and thought they had someone they could get some money out of and since I was from Simpsonville, Ky. seemed to indicate I was somewhat of a "redneck" and they were not entirely wrong.

When it came time for the award I had dressed in a beautiful rose red wool suit with a gray fox collar and high heeled shoes. I tried to look as elegant as I could because I wanted them to know that the Saddle Horse trainers could stand up with anybody, because they really did not know too much about us. Well, imagine my shock when they announced they were ready to give me this trophy and up stood Eddie Arcaro who was to make the presentation. As he handed me the trophy, we both laughed. Finally everybody at the convention was laughing. You talk about "Mutt and Jeff!" That is really what we looked like. It was gratifying that two years later Randi Stuart was named for this same honor which was really breaking the ice because she was an amateur and within three years, The AHSA had recognized two women riders from the Saddle Horse industry.

It was the custom of the United Professional Horseman's Association to present its trophy to the winner of the UPHA Championship class at the annual convention. In 1978 14-year-old Shauna Schoonmaker, riding her good horse The Deputy had won the class. This was before the class was divided into the Junior and Senior divisions. The convention was held that year in Nashville, Tennessee and the Schoonmakers and I were in attendance. I noticed that Redd was very nervous. I had been told that he was going to be honored and I thought maybe he had gotten wind of this.

I explained to Shauna and her mother that Redd always reads the speech introducing the winner of the UPHA Championship and I said, "He is really good at this and sometimes he makes you want to cry." Redd gave his speech for Shauna and presented her with the lovely trophy emblematic of her big victory. Soon Redd rose and started to make another speech. He was pretty devious in his presentation talks, he could talk for five minutes and never tell you who was going to get the award, which is what he proceeded to do. Then he said, "she." I thought, oh it was Donna Moore. Finally, they were going to recognize a woman as trainer and he stopped talking and reached over and grabbed a glass of water and said, "This is hard to do." He finished his speech and the last sentence was, "And the UPHA Trainer of the Year is my mother, Mrs. Charles Crabtree." Talk about a surprise! I think that anybody who receives awards like this given out by the AHSA, UPHA, and the ASHA are always surprised. If you work hard enough to deserve one of those honors you do not have time to sit around and think about whether you're winning anything.

Winning is the aftermath of a concentration of hard work and dedication, so I think I speak for everyone who has received awards to say that they are always a surprise. In 1994 they designated Donna Moore to receive this same award. She is a wonderful trainer and unsurpassed in her ability to select a nice horse and train it. The honor was a long time coming for this very deserving woman.

I was frequently asked in the early days how I became recognized in the horse business. I told them, "In my case I did the best I could. I kept my eyes and ears open and my mouth shut. Then I would go in the ring and beat the heck out of them." I think this is what Donna Moore has done because she has risen to a place of great prominence as a trainer of the American Saddlebred.

The first time I ever really met Donna was when Charlie and I went up to Knolland Farms where she and her husband Tom Moore were training for Ed Jenner. We went on a buying trip. We went into the stable and there were two little yellow-haired girls with a Hackney pony and they were pretending that it was a great big show horse. They were giving it the show horse treatment practicing bandaging it's legs, grooming it, picking out it's mane and short tail. They were absolutely adorable. Those were the two girls now known as Melinda Moore, a trainer in her own right and sister Melissa. So that family of four are unique in our business. A lot of people thought the Crabtrees were unique and perhaps we were, and now here a family of four absolutely tops in the profession.

Donna is a great story teller. One of the most memorable stories she told was when she and Tom were first getting established in the business and they were at Knolland Farm. They had the champion stallion Valley View Supreme and they had two mares who needed to be bred on the same day. Donna said they could not afford to have the veterinarian come and gather semen to impregnate the second mare. They had one of those long plastic examining gloves that came above the elbow and thought they may be able to put this on the stallion and collect the semen. That afternoon they led the mare outside since they did not have a breeding shoot. Donna was holding the mare and Tom was trying to manage the stallion. Just as Tom put the plastic glove on the horse, a breeze came up. This flapping glove scared the horse to death and he leapt away from the business at hand and took off for the barn. Tom grabbed the lead shank trying to hold the horse back, but the horse had a head start and Donna said all she could do was stand there and hold that bewildered mare and look across the hill and see that horse out ahead of Tom racing back for the barn, and Tom with his big long legs taking giant steps yelling, "Whoa, damn it, whoa!"

As the saying goes "When you're hot you're hot" must be true because about this time it seemed everybody was calling up to do an interview. This included, believe it or not, *People Magazine*. It had first come into existence and was not the sensational magazine that we can consider it now. Newspaper writeups and our local Sunday supplement ran half of that issue about the lady from Simpsonville who was in the *Louisville Courier Journal*. Then there was a very nice article in *Sports Illustrated*, and a nice article in a magazine that failed later (it was just too fancy to last). There was *Southern Living* and inclusion in several books from England and one from France. Well, this was awfully gratifying. When I would talk to these people I would try to tell them that the women were becoming a force to be recognized in our business and that I was not at all a unique person because by that time many of these young people who had started out in equitation had worked their way into training. I think it was many years before women got their just rewards in showing horses. I guess that is the natural evolution of things. You not only have to prove it one time, you have to prove it over and over to make people accept something that is new in any sport. I do not think we were quite as revolutionary as the young lady who tried to get in the Citadel, but women were not in the majority at that time and maybe we never will be.

The honors were not always that great for me. I remember that in New York I would go up out of sheer boredom and sit in the press box, that is where my friend Alice would be, and we would talk in between events at the National Horse Show. There was a man there who wrote a horse show column for the *New York Times*. He was very nice that first time I had won. The judge that year was Bob Mannix who was an excellent teacher and we felt the same way about riding, so it was not unusual that he thought my rider was the best. The next year, when he brought his rider, naturally I thought his rider was the best, because there were not many really top riders at the time.

That third year I used to stay with Alice when I went up to the New York show. She said, "Helen I guess someone else is going to tell you about this, so I have kept this article for you, written by this New York Times writer." The jist of it was that my rider had won when Bob Mannix was the judge and the following year Bob Mannix's rider won when I was the judge. The implication was heartbreaking. I was absolutely furious and said, "Alice, can I make this columnist make an apology?" She said, "No, Helen, it is just an opinion. I do not think anybody will pay attention to it." But I paid attention to it and it stayed with me a long time. It really hurt to have my honesty questioned. After the next four years my riders had won the Championship at the Garden. This man was still up in the press box and I said, "Remember me? I am Helen Crabtree. I am the one you thought was playing favorites and I hope you noticed that my riders have won under a varying group of judges." Ordinarily the press was very good because our sport was rather new and for many years publications kept the horse shows on the society page. I think one of those reasons was the Illinois State Fair and one of those other shows referred to themselves as Society Horse Shows, so that is how we got stuck.

When we raised a beautiful black colt that looked like he was really going to take his place in the history of our breed, we maintained him as a stallion and I named him Harlem Globetrotter, not only because I admired the ability of these athletes and their entertainment value, but most of all, I thought maybe that name might get us pushed over to the sports page where we belonged.

In 1989 the UPHA introduced a new trophy for sportsmanship and I was the lucky first recipient of that award. Since I believed so much in the development of the young riders as good citizens as well as good riders, it was gratifying to me that this element of my involvement with horses and riders would be recognized. I think that anyone who has since won that award treasures it as much as anything they have ever received.

Another stride forward for the recognition of women in our sport was my inclusion in the very first Kentucky Horse Council representing the American Saddlebred. That was a wonderful experience and I met some really great people there. I stayed there several years until I got so very busy writing the book *Saddle Seat Equitation* that I just could not take the time out to drive over to Lexington to our meetings. I wrote a letter of resignation and asked if Redd Crabtree could take my place. I am sure they would have taken him anyway, but I wanted someone who was articulate and could fight for the American Saddlebred in a logical, effective way. I thought it was pretty classy when I said, "I am resigning because I have literary commitments." Now that was pretty good, I thought. Whether I impressed them or not, I do not know, but they were kind enough and smart enough to ask Redd to take that position for the American Saddlebred. He served on that committee for many years and did yeoman service for our breed, traveling to New York and all around. I would like to say right now that almost without exception the people who have risen to the top in the Association of American Saddlebreds have done so through their willingness and desire to promote our breed.

Randi Stuart Wightman, president of the ASHA is a very good example of this and those who have gone before her. These people knew that one does not work for personal honors but they work for the betterment of our breed. Not to quote too much of an obvious cliche, but they do put in their time and work extremely hard to promote our breed and get the recognition these wonderful horses deserve.

Several of my awards over the years remain constant in my memory. Almost without exception I remember the ones with the hilarious side to them. In 1984 I was inducted into the St. Louis Horse Show Hall of Fame. Charlie and I both had been named and were to have received that award together the previous year, but I had a roaring case of the flu, so Charlie went up and was inducted into the Hall of Fame. The next year I went. Gussie Busch of Anheuser Busch fame was a great horseman. I think those beautiful Clydesdales in their ads reflect what Gussie thought of horses and although he never had Saddle Horses, the closest was the harness horse his niece Sallie Busch Wheeler had. It was customary for Mr. Busch to drive the inductees into the ring in a coach and four. This was fine. I was sitting in there with Marion Brown, who was the actual recipient in 1984. We started up and Mr. Busch entered that small ring in Queeny Park. Not only was the ring small, but the entry gate was small too. I think there were only inches to spare on either side of that big coach and here he went top speed. I was hanging on for dear life because I thought at any minute we were going to crash. Later I was told by Ruth Pfeffer, who is president of that horse show that her experience with this was that Mr. Busch wanted her to sit up beside him on the box and he handed her a pill box and said, "Now keep these at hand because I may need them." They were nitroglycerine pills to be used in case of a heart attack. Here was this man practically exceeding the speed limit, ready to have a heart attack at any moment, and there we were sitting in the coach waiting either to be demolished or to be honored.

In 1975, much to my surprise I learned that MacMurray College was going to confer upon me the honorary doctorate of applied science. This was indeed a single honor. I was not only surprised, but was gratified. Here was an institution that realized that all of our talent was not in the seat of our breeches! This applies to so many people active in this show horse business today.

It was a happy time for me when my two sisters attended the ceremony at the college, both of them having been students there. Sadly my parents had died before this honor I received which I think would have meant so much to them. But at least I have this wonderful picture of the three Kitner sisters. I believe it is the only one we ever had taken together. One gets busy and does not live by the camera rather by the clock. I went up and was introduced and stood where I was to receive my honorary doctorate and move the tassel from one side of the mortar board to the other. Who should be reading the encomium but Waddy Applebee, my very first boyfriend when I was ten years old.

I will always remember that day with gratitude towards MacMurray College for honoring me, for being something I would have given my life for permission to do.

I will not bore the readers with a listing of all of these wonderful honors that I gained throughout my life, but if there is anyone still left who had anything to do with those awards I want to thank them all and say they have not been forgotten. Every nice thing that ever happened to me, and certainly the funny things that happened, stay so bright in my memory. While I cannot train anymore because of my eyesight and now I can barely see the horses in the ring, the memories are so important to me and always will be.

Famous ringmaster, Honey Craven; Helen Crabtree, judge; and "Whitey" Kahn, Judge at Eastern States, 1966.

"Admiral" Crabtree and ringmaster at Indio California show.

Helen Crabtree.

Helen Crabtree and pilot in search of Mt. McKinley, Anchorage, Alaska, 1981.

Graves in Russian cemetery, Alaska, 1981.

2
Judging After Move To Simpsonville

Judging was very important to me. After we moved to Simpsonville, we had become a very large stable. With the number of horses and the organization we had, it was easy for me to get away. Charlie did the teaching when I left to judge. I had assistants Debbie Wathen and Debbie Basham, as she was known then, was my first assistant. She is a wonderful horsewoman who had several World's Championships riding in equitation and on gaited ponies. She knew my ways and I always had assistants from that time on.

When I was out of town, Charlie, Redd, Charlie's assistant and my assistant worked the horses. We all trained the same. Charlie was a wonderful lesson instructor so when I left to judge he took over the teaching of the riders. They loved it. He had a little different approach. Theoretically, we were the same, but it was probably refreshing to hear something taught in a different way, although we were all saying the same thing.

The assistants never taught the riders. They trained my horses and the customers' equitation horses. Charlie and Redd, or both of them, worked the open horses and the amateur horses and ponies. So we had a wonderful set up. It did not take long for the number of riders to outgrow our accommodations, so we built a very big garage with living quarters above it. This could accommodate 16 riders who came to stay all summer and during vacation. We had two boys there, David Sheck and Eddie Lumia, who stayed in Redd's vacant cottage so it worked out well.

I loved judging. It was a very good thing for our business that I had an opportunity to see a lot of horses that we would otherwise have never seen. Those undiscovered stars that were not advertised for sale (which were always priced out of reason). As for the good prospects, if you really knew what you were doing one could find the hidden stars. Therefore, I bought a lot of horses from the entries I had seen in judging.

Judging was really fun. I judged all over America, from one coast to the other. From New York's Madison Square Garden to Del Mar, California right on the coast, down to South Africa and of course many shows in Florida. Even in Canada and then on up into Anchorage, Alaska. I went there, not to judge a show, but on the invitation of the Midnight Sun Riders Club of the Elmendorf Air Force Base. This was after the big earthquake in Alaska, so it made some of the travels rather interesting.

The rider I enjoyed the most was a very heavy set, very earnest woman in her mid-forties. She had a very heavy set, very earnest palomino mare that she rode. This woman would do everything I would say. She was not particularly adept at it, but she tried. The final day I was there, she came to me and said, "Mrs. Crabtree I have something I want to ask you. It has been such a desire with me all my life, I wonder if you could tell me if there is any chance that I could go to the lower 48 and open a stable?" Well, talk about scrambling for words! I thought, "This dear woman!" I told her, "Honey, had this been ten or 15 years ago I am sure it would have worked, but right now the teaching stables have proliferated so much and the competition is so great that anyone who has not established themselves in the show ring in the "lower 48, as you call it, would have a very tough time." So I got out of it that way.

The most fun of that clinic was not the clinic, but the fact that Sharon Lewis, mother of Ruth Anne Lewis went with me. We flew to Anchorage and took several trips around over the Seward Bay where the earthquake had been so terrible that the sea water had come in from all around. The trees were standing but they were all dead. The mountains were hovering right over your shoulder.

I remember being in a jeweler's shop in downtown Anchorage. I had wanted to get a real Alaskan gold nugget to make a tie tack for Charlie. As I was looking over the assortment, I glanced out in front of this store to see this very steep mountain rising straight up. I said to the clerk, "It is fascinating that everything is really close." She said, "Everything is close here but everything is far away." I said, "What do you mean?" and she explained, "You see that mountain, can you see the top of it?" I said, "Oh, yeah, I can see the top of it." She said, "If you were up there you would never be found." That was how hazardous and how dense the country around there was and how precipitous it was. The ravines were huge gashes in the earth. I suppose maybe the earthquake had added to the terror inspiring mountains around there, but it was a forbidding place to be.

Cars were another thing in Anchorage. Not too many people had them. It seemed everybody flew planes. As the old saying goes, "You can't get there from here;" Well, they couldn't! So one day I said, "We have looked and looked and tried to see Mt. McKinley and it is so shrouded in fog we haven't been able to see it." The man spoke up and said, "Let me take you up in my plane and perhaps it will be a good day and there will be a crack in the atmosphere and we'll be able to see it because it is well worth your seeing."

Sharon and I helped this man push his flivver plane out of the garage. I thought, what are we doing? Then I realized this is normal for these people. They do it all the time and I suppose a light little plane like this could land on an iceberg if it had to. So off we went and unfortunately we were not able to see Mt. McKinley. What he did do that was so fascinating, was flying so low over a large glacier that I had the feeling if I could have rolled down the window of this little plane, I could reach out and pick my own ice cubes. The glaciers were veined in brilliant dark blue. We asked our friend and pilot what these were. Was it the algae in the water or what? He said, "No, they are pressure veins, the movement of glaciers cause the pressure, colors the veins in the ice into that deep gorgeous blue." That is what I remember most about that particular trip to give the clinic.

I am not sure if the people who attended the clinic got as much out of the clinic as we did from the visit to Alaska. I did ask them how they went about riding when it got so dreadfully cold. Were the barns heated? They explained that there was a little heat in them but when it is that cold they go out in the middle of the night and with heavy mittens on their hands place them over the horse's eyes until the moisture melts and they could open their eyes.

It was an interesting experience to say the least. I have always wondered if that lady with the fat palomino mare ever realized her ambition to open a stable somewhere. For her sake, I hope she did, because I never saw anyone want anything as much as she did. The judging was a lot of fun, as I have said earlier in this book, because I got to see so many of the horses that later became ours. I judged a great many divisions. I am almost embarrassed to say I did this because I feel people sometimes think the more divisions you have, the less you know. It seemed I worked into this gradually. I had judged Saddle Horses and ponies. Then because of the driving exposure with the Hackneys, the Shetlands, and the fine harness horses, I had a card in Hackneys. Then the National Show Horses asked me to take a card. The Arabian people said, "We want you to judge us." I said, "Oh, I don't know whether I am qualified as I do not train Arabians." But what happened was that in the latter part of my teaching years I started taking guest riders and a great number of them were on Arabian horses.

One of my most hilarious judging experiences was when the Miniature Horse breed had just been developed. The most difficult thing about judging the Miniature Horse was to keep from calling them ponies, because really that is what they are, the descendants of the Shetland Pony used in the mines. When that became archaic, people were stuck with the animals, so very smart promoters in Tennessee thought they would develop a breed based on height and a few other points and call it a breed.

At the first show I went to, I said, "I don't know anything about these animals." They said, "Well Helen, you judge horses and you have judged all breeds." They don't dare say ponies, "We think you can do it and won't you please judge the show? It was in Murfeesboro, Tennessee. I went there and the first thing I saw was unforgettable. I had not yet parked my car and here came a station wagon. I thought, hey, that would be great. These things are so little they could fit into a station wagon. Well, let me tell you, they did. Only in this case the tack trunk was in the back of the wagon and the little horse was up in the front seat next to the driver. I never got over that and printed on the side of the station wagon it said: Every Yard a Farm. The following year I was asked to judge a futurity. This meant weanlings!

Then I got into the National Show Horses in the very beginning.

This breed is the combination of the Arabian and the American Saddlebred. They had very stringent rules. I have always believed in judging by the rule book, and if it says that an animal is a country pleasure horse and should trot below level, that is what they mean. I think it should. This business of buying an ex World Champion to turn it into a pleasure horse so somebody can get a blue ribbon is not my idea of what to do, although I see it done a lot. I am not complaining, let people do what they want. We are retired now, although I can still have an opinion. At the time, I was still fully in it and this was one of their early shows being held in Ohio.

I was there to judge. Remaining uppermost in my memory is the country pleasure class. I guess I did an adequate job judging. I didn't hear any comments aye or nay. So I considered myself to be doing pretty well since they knew more about this breed than I did. It was still really an invention then and everyone had opinions as to what they should be and a small committee had written the rules. There were more people who didn't believe in the rules than those who did.

So anyway, here came a country pleasure class and this horse was just beautiful. All the motion in the world, well ridden by an attractive lady. I thought, "why in the world didn't they read their own specifications?" The rules definitely said that the country pleasure horse should never trot above level. So, I dutifully tied the horse out of the money, this high-going elegant looking horse. Later on in the day I found that horse was undefeated in country pleasure! It was ridden by the wife of the chairman of the whole idea of the National Show Horses. That is when I decided that I did not want to judge them anymore if they were going to write the rules one way and judge another. I did not agree to ignore the rules popular or not, they wrote the rules and that is how I judged. I did judge their national finals.

In fact, because so many breeds held their national finals in Louisville from year to year, I judged the national finals of many breeds, the National Show Horse, the Arabians in equitation, and the Morgan Grand National which I judged several times.

I judged "Louisville" once and that's a heart breaker for me to stop, look back, and remember because I had a class to judge which was the most difficult thing I ever did. My right eye had been removed several years before, but I was certainly still very capable of judging. Many professionals, doctors, artists, all sorts of people manage with the sight of one eye because one has more than half vision. Macular degeneration had begun to set in my other eye, so I realized this was going to be my last season to judge and that I would just arbitrarily stop.

All of the riders knew I had lost my right eye, so I had to have the ringmaster stand on my right side. I told him to stand on that side and to keep riders off us because they think I can't see. The first way of the ring they're going to run us down if we make one step out of where we are standing. So we finally shooed them back to where they were supposed to be.

One of the preliminary classes will forever stick out in my mind. When one judges, the greatest thing that can happen is to have a fine group of horses and riders, that all the owners are good sports, that the best horses work the best, the worst horses work the worst, and that every decision is apparent.

In this class this was not the case. There was a young girl on a nice going pleasure horse, and a tall young man on a three-gaited show horse. Both in the same class and both riding exceedingly well. The rest of the class tied itself. Here were two top riders. I had always liked the individual test of changing horses. In order to judge changing horses, one must have a good memory. One judges the class not by how the riders look after the change of horses. That would be unfair. The quality of the horse would dictate what the rider looked like. One must remember how rider A rode the A horse as compared to how rider B rode the A horse, and vice versa.

I guess that was the tough thing for the audience to understand. Because when I asked these two riders to change horses, here was the boy who had been on the hot shot walk-trot and ridden it very well changing to the very nice pleasure horse. The young girl changing from a pleasure horse to what looked like a fancier horse than her own. I thought, ooh, I know what this audience is going to think. They are going to think this is terribly unfair that this boy has been taken off his fancy horse and put on a pleasure horse and this girl has been taken off her pleasure horse and put on something nicer. That was not the way I judged it, but the terrible part of it for me, was that these riders were so close. Both of them did a wonderful job, but I had to satisfy myself. I knew it was the last time I would judge Louisville and except for one show the last show of my judging career. I would live with that difficult decision the rest of my life.

To me the boy did not ride the pleasure horse as well as the girl had ridden that horse. He appeared to ride down to the horse. Of course the crowd had been screaming for the boy. That was back when few boys were riding. I just wanted to go to the microphone and say, "Let me explain this", but of course I could not. That was a very sad thing for me and it stuck with me much longer than all of the other wonderful classes with the great horses, great riders and the great things that I will always remember.

One of the lesser horse magazines had a woman editor and I won't describe her any further than to say she was neither qualified to comment on judging nor did she have the character to control her bias. The magazine came out with its State Fair coverage and said, "When the equitation came along all hell broke loose." That comment really hurt my feelings. I am sure I judged badly from time to time, but this was a very hurtful thing to do because it was at the very end of my judging career.

The final show I was to judge was the Morgan Grand National. I had judged this show so many times in the past, judging all of the divisions. They had several judges and I was judging equitation only. It was a very interesting show. It was my first introduction to Tom Caisse who will always remain very high in my book. He, along with Cecile Hetzel Dunn, were two of the judges. When not judging, the extra judges were invited to sit in center ring and partake of the finger sandwiches. So I was there and picked up a sandwich and was about to put it in my mouth when Tom Caisse jumped up and said, "Helen put down that sandwich!" I put it down. I thought maybe he saw a bug on it or something. Well, with that he grabbed my arm and Cecile grabbed the other one and they marched me out in the middle of the ring, handed me flowers and proceeded to say some of the nicest things that have ever been said about me and about my judging career.

What a wonderful thing for those two judges to do. The audience stood, cheered, and applauded. This took care of the nasty remark in the horse magazine. Shortly after that the judges left and walked up the ramp together back to the stabling area. Who should be standing beside this ramp but this nasty woman who had made the crack about me in her magazine. I looked over. I

Our bus group at Krueger National Park.

Rondavel.

Port Elizabeth Clinic.

Elephant charging.

Victoria Falls.

could not resist it, and said "Did you hear all hell break loose in there?" and she said, "I didn't write that; I never wrote that." Well, of course she did, but that was the only time anything nasty, that I knew about, had been written about my judging, for which I am forever grateful.

I think some of the most interesting things that have happened to me have happened in judging. Some are very funny, some are sad and all are nostalgic. One of the best parts of judging is the chance to see so many parts of the country that one would never observe and some in foreign countries as well, because I judged in South Africa and returned to give two clinics. Perhaps the first time I went to South Africa has to be one of the funniest experiences of my life.

I had been totally unaware that there was a Saddle Horse Registry in South Africa and it was rather a strong group. Their Grand Championship, which compares to the Kentucky State Fair here was held in Bloemfontein in their mid summer which would be in our mid winter. So when I was invited to judge, they also invited me to bring Mr. Crabtree along or any other friend I would like to bring with me. Well, of course it was Charlie I wanted to go with me and of course Charlie immediately said, "No." So this went on and I tried to attack the "no" from every angle I could think of without actual physical combat. Finally, it was the last day that he could get the passport and shots and everything else that would permit him to go to South Africa. For the second time in my life, I pitched a tantrum. I really cried and I begged and I hung around his neck and he got so disgusted that he said, "If you'll just leave me alone I'll go." So thus began one of the most interesting parts of our lives.

We found that Pep Peppiat, a good friend and trainer in Lexington, had judged the Bloemfontein show the year before. So I called him, which was a very wise thing to do, and asked him if there was anything we should know about the trip. He said, "Yes, Helen, be sure to go several days ahead of the show and go to Krueger National Park and other places that might be of interest to you, but don't miss the opportunity to see those wonderful things." So that was exactly what we did.

In due time we took off for O'Hare Field which was our departing point to go to South Africa. Now just before this I had gotten one of the most beautiful purchases I ever bought. It was a black twill wool pantsuit and it was an exact replica of an Admiral's suit. Peppiat said, "You'll be leaving in the wintertime when it's cold and arriving in South Africa when it's hot, so don't weigh yourself down with a lot of clothes." So I thought, here's the wonderful, thing, I can wear this outfit to travel in and then take off the coat when it gets hot or change the turtleneck sweater to a blouse or something lighter when we arrive.

This seemed like the logical thing to do so when we arrived at O'Hare our flight was called and we started down toward the long runway to board our plane. As we walked along there were people coming off of a plane and it was quite apparent that they were staring at us. I began to feel very uncomfortable and Charlie said, "Helen, those people are looking at us." I said, "Oh Charlie I don't think so." He said, "They are." I looked back and here was this man completely turned around walking backwards still staring at us.

Then it dawned on me that the week before our departure, President Johnson had appointed two lady Admirals, which was revolutionary at the time. Well, it was obvious the proletariat thought they were looking at one of the lady Admirals. Of course I had on my ever present turtleneck which if anybody knew regulation apparel for the Navy would realize that a white shirt and black tie was the proper attire, but that suit was so authentic that I'm sure that's what people thought.

The trip itself was tremendously long. I have never been able to recall the tail numbers that identify planes, but this plane was the largest of its time. We were taking a direct flight from Chicago to the Northwest coast of Africa so it had to be a big one and it was. We managed pretty well. It was very tiring but we found out that on the seats we could put the armrest down and sort of take turns lying in each others laps to relax our muscles and get through the long nights. We did finally arrived in Rwanda, Angola on the Northwest coast of Africa. This was a stop that did not permit anyone to get off the plane. It was against regulations. I was so excited about being in a foreign continent that I couldn't stand it, so I pleaded with the flight attendant to let me walk down the steps and asked her to let down the steps and I explained, "Your idea of disembarking from the plane is to step off. Now I won't step off-you hang around my waist and I will bend over and put my hand down on the ground because I want to say I was in Angola." She laughed and said, "Well, O.K., we can do that." So I can honestly say I was in Angola albeit it was only my hand, but at least I did touch the ground.

Then, in short order we took off and flew to Johannesburg and that was a fascinating experience. As we lowered our altitude for about a hundred miles we saw something that resembled big gold colored rectangular piles of dirt. We knew Johannesburg was famous for the gold mines. I think most people did not know they stretched miles and miles before you got into the city. These symmetric rectangles were the tailings from the gold mines. The vein was very strong and it was not concentrated just in the city as we had thought.

Some of the wild animals we could not identify but you can surely identify a giraffe from an airplane. It was in a high state of excitement when we got off the plane in Johannesburg. We spent the night there. The next morning we took a flight to Krueger National Park and Animal Reserve where our stay had been arranged through the South African government, so we were very privileged. We did not realize how privileged we were until we got our accommodations and the little dwellings were replicas of native huts which were called rondavels. They were round buildings with a pointed straw thatched roof. One of those huts had air conditioning, and guess who got it. We did, and we were thankful because it was very hot.

The next day we were introduced to our driver who drove a Volkswagen bus which carried five people in addition to the driver. He was a fascinating man in his southern khakis, his little khaki cap and the knee socks. He was an Australian who had served in World War II as had Charlie, and the husband of the Austrian couple who were very nice. He was an Austrian film director. His wife revealed they came to South Africa quite often trying to keep up with the frequent changes in the government. Our fifth person was a German communist who was just absolutely awful. This man was a real pain because he had been in World War II. He claimed that he did not believe in it and that he didn't think Hitler was right at all, but he had been dragged in as a 17-year-old boy, which none of us of course believed. When he did talk to us it was in a very degrading way and said that the Germans knew everything and the Austrians and the Americans knew nothing.

As time wore on his reference to the war was really getting to our driver and it looked as if they were about to come to blows. He kept telling us how bright the Germans were and how dumb the Americans were. Finally I could stand it no longer and said, "Well, you may be right, but we've just put a man on the moon. Now, when you get one up there I'll give you my address and you be sure to let me know." That cooled him off a bit, but from that time on it was very touchy.

One evening we went out to a place in the forest that served dinner. This was a beautiful experience as we sat on the verandah. Waiting for our time at the table we looked down a broad expanse of a stream that headed right into a rising moon.

The trees in South Africa are not the same color of green as the trees here. Everything was a blue green, a thrilling color. The leaves were separated, large, and fat so that when the moon came up it silhouetted these trees along the stream. I shall never forget this sight. It was one of the most beautiful sights of my life.

While we were in eating, we noticed that our driver and the German had gone outside and fearing the worst we all rushed outside. They were squaring off. We separated them and told the German if he didn't behave we were going to have the authorities eject him from the park. From then on he did quiet down. He spent his entire time taking pictures. I don't think he saw anything in the park, but he got a lot of pictures.

The animals in the park were fascinating, but what I feared most was seeing something being eaten. The animals that we saw all had their bellies full and were resting. Like the lion pride we saw lying quietly under a tree just looking at a group of wildebeest, their main source of food, calmly walking by within charging distance. Our driver explained they were safe as long as the lions bellies were full. Now when they get empty and they're hungry then they go out and look for food. Then some poor wildebeest would be the next dinner for those lions.

We saw all kinds of animals there. I think the most entertaining were the monkey and the ape. We were told to be very careful about them and keep the van windows rolled up because they would try to jump in and grab anything we had. They learned that people carried snacks and that sort of thing with them and they could really bite and be pretty tough. Also we learned the king of the jungle was not the lion, it was the elephant. They were to be the most feared. We saw a few in the distance and we wisely viewed them that way.

One had to be careful, we found, because if one admired anything South Africans had they wanted to give it to you. So you had to be careful not to admire something of embarrassing value because I'm just afraid you would find it in your knapsack before you got out of there.

In short order we were in Bloemfontaine and the horse show began. It was interesting in that it was on a show ground that had a big grandstand, double tiered wooden, like our grandstands at the race track and I guess this was a race track of sorts, except instead of a race track they had a ring for hunters and jumpers. In our area this would be described as an outside course.

The novel thing for the Saddle Horses was that they showed on a cinder track that went around this entire hunter course. When the horses first came in, I realized the track was very hard. I could hear the shoes go "clop". I thought, "Oh, good grief we'll never get through a class because all these shoes are going to fall off." I don't know how long the clinches on those shoes were, but I do know that we didn't lose a shoe the entire show.

There were about two horses that were really quite outstanding but it was so hard to judge them because they would just disappear out of sight. I felt like the Lone Ranger standing up on a hill —peering out over the vast west trying to find an Indian, because every once in a while there would be no one in front of me.

Then the announcer would say, "Here comes Johann, now everybody clap for Johann." Then when somebody else would come by he would ask the spectators to clap and cheer for each one. The audience replied with great enthusiam. The announcer was a cheerleader of sorts. This was disconcerting. At first I thought, "Oh, dear, this man is picking out his friends, but he did it for everybody in the class.

When the horses lined up in the saddle classes which were first, and after I turned in my card, the ringmaster would gather up the ribbons. The ribbons were not like our rosette ribbons. They were garland ribbons that wrapped around the horse's neck like a necklace, rather than handing it to the rider or hanging it on the bridle.

The announcer would announce when the ringmaster first went out, "Now first place will go to..." and he would start to walk toward one horse and rider and the crowd would go "Aah" and he'd jump back shaking his head and aim towards another entry. This was a lot of fun because the audience didn't really clap for the exhibitors when they lined up, but they had a barrel of fun, clapping and yelling when they thought the horse they liked was going to get the ribbon. Finally they would hand out the ribbons and the class would be over. I had become rather used to this.

Then came a fine harness class. The expense of purchasing the harness and buggy in this country, as the duty would be almost 100 percent, added to import, made it difficult to afford. I remember there was a shiny new Houghton, a lovely mare turned out in A-1 condition but the mare could not step over a corn cob. The overall appearance was just grand. She was pretty as a picture. Then I walked up and here was a little horse kind of short in the neck, big in the head, no mane and her rear end completely covered by an enormous full false tail which was not quite up in the crupper like it should have been. No wonder this entry impressed me in an odd manner as I was looking at a horse I'd previously judged in the three-gaited class.

However, this mare could trot as high as her chin. When I closely looked at the buggy the high going horse was pulling, I realized that the shafts were gas pipes and that there were four bicycles wheels and the rest of the buggy was made of sheet metal. I was stunned and it tickled me so that I happened to look up in the stands at Charlie and then I looked down very quickly so as not to laugh, but it was really laughable. It was not to make fun of anyone, but it was such a departure from what we were used to.

I later found out that people did this because they could not afford the duty on the buggy so they made their own out of something. If it broke, they could take a welding iron and put it back together. This made a lot of sense to me and after that first encounter it was not uncommon for me to see such buggies.

That entire show was an experience. We were entertained every evening. The people were just wonderful. When the show was over we had been invited by a saddle club in Port Elizabeth, which was several hundred miles south of Johannesburg. It was Mr. Bolton who invited us on behalf of the club. I believe he took *Saddle & Bridle Magazine* and had read about the doings of Crabtree Stables, and the fact that outside riders came in and studied with us and they were responsible for inviting the two of us to come down to give a clinic to the Port Elizabeth Saddle Club. Charlie was rather reluctant to do this. I do not know why, he is one of the best clinicians I have ever heard. He has always been very modest about that. The two of us spent two entire days giving the clinic. The people were anxious to learn and were very grateful for everything we did. The club was doing a tremendous service to improve and popularize the American Saddlebred in South Africa. The Bolton family sent their son and daughter the following year to ride with our stable that show season. Mr. Bolton later came to the United States and became very good friends with the Willimons and did business with them. Our time with the Port Elizabeth Saddle Club was very interesting and a lot of fun. Anytime you can get a group of people together who want to learn, it inspires you to do your very best. We almost wore the people out with the sessions. We just kept going.

From Port Elizabeth we went to Durban, which is on the Indian Ocean. It was a shoe manufacturing town. We were told there was a new park which was Addo Elephant Park that we should visit. We had been provided a car. This thrilled Charlie to death because it was a right hand drive which he had not driven before. I sat beside him trying to remind him when necessary to keep on what was, to us, the wrong side of the road. When we arrived we went to a couple of museums and to the elephant park.

I must say this was a disappointment. When we drove into Addo we only saw the back end of a scruffy ostrich racing away from us. That was about all we saw until we got to a place where there were some huge fences put up constructed with steel cables and huge timbers. The timbers were square and larger than telephone poles and looked very sturdy. I had a camera and I wanted to get a picture of the elephants which we had just seen winding through the forest. This was just the time our park brochure had said the elephants would gather there to drink.

Wanting to get a picture I kept getting closer and closer trusting the fence, not heeding Charlie's warning, "Now Helen, don't get so close." Well I should have listened because I got a little too close. The next thing I knew, this huge elephant had charged the fence and he was going a mile a minute and bounced off of that fence.

I had learned my lesson in a hurry. I ran back to a raised observation post. A pile of dirt wide enough for several people to stand on. When I got up there I was standing next to a tough looking man and the rudest little girl I ever saw. She was running and screaming. You could not hear anything. I tried to stay away from her where you could see the elephants, but that was an impossibility.

I thought, "Here I am thousands of miles away from home and this is my only chance to strike a terribly rude child," an impulse I had successfully swallowed for many years. As I got ready to draw my hand back, perhaps sensing this, the father turned to me and said, "Why Mrs. Crabtree what is a famous horse lady doing in Addo Elephant Park?" I nearly fainted. How did this man know who I was? The only explanation Charlie and I could imagine was that he had attended the Bloemfontein Horse Show or the clinic in Port Elizabeth. That is about as close as I ever came to attacking a student and I was never tempted again. This really made an impression on me. The man attributed my shocked look to being recognized and I knew in my heart he had saved the day for me, no matter what I thought of him.

From there we went back to Johannesburg. No matter where you went in South Africa you went back to Johannesburg or landed in Johannesburg. We went to Rhodesia and to Salisbury the capital. As we got off the plane, much to our surprise we were being paged over the outside loud speaker and went in and heard the distressing news that Charlie's middle brother had passed away.

Being in South Africa, the planes only flew twice a week at that time and there was absolutely no chance to get back for the funeral. There was nothing to do but stay. Charlie made the necessary phone calls to express his extreme sorrow. It is strange since we travel so little out of the states that this would happen while we were out of the country with no chance at getting back.

What we had seen so far in South Africa had been top drawer - the dignitaries, the high living and the beautiful homes. We knew there was a middle class. We asked to go to this man's house who was a former employee of Ashland Oil Company in the United States. When his boss heard, through Mr. Stuart of Skelly Oil Company that we were going to be traveling nearby he suggested giving us this man's name because he lived in a suburb of Salisbury and would love to entertain us. So we spent a night with him and it was certainly a different lifestyle than what we had been treated to. The people were very nice and the living was very simple. We wanted to go into the rural farming area because we were good friends with Cynthia Wood and Dale Duffy of California. Dale had said, "I want to go back to South Africa. There is a gentleman there who had a farm in the Transvaal and I'd like to take you out to it." We met Dale and went out into the country where we met this nice farmer and his wife. One of the decorations on their front porch was an elephant tusk. Somewhere in our belongings there is a picture of Charlie trying to lift this elephant tusk. He thought he would just lift it up for a picture. Strong as Charlie is, he could not budge the tusk.

The next day, the man whose farm covered the acreage like the Texas farms, took us out for a drive in his pickup truck. I sat up front with him. Dale and Charlie were seated on wooden chairs in the back of the truck. I have never been very good with math or cared that much about it and I looked down to the speedometer and it registered 90. We were going to throw these people right out of the back I thought. Well, it was kilometers instead of miles, but it was still quite fast. The main things he wanted to show us were these small kangaroo-like animals who lived in the ground in burrows much like the prairie dog colonies in our western states.

The electricity on the farm was provided by a generator which ran until nine o'clock at night. I, being a terrible insomniac, was accustomed to reading myself to sleep. At nine o'clock when we went to bed the lights went out. I asked if they had a flashlight and I remember reading myself to sleep with it.

Then the next day we got back to Salisbury where one other person and the two of us went in a small plane to Victoria Falls. For some reason no one else wanted to go because the tribes were fighting and Victoria Falls was the line across which they were shooting at each other. It was a rather adventurous thing to do. I told them, "If I am going to be shot, I'd just as soon be shot in South Africa as in North America." Charlie said, "Well, let's go," and it was a marvelous sight. We flew over the falls and landed. From there we went to a small restaurant near the falls which only had three diners in it, those three being Charlie, Helen and the other passenger. After lunch the restaurant allotted us rain gear, because in order to see the Falls from the front we had to walk about a mile into the dense rain forest which obviously was the result of the Falls and the massive Zambezi river rushing to the Ocean. The restaurant proprietors sternly warned us to stay on the Rhodesian side of the river as the Zambians would shoot anyone who ventured to their side.

We came down through the forest, saw the Falls from there and got a paddle steamer that took us up the Zambezi River to see the hippopotamus colonies sunbathing in the middle of the river and that was the last of our big adventures. Having convinced ourselves that no native would want to shoot someone from Simpsonville, Kentucky, it was only on the return flight to Salisbury that the obvious question of, "How would anyone know that we were from Simpsonville, Kentucky?" occurred to us.

After that we went back to Johannesburg and flew from there to Zurich, Switzerland. We stayed in Zurich which is really a beautiful place, and we traveled to one of their famous ski resorts. We had no ideas of skiing, neither of us being skiers. We did take the ski lift which was a huge thing that accommodated 20 or 25 people up to the top of Mount Rigi. The view and magnificence was something one would never forget. This is rather a quiet existence but what we did later that night was out of character for the prosaic Crabtrees. We went back to our hotel and I must say that the food there was delicious and one of the main things was the economical price of their caviar. We felt like royalty, stuffed with caviar.

Then what should we do? That afternoon walking down the street, Charlie had said, "Oh look they're advertising a dirty movie with an arrow pointing downstairs." I said, "Oh, good Lord." That night he asked, "Is there anything you want to do?" I said, "Now look, I'm like any other wife in the country who's never done this. I have always had a curiosity about X-rated movies." I said, "Let's try that movie, we do not have to stay, I'm just curious about how those things operate."

I felt like someone else skulking into the doorway that opened to a flight of stairs and into a darkened room. We got there just as the movie started and I looked around at the weird people seated there. It was enough to give you the shakes and I was not sure I wanted to stay. Charlie said, "Now you wanted to come here, now watch." So we watched about five minutes and I said, "Now, isn't this enough?" He said, "Yes," so we left. This is my shameful admittance as to what went on in beautiful Switzerland.

We flew from there into London. This was rather disappointing because we had not been advised as to the right tours to take. All of the things we missed we had wanted to see. We had signed up to see the Tower of London. Being a country girl from Illinois, I thought the Tower of London would look something like a silo. I hated history, geography or anything else that had to do with that sort of thing when I was in school. Of course the Tower of London is an actual city. I did get a little tired of all the beheaded wives of all the kings. The crown jewels were awe-inspiring and the fact they were so big they did not look real. Our most memorable thing was riding on the double-decker buses, and it was so much fun.

We were there the two nights. One day the most exciting thing that happened to me was when we got back to our room. We were staying in the famous old Grosvenor House. We went up to our room. The twin beds must have come from the army. They were extremely narrow. The covering was a down comforter that wasn't much wider than the bed and kept slipping. I looked frantically for safety pins, anything to hold my covers in place. I spent the entire night retrieving the covers off the floor.

The next morning I thought, "I'm going to take a bath, no showers, just a bath." I went in and there was this big long thing that looked like a horse trough sitting on a tall base and it was huge. I disrobed and was waiting for the tub to fill up. I thought it was too dark in there so I punched the button on the wall. Well, it was the bell for the butler and I heard this surprised voice outside say, "I didn't ring for you." It was Charlie. Fortunately, he had answered the door or the man may have come into the bathroom. I don't know if it was a safely device in case somebody tried to drown in this fool horse trough.

The next morning, we boarded the plane for our return by way of New York then home. We had an experience that I would not trade anything for. I am so thankful Charlie went with me because experiences like that, particularly the first time, should be shared.

Second Trip

Two years later I got a call from the Bloemfontein group asking for me to return to conduct a clinic. I had enjoyed my previous trip so much and knew my way around a little bit, so I was glad to return. At that time I had been visiting with Marsha Shepherd at Bobbin Hollow Farm in Mass. She was then married to an airline pilot. When I mentioned this trip I said, "Marsha why don't you go with me" she said, "I can get the family airline rate and I would love to go."

When it was time for me to go, I checked on my passport and realized it had expired. I did not know what to do so I called my congressman Mitch McConnell. He said,"I'll get it for you and I will get it to the gate where you depart." I was going to meet Marsha there and I had told the South Africans that I was bringing this gorgeous blonde lady who is a very wonderful horse women, you'll be so happy to meet her. Of course they were in a high state of excitement to meet her.

When it came time to go, Marsha did not arrive. I had gathered up my passport so I was a legal passenger. When I entered the plane, I noticed a large portion of the plane had been boarded up with just raw boards. This was when the apartheid problem in South Africa was really heating up. I wondered what in the world was going on. They are carrying something on this plane. This was my own idea, it is not an accusation. It was just a wild idea in my own mind that this plane was carrying contraband.

It did greatly reduce the seating capacity, which explained Marsha's absence. We were all really crammed in. My seat was at the very end of the section directly underneath the movie. If you want to sleep under a movie in that first row, there is just no way to do it. Plus the fact there was this young couple with a baby who were constantly changing its diapers seated directly behind me; which in those close confines was not a pleasant atmosphere to be in. This time I had taken a raincoat with me and I thought I am going to try to get away from all this stuff to get some sleep on the floor and snuggle against the wall right under the movie which by that time had stopped.

I no more than got down and situated or thought I was, only to discover that I was lying not six inches away from the diaper bag.

Well that did it! I went down the aisle to the flight attendant and said "Look," explaining the situation, "This is impossible, I have got to get some sleep. These people are nice enough, but they have this baby that wears diapers and since you do not throw diapers out the window I am just stuck." She kindly found me a couple of seats, one which the arm folds down, and said, "Here, come up and you can lie down on these two seats." So I did.

Just in that short space of time, since my last visit the SAS, which was the airline for South Africa, had built their own little landing strip out in the ocean which absolutely boggled my mind. I'm easily boggled as you may have discovered but not being a student of oceanography I assumed the ocean was miles deep everywhere, not realizing there were peaks that were rather close to the surface such as was the case here. This was out in the middle of the ocean. We landed there on the island which was named SAS. After that terrible night, I felt grungy and wanted to take a shower and brush my teeth, just do something to make myself feel better and more presentable.

We entered the little primitive sort of waiting room where we sat while they refueled the plane. In the restrooms there were obvious signs that said Do Not Drink the Water-This Is Sea Water. I had carried my toothbrush in a little carrying case off the plane. This is how alert you are after a night dodging diapers and everything else. I proceeded to whip out my tootbrush and stuck it under the tap loaded with toothpaste and put it in my mouth. It was the worst taste one could ever experience by brushing your teeth with sea water! I had no way to get this taste out of my mouth. Finally I rinsed my mouth as best I could and rushed out of the bathroom. The first of the personnel I could see, I asked if they had any plain water to wash out my mouth. She said, "What did you do, brush your teeth?"

Shortly we were in the air again on our way to Johannesburg. I was met at the plane by the officials of the South African Saddle Horse Society. They were extremely proud to have found an antique auto. It was a four-seat convertible and drew a lot of attention wherever we went. As we entered the show grounds we stopped by the grandstand and I looked up to see a bed sheet with flowers painted and the inscription in big black letters, "We love our Helen." These people were like that. It was not just me, it was anyone who came to South Africa to support the Saddlebreds. It is impossible to match their hospitality. They are truly wonderful people.

The clinic was successful in every aspect because they had people enter of all ages, not just young people. It included riders on Three and Five-Gaited horses and Fine Harness horses (how to fit the harness and proper driving techniques). We had a marvelous three days of clinic. On the final night they had a banquet. They said, "Mrs. Crabtree will you come forward? We have something for you," I thought now they're going to give me South Africa and the man proudly held up a green man's sport coat. He said, "This is the official jacket of the members of our organization and we are making you an honorary member of our Saddle Horse Society." It was one of the nicest things that ever happened. I thought this was a man's jacket they are putting around my shoulders and I feel like I have just won the Masters' Golf Tournament. That was the way people did things there.

I went to the capital, Pretoria. This was a very interesting place. It was the center of the diamond district. I went down to the Kimberly Diamond Mine. I could have gone down into the shaft where they were digging the diamonds, but I wasn't too thrilled at going too far underground. We went to a certain level where we saw the diamonds being separated from oily black mud in a sluice box. Surprisingly, a good days crop of diamonds could fit in the palm of one's hand.

The Jacaranda trees that lined the avenue that went into the capital were in full bloom and were just beautiful. I remember that and the lovely people with whom I stayed because when the clinic was over I had two days to wait until the next plane. The flight back home was into New York and a very dull flight from New York into Louisville.

I can still remember parts of those trips that I thank the whole industry for letting me be a part of, and getting in on the ground floor of the interest in horsemanship or equitation whichever you want to call it that has evolved into the international every other year competition. So little did we know what we were doing when we started out, but it developed into this great competition which is a benefit to the Association here and the Saddle Horse Industry in South Africa.

Four years later I made a final trip with Bud and Cindy Willimon of Simpsonville, Kentucky. Bud had arranged to supply used tack to the people of South Africa through Mr. Bolton, and at his invitation the Willimons invited me along which was fun because I wanted to see it again and see the people. We flew directly by way of SAS into Johannesburg where we hired a car and did a lot of driving. We went on to Port Elizabeth and stayed at the Bolton's home. Bud gave a shoeing clinic and I worked again with a few riders from previous visits.

From there we drove to Cape Town. Our adventures along the way included stopping at an ostrich farm. Cindy didn't back away from anything. When they offered her the chance to ride an ostrich, she did so. I had been offered the chance to ride an ostrich when I judged at Bloemfontein. They said it was customary for the judges, but at that time women judges wore skirts nothing like the pants suits. I could see myself hanging around an ostrich's neck with my skirt blowing up in the wind. I politely declined that time. Here was a time when I could have done it. Cindy being so brave, she took the ride. The most daring thing I did was to stand on an ostrich egg and have my picture taken.

We stopped on the way to Cape Town at a lodge. As we went outside, the stars looked as if you could just pick them right out of the sky. This was the most incredible sight. What I questioned was if this was an astronomical phenomenon or the time of year? The Willimon's and I have talked about this midnight blue sky and the huge stars that seemed to hang within reach. It was absolutely awe-inspiring.

We drove on to Cape Town. There was a huge cave right in the Cape. This was after the loss of my right eye. I felt that the darkness of the cave would be too much so I decided not to go down in the cave and instead waited outside.

When Bud and Cindy came back, Cindy was as green as lettuce. I had never seen a human being so green. We concluded she had gotten a bad hamburger at lunch. We later learned that this was Cindy's first indication that she was pregnant with Dakota, who is now quite well known in the horse business and one of our grand young riders. Cape Town was truly an experience and the Willimon's were so very kind to include me. If I did not thank them adequately then, I want to do so now.

Charlie, "Dr. Livingston, I presume."

Bud and Cindy Willimon with Helen on South African trip.

Cindy Willimon riding an ostrich.

Reagan Inaugural Parade

Shortly after the 1980 Presidential election, we received a call from the President-elect Ronald Reagan's chairman of the inaugural parade inviting the American Saddlebreds to march in the parade.

I asked how many horses and riders were needed and he told me that eight was the general number. "Can you accommodate sixteen?", I asked. I was assured that we could bring that number, as Reagan was most anxious to have our breed in the parade.

A lover of horses, Mr. Reagan had been very disappointed when he had been turned down by whoever his staff first contacted, with the excuse that the show horses would never tolerate being sandwiched in between high school marching bands. "Please tell Mr. Reagan that we will be there with 16 horses ridden by young riders and one very proud teacher and trainer." In order to really prove the versatility of our breed, I borrowed the very handsome five-gaited stallion Light Speed from Mrs. Jean Nalley of Louisville for me to ride. I tried to get riders and mounts from areas representing all of the United States.

What a honor this was! The ASHA had a beautiful banner so we added two more girls in proper show attire to head our group.

Remembering the poor poet Robert Frost, who became so cold at John Kennedy's inauguration that he was unable to speak, I cautioned everyone to dress warmly. We even invested in electric socks and any device short of bourbon to keep our riders comfortable.

I had bought a gross of granola bars to feed the riders when we assembled at the mall to await the beginning of the parade. We had not fed the horses that morning and I had asked all riders not to eat or drink. Not only were we determined to be the most handsome group, but the most sanitary!

As luck would have it, that inaugural was the warmest day in history. We all turned off our electric socks and proceeded to wait. The parade was held up a long time because outgoing President Carter was orchestrating the news of the hostage release in Iran. Yes, there is more than one way to rain on a parade!

Finally we were on our way with marching bands ahead and behind our magnificent group. As we headed up Pennsylvania Av-

Reagan Inaugural Parade, January, 1981.

Reagan Inaugural Parade, January, 1981.

enue, I was so overcome with patriotism and pride in our group that the particular moment rushes back overtime. I think of that day and our participation in history on the horses that almost missed the parade.

1981 Salon Du Cheval Et Du Poney

The French Minister of Agriculture called in the early summer of 1981 to invite the three Crabtree's to come to Paris as the guests of the French Government.

The occasion was the production of the Salon Du Cheval Et Du Poney. This was a showcase of every breed of horses to be held in Paris during ten days in December.

It was impossible for Redd, Charlie and me to leave our business, which involved over 100 head of horses.

The minister remembered our family from the New York National Horse Show in Madison Square Garden. In fact he pointed out that he had especially admired a chestnut mare I had ridden to win the Championship. Of course, in my usual impulsive way, I told him that I had won a few times with a bay gelding. I had completely forgotten winning with Cathy Noble's grand gaited mare, Stonewall's Sound of Music! Which proved the point that the young riders competing in the equitation finale took precedence over all else.

Consequently, I asked if I might bring three five-gaited and three three-gaited horses with young riders. The number of us who flew to Paris increased to twenty. I had gotten horses from Kentucky, Idaho and North Carolina. One of the horses could not make the flight, so it was a group of three five-gaited horses and two walk-trots.

Knowing that it is very hard for Europeans to understand our high-headed, high-stepping breed, I was rather apprehensive about our first exhibition. I had learned from T.V. that whistling at European sporting events is a sign of derision. Knowing this, I asked that we simulate both a three-gaited and a five-gaited class and I would act as judge.

As the first horses entered, I asked the French ringmaster to explain to the audience that unlike the jumpers, our horses liked it when the audience applauded and whistled! So we cut any possible detractors off at the start, and before the week was over, the area around our exhibit was so deep with curious spectators that the grooms could barely get in the stalls.

My memories of the sloping avenue winding through the Arc De Triomphe, with the yellow headlights and red tail lights glowing like a shimmering ribbon, remains vivid to this day.

The Louvre Museum was marvelous, but the first view of the "Winged Victory of Samothrace" on the platform leading to the main stairs, evoked such a burst of emotion that I could hardly climb the stairs. The happy circumstance that the visit to the Louvre was on my 65th birthday added gratitude to my awe.

Chartres Cathedral was heroic with its stone entry worn down by the knees of worshipers over the centuries, and made us feel somewhat gauche with our bicentennial. The magnificent rose window and the sandstone carved stations of the cross live forever in my memory. The ruins of the Roman Aqueducts on the way brought to life the phrase: "All Gaul is divided into three parts" - a phrase that had meant absolutely nothing to me before.

I love the French National Anthem and, remembering the native tongue, I taught all who did not know the French words.

All of our horses and riders were stars, but Mary Lou Gallagher and her unbelievably high-going Lad O'Shea brought down the house every night.

On the last morning I went out to Longchamps race course. The ground fog barely revealed the horse barns behind the track. Graceful elms, tall in the soft morning light, crowned the scene that lives in my mind just as vivldly as it took my breath 15 years ago

The horses and people returned tired but well and happy. We had memories to last a lifetime.

3
Achievements

I went up to the Simpsonville post office to get the mail. I used to read the mail in the post office so I could throw away the trash which was two-thirds of what mail consisted of, then and now. In glancing through the mail, what to keep, what to throw away, I saw this envelope and it was from A.R.I.A.. At that time of year every organization that needed money was sending out what I call begging letters, so I looked at the A.R.I.A. which meant the Metropolitan Opera to me and I thought are they going so broke that they have to seek contributions? I opened up the envelope- then I had to laugh. It was from an organization I did not know existed, in fact it was a very new organization called the American Riding Instructors Association located in Cherry Hills, New Jersey and in its second year, having its annual convention. It was bestowing upon me the honor of Master Instructor — what a wonderful honor.

I found out this was quite a large organization with very few being Saddle Horse instructors. These people were interested in any phase of good horsemanship. I really enjoyed meeting the group because they were very interested in an explanation of Saddle Seat, not as a form, that was simply an appearance, but the nuts and bolts of the whole thing. A mental approach to the control of the horse not only through the body but mainly through mentality. To them it seemed that the horses were very high-headed with extreme action, obviously very different from the hunter and jumpers.

The talks were well received and we had wonderful discussions back and forth over the next three days. That was one of the nicest surprises I ever got. If it were not so difficult for me to travel now I would enjoy their annual convention. As it is, I might wind up in some elevator in some hotel and not be able to see the proper floor. I might go up and down for an hour before anybody found that crazy lady who was playing with the elevator.

George Morris, Helen Crabtree, Sally Swift and Denny Emerson, American Riding Instructors Assn., early '90s.

Alan Balch and Helen Crabtree.

Lifetime Achievement Award, Jimmy Williams and Helen Crabtree.

I had known Jimmy Williams for many years. We inherited Lindy Patrick from him. She was predominately a hunt seat rider, a western rider and a dressage rider. She rode a horse just about any way you could ride it and she had won the finals in all of those seats except the hunt seat. Strangely enough, she had a tough mare to ride. Lindy came to us hoping to win the Saddleseat AHSA class which she did. So we knew Jimmy and greatly respected him because you mention his name on the West Coast and it was like you were speaking of a deity and he was deserving of this high respect because he concentrated mainly on the hunters and jumpers and the western horses where he was extremely superior. He was such a consummate horseman that the Saddle Horse people went to him when they had a problem. He was a great man on how to bit a horse, what a horse was thinking, and how to think along with a horse. The AHSA instituted a new award, it was the Jimmy Williams Award named because he was the first recipient. The trophy was a very large shiny mahogany board with a full size silver cowboy hat hanging on one corner, then a silver border on the bottom of the trophy showing Jimmy on the various types of horses he trained. Charlie had gone to get the mail at our little post office and when I came to the stable later he said, "Helen have you seen your telegram?" and I said, "What telegram?" and he said, "The one over there on the desk." Then I said, "Do they still send telegrams?" and he said, "Helen, go read that telegram." Well I did and was absolutely thrilled to read that the AHSA, in appreciation of my years of work, had named me the recipient of the Jimmy Williams Lifetime Achievement Award.

What more could anyone ask than to be honored in this fashion for a lifetime of service and enjoyment. I do not think I have ever been so grateful. I read on and it was a very nice personal message by the president of the AHSA and what he thought of the recipient. The final sentence of the telegram said, "And we can think of no one more desiring of this award than you, Mrs. Crabtree." What a hoot that was! I laughed until the tears ran down my face, obviously it was a typo error but one of the funniest ones I ever read. I had not fully recovered from that until Nancy Crabtree called and said, "In the USA Today there is something about you." At that time I was 75 years old and it was not bothering me a bit. I was active in everything, still showing, still training. So it was just like another day in my life.

Nancy came down with the sports section of the newspaper. In the colored section across the top, highlighting some points of what is happening that day was about me. This brief mention said the AHSA was honoring me with a Lifetime Achievement award to Helen K. Crabtree of Simpsonville, Kentucky. Then it said Crabtree, 80, well I do not remember what else it said but I thought 80! I am thrilled to death to get to 75 and here they were calling me eighty. The award had to be the highlight of participation in riding and training horses and riders, no matter what breed. To be honored by not just people in your own area of the AHSA, but to have all seats honor you was more than I ever expected.

There were three honorees that night. The first was a young boy who was honored for his good sportsmanship and good riding. He was a young teenager who overcame his shyness with just the thrill of the honor. His talk was extremely interesting. Then came a lady, and she too was overcome with the honor. In fact, she started thanking people and could not find any place to stop so she thanked people for ten minutes. We all loved her because we knew that this was just a manifestation of what being honored by the AHSA meant.

Then came my turn. Alan Balch, whom I had met several years ago when he was manager of the Santa Anita Horse Show, which I frequently judged, introduced me. He had called me to tell me I was going to get this award and to be prepared for it. He told me I would have to give a talk and I thought, Oh heavens, what will I talk about. Talking has never been a short suit of mine. So I wrote a speech. When I got up, it was not difficult to thank the the president of the AHSA and to kid them a little bit that I was the most "desiring" person of the honor, an honor that I did not even know existed. Then I started to read the speech and discovered to my horror that with the light on the podium there was no way I could read that speech. Alan tried to hold it for me and finally after two minutes of faltering around I said, "Oh, forget it," and I just stood up and talked. I told the people about our early days of finding out what the AHSA was and finally entering into it not only to be recognized but hoping we could have some input. This had all been accomplished beyond our wildest dreams. The AHSA is just as interested in the Saddlebreds as the hunter and jumper and any other breed. It was a wonderful night, we all wound up laughing until we cried!

4
Girls At Dayton Show

I want to talk about an occurrence that was kind of a heartbreaker for me, but when you believe so strongly in something then you stick with it. We had taken several young people to the Dayton Horse Show. I had five riders there and we stayed in a small town on the outskirts of Dayton at a nice motel. We went to the show grounds and I had left the riders at the motel with all of their luggage and I said,"Now stay here and take care of your luggage. I am going to the grounds to get the horses settled."

When I got back to the motel the front desk called me and said, "Mrs. Crabtree didn't you have some young riders here?" I said, "Yes, there are five of them." They said, "We are a little concerned because one of them called and asked if there was a movie in this area, and we are afraid they have gone to this movie and there is no way to get there but by walking along the side of this country road and this is not a nice section of town."

I was horrified. Not only had they left this one girl to unload all of their suitcases which I could have crowned them for, but they had taken off to go to the movies. Never realizing of course, the peril they were in and they were in peril. Debbie Basham was my assistant at that time and if you stamped your foot, Debbie would jump four feet in the air. And she could get very excited and she knew I was mad as hops. I called every movie house in the area and asked if there were four little girls there, but nobody knew anything about them. I said, "Well give me the addresses and we jumped in the car and we went to all these movie houses and I think there were about five of them. I found out how to get into the movies for nothing, because you get as mad as I was and as nervous as Debbie was and you just barge on in and say you are looking for four little girls. We looked and looked and could not find them. I was desperate by this time and we went back to the motel and called the desk and told them, "We have gone to these movie houses and these children are not there." They said,"Wait a minute there is one more that is a little further away and maybe they are there."

Well, by this time I was so upset that I was about to cry from being mad, afraid, and nervous. You name it, that was Helen and of course Debbie was shaking in her shoes. I said, "Come on Debbie let's go" and we jumped in the car and raced down to the movie and sure enough here the four sat next to the front row. They looked like four birds on a telephone wire gazing up at the movie and I will never forget its name: *Sargent Pepper's Lonely Hearts Club Band*. I stamped my foot and called one of their names and they all looked and suddenly became about two feet high. I said, "Come here!" They followed us. On the way back I was so upset because I believe so strongly that my primary job is to see after the health, development, and safety of these kids. The fact that they all became good riders was secondary. That was the way our whole stable operated. In the car I said, "Now look, you are gone. You know you have broken these rules. What do you think that anyone driving by would consider you were? I will not use the word, but you know. Why somebody did not come by and abduct you girls I do not know. On top of that you left the one girl there to unload all your luggage, which was not fair. Now Jim B. Robertson is a very good teacher and I am sure he will have room for you and if you do not know how to get in touch with him, I will look up his telephone number, but you are gone!"

We got back to the motel and Debbie was shaking with the enormity of everything that had happened and everything that was going on. Finally she broke into hysterical laughter and said, "Mrs. Crabtree, do you realize you did not put on the pants to your pants suit?" Well, there I had gone in the top to my pants suit and pants liners so I was covered up, but here they were, these white nylon things. I think I was really moving so fast that nobody really noticed, but anyway I was just aghast at what I had done and Debbie was still shaking and finally we were both laughing.

About that time the phone rang and it was Mrs. Schoonmaker and she said, "Helen, what in the world is going on? Shauna has called me and she is hysterical. She says you're kicking her out of the barn." And I said, "Well, Barbara that is what I have done." I told her what the kids had done and how terribly dangerous it was and it was not just that they were disobeying rules, they had done a stupid and incredibly dangerous thing. They could have all been killed. She said, "It is just awful. We just bought Warlock and I just do not think he will be the horse with anybody else that he is with you, and Shauna wants to stay so badly."

When she said Warlock I guess a little venality crept into my being and I thought, "Oh, I do not want to lose that horse." The other horses were wonderful too, and these were grand kids. I loved them all. If they had not learned to behave and take care of themselves by then it was going to be too late if I did not do it for them. I said to Barbara that I would keep Shauna but the others had to go. So they did.

Somebody said, "But Helen those people were all millionaires". I said, "What does that have to do with it? They are girls first and customers second."

Reunion at Kentucky State Fair week. Charles and Helen Crabtree and Bill Munford — Hall of Fame, 1989.

5
Beginning Of Reunion

On August 23, 1989, one of the most wonderful things that could happen to anybody, happened to Charlie and me. Jennifer Turner Joiner, who is one of my former assistants, and the mothers of two of the girls I had bounced out of the barn at the Dayton show, Caroline Perry, Nell Perry's mother and Barbara Friedman, Morgan Friedman's mother got together and organized a reunion of the Crabtree riders without my knowing it until the very last moment. The reunion was on Saturday at the Kentucky State Fair. The luncheon was held at noon and around 100 riders attended. Some of them showing at Louisville, others came in who were not. Among them, my first assistant who was my student at MacMurray College in 1940, Ruth Kauffman, who became Ruth Palmer when she married R.S. Palmer. They are a very wonderful couple who have done so much for the horse business in Missouri. I was never so proud of any group in my life. They had all grown up into lovely people.

I had one boy and he said, "I feel like a fish out of water. I always admired the Crabtrees. It was always such a work house, I thought Helen's name was Redd Charlie Helen before I got to the name because everybody was always in such a hurry." Each one of those young people got up to speak. I thought, well here was a girl Bev Anderson from Tulsa, a good rider but not really a dedicated equitation rider. So we got her a nice little hot bay mare to ride so she could accomplish something in the training of that horse where she would have had a difficult time winning in competitive equitation championships. So at one of the shows I reminded the riders of the test of the individual workout. This test calls for the rider to make up their own one minute workout and hand it to the judge, then go out and do it. I said, "The main thing I want you all to do is there is going to be a great temptation to try to be very spectacular, but make darn sure that whatever you write down is something you can do, because perfection is better than a big splash and a big crash." I asked everybody to bring their workout and put them on the tack room table. I picked up Bev's workout and she said, "I will do a sandwich figure eight at a canter on the first circle, a trot on the second and third, and a canter on the fourth, I will leave the line-up and I will aim for the mid point of my intersection and I will miss it by four feet. Then I will try to take my left lead and get a cross canter and the mare will go straight to the wall. I will whirl her around and in doing so I will get a total cross canter and I will stop and try to trot, I will get the trot but my circle will be about three times as big as the first one." Well, you would have to laugh at that. Bev was so funny and that was exactly the way that mare would do figure work. She was a little devil about it. Bev was one of the people who came back to the reunion. Do you know what she was doing? After graduating from college she was helping to design off shore drilling rigs and in a recent conversation she is now forming her own company to design these rigs for the oil industry. Can you believe that?!

Then there was Kristy Grueneberg who had taken over a brass foundry when her father had passed away and not only was running it successfully, but had developed a revolutionary process with brass. I am not writing about going in a department store and selling cosmetics. These were kids that had wonderful brains and used them. I think that riding had something to do with it. The competition, learning to deal with situations that arrived unexpectedly, and the persistence it took to be good, the joy of doing their best, which was all anyone was ever asked to do, certainly had wonderful results. I had so many letters from people who could not come to the reunion. Every one of them said, "We feel that whatever we have accomplished, our years spent in riding have contributed so must to the success of what we are doing now." What more could you ask? Think about it. Here were two of those ladies whose daughters I had bounced out of the barn. They knew it was well meant. I think it was their way of saying, "Helen we understand what you did and we agree with what you did." I had never known how the parents and riders felt about my Dayton decision. I felt very badly about it because I loved those girls, but they had to learn and they did.

One of the dearest persons there was our cook, Hattie. A delicate little lady whom the girls adored. Hattie looked so proud and so beautiful in her white satin suit and her dark brown face shining with joy and excitement. As the talks came to her, I was concerned that Hattie might be embarrassed to speak. Not so! Hers was the most heartfelt of all because she said, "I am so glad to be here with my girls. I will never forget them and I will always be a Crabtree girl myself." Unfortunately, three years later Hattie passed away and she has been missed ever since by anyone who was ever at Crabtree Farms. With her cheerful smile, she took care of everybody just like we were her children. What a wonderful person she was.

Many who could not attend sent flowers and letters. It was a afternoon I never wanted to end.

Charlie and I went back to the hotel in an absolute euphoric state. It was so wonderful to see all of those riders and owners that we have had over the many years. That night we went back to the show hardly able to see what was going on because it seemed every two minutes someone was coming down to talk to us. The other trainers were so kind to say what a wonderful day it must have been and how much they enjoyed seeing the former riders. When Linda Fischer, a former rider, came to ask me to come to Redd's skybox, I dutifully got up and went with her. And she said, "We need Mr. Crabtree to come with us." "Honey, he does not go to the skybox because he does not like to look at the horses from the end of the ring," I explained. Then she said, "Mrs. Crabtree, you must come. Something is going to happen," and I said, "What is wrong?" and she said, "No, I am going to have to explain that you and Mr. Crabtree are being inducted into the Hall of Fame and the presentation is about five minutes away."

This was almost more than I could stand. The afternoon was enough to make us happy for the rest of our lives and here came this signal honor. Then Linda raced back and got Charlie and said, "You must come. It is time to go out in the ring." We went out with Bill Munford, the show manager. We did not hear a word the announcer said because that was such an honor and we were in such a state of shock that what was being said went in one ear and out the other. One cannot believe it is happening to them, to be recognized by your peers and to be put on that honorable list at the World's Championship Show.

I had carried out of the ring a long florist box. It had been given to me as I entered the ring and it was so cumbersome I handed it to Bill Munford. The box was obviously filled with long stem roses. I said to Nancy Crabtree, "Would you and Redd like to have these. I know these are flowers and we are just loaded with flowers from the reunion." She looked at me in astonishment and said, "Oh, Gran read the note." I opened it up and the note said "Loved you then, I love you now and I will always love you, and it was signed Redd. So that was the end of a perfect day in every respect.

A Special Day For A Special Couple October 1989
by Joseph Pfeffer

They came from all over America, and from all walks of life, Some are married and have families, some are still single. Some confine their contact with the horse world to reading magazines and occasionally visiting shows, while others are major names on the present day American Saddlebred show scene. But they all have one thing in common, and on Saturday morning, August 26 in Louisville, they seemed transported in time and suspended in space: they were all, for at least one more time, Crabtree riders.

August 26 - the biggest day of the year in the Saddlebred world because it culminated in championship night at the Kentucky State Fair was special this year for another reason. Two former "Crabtree Moms," Caroline Perry and Barbara Friedman along with one ex "Crabtree Girl," Jennifer Turner Joyner, had conceived the idea of a unique way to honor one of the true living legends of the Saddle Horse world. Several years ago, they had been struck by an amazing similarity in the way former riding students of Helen Crabtree had described their experience with her and the effects those experiences had on them: Helen, and Charlie as well, had been important determining factors on the course of their lives. Not only had they learned to be superb riders under the Crabtree tutelage: they had learned lessons for life, difficult to describe but impossible not to see, that seemed to add a special and unique dimension to their lives. In a very real sense, because of their "Crabtree years," their lives seemed elevated to a plane they could not even have imagined without those experiences.

So Perry, Friedman, and Joyner went to work, and after a three-year period found themselves with an almost unbelievable guest list of 90 former students and family members, 85 of whom actually showed up at the Executive Inn for brunch on a muggy late summer Louisville morning. To mention them all here would take up most of this column as well as run the almost certain risk of leaving several people out. Suffice to say they spanned the decades and the generations of Crabtree riders.

From the "Memphis era" in the late '40s and early '50s, there was Stanley "Hi" Petterer, now in the Thoroughbred business in Lexington and one of only three male former riders at the brunch.

From St. Louis, where both Helen and Charles Crabtree really began their professional careers, came the "two Ruths," Palmer and Pfeffer, both of whose associations with the Crabtrees go back more than 40 years. Ruth Palmer was Helen Crabtree's student at MacMurray College in Illinois, then went on to be her first assistant at the old Riding and Hunt Club in St. Louis. Ruth's husband, the veteran St. Louis area trainer R.S. Palmer, was in attendance at the brunch. R.S. noted that, while others had remarked on Helen Crabtree putting horse and rider together, and putting together correct form with aggressive, competitive horsemanship, she had put something else together for the Palmers: she put Ruth and R.S. together, and their marriage has lasted four decades and is still going strong,

As for Ruth Pfeffer, she identified herself as one of several "older riders" Mrs. Crabtree took on as a kind of new project in the early 1970s. Among the others was another St. Louisan, Jean Fetner, a noted artist as well as an outstanding horsewoman, who could not be in attendance at the luncheon but who sent a sculpture in her absence.

But the day really belonged to the "Crabtree girls," a talented, vibrant group of young women who now range in age from their late 20's to their mid-40's, an extraordinary group of riders who began with the Crabtrees at Rock Creek in 1954 and did not stop winning championships until some three decades later, when Helen Crabtree retired from the active teaching of young riders, though she still maintains a busy schedule of teaching "guest riders" and conducting clinics around the country. Many former "Crabtree girls" are now married, and a surprisingly large number are in professional positions of one sort or another. A handful are professional horsewomen, including Debbie Foley, Liz McBride, Debbie Basham, Lisa Rosenberger, and of course Ruth Palmer. They seemed as fresh and full of life on that Saturday morning as they ever did during the headiest "Crabtree days," and the special quality of poise and social grace they learned at Crabtrees was stamped on every one. In terms of when they rode with Helen, they ranged Ruth Palmer to Ruth Anne Lewis, who rode in the early '80s. In terms of involvement with horses, they ranged from Beverly Anderson, who won top equitation awards in the early '70s and had not even been to a horse show since 1976, to Mary Gaylord Conatser, who got up at the brunch and nervously asked to speak her piece early because she had to be over at the Fairgrounds showing at one o'clock.

Riders like Linda and Karen Fischer, Cathy Noble, Lisa Rosenberger, Linda Lowary Price, Amy and Judy Barmeier, and Shauna Schoonmaker Edwards recalled the high-spirited days of the Crabtree Farms dormitory, when Charles Crabtree turned into a kind of housefather, never turning off the kitchen light until he was sure all the girls were safely back where they were supposed to be. Because of the family nature of the gathering, and because, as Shauna Schoonmaker noted, the married ones wish to stay married, the "girls" toned down the retelling of what one of them called the "juvenile delinquent" stories. Even so there was some interesting stuff about an old pair of jodphurs that some of the girls used to stuff with paper and then put riding boots on. These jods were placed under the bed of unsuspecting new recruits in the dorm, in order to make them think there was a man in the dorm. The fun and games were all part of the scene, all part of what gave the Crabtree entourage in those days such a family feeling.

There was strong representation from those riders who today provide living proof of the Crabtree legacy, Randi Stuart Wightman had just won the amateur five-gaited world championship the night before with Admiral's Mark, while Mary Gaylord Conatser would go on to win the ladies world championship with Santana Lass on Saturday night. Among the other very active horsewomen in attendance were Mary Lou Gallagher, Andrea Walton DeVogel, Kathleen Lyda Berger, Wendy Wagner Johnson, and Linda and Karen Fischer whose family for years provided local support and at times a kind of "home away from home" for out-of-town Crabtree riders.

The event's most emotional moment was provided by Lynne Girdler Kelly, one of the original Rock Creek riders and Helen's first AHSA Medal finals winner. In her showing days, Lynne Girdler gained fame beyond the Saddlebred world by showing the black gelding Storm Cloud to both equitation and junior exhibitor championships. It might not be stretching things too far to say that Lynne Girdler, Helen Crabtree, and Storm Cloud really started the modern era in Saddle Seat equitation; they were certainly "present at the creation."

Lynne sat next to Helen Crabtree at the head table. When her time came to speak, she was too overcome with emotion to do so. Mrs. Crabtree, never at a loss for words, simply said that Lynne Girdler was her dearest and closest friend. The two women then collapsed into each other's arms, with Helen simply saying, "this says it all."

Amidst all the telling of humorous stories, almost everyone in attendance tried to capture the special essence of the "Crabtree experience." Some spoke of Helen's "perfectionism," others of her uncanny ability to match horse and rider, still others of the laser sharp mind that never let you rest or lapse for a moment. Nearly everyone spoke of the teamwork between Helen and Charlie, and the way they complemented each other. Many outside the Crabtree circle may not have been aware of what a superb teacher Charlie Crabtree was. One rider noted how refreshing it could be when, after a particularly demanding session with Helen, she would go to a show and Charlie would say, "Forget all that stuff about your legs. Just get in there and ride." Helen noted that Charlie was every bit as good a teacher as she was; the only difference between them was that Charlie had the bad habit of telling riders everything he knew in the first lesson. "In order to make money in this game," Helen said she told him, "You have to kind of stretch it out a little."

Through it all, it was abundantly clear that Helen Crabtree is one of those rare individuals who touches and transforms every life she comes into contact with. At the luncheon, she got credited with everything from Lisa Rosenberger's career as a professional trainer to Amy Barmeier's Ph.D. in psychology, and much else in between. Perhaps Helen Crabtree's greatest talent is first to bring out the very best in each individual, and then never to let her or him be satisfted with anything less than that "personal best." This is why her riders always had a unique aura of excellence, competitiveness, and aggressiveness, without ever being accused of lack of sportsmanship.

This day, which began with the reunion brunch and ended with their induction into the Kentucky State Fair Hall of Fame, was indeed a unique and special one for Helen and Charles Crabtree, reflecting the unique and special position they have occupied for some 40 years in the American Saddlebred world.

6
Perfect Attire? Don't Be Too Sure!

"You're not going to put that shoe polish on the jods, are you?", Charlie asked me. "No, I'm going to put it on this girl's leg" I replied, "and bring me a new roll of friction tape."

This was not a scene from a hospital emergency ward, it was a near disaster at the American Royal Horse Show in Kansas City.

It was championship night for the equitation riders. Seven of our riders had qualified. Six were seated on their horses, back numbers in place, attire correct with the black suit and formal accessories. All were there but one girl who was late because she discovered that her cleaner's bag contained only the riding coat and no jods. Frantically she was searching for her roommate's black jods when the other riders left the hotel. Apprised of her predicament, we were holding her horse saddled in the aisle, and the other riders had wound their way up the circular ramp at the old Royal arena. Only a sheep - herding exhibition now preceded the equitation championship and it was well on the way. I said a silent prayer asking for dumb or stubborn sheep to delay herding into the final pen.

At last the rider raced in, waving the borrowed jods. She went into the dressing room to remove her slacks to put on the formal jods. There was an anguished wail and I raced into the room to find our girl completely dressed but immobile. The pants were long enough but were dangerously tight. Her roommate was about as fat as a golf club and this poor girl was afraid to move.

"Take tiny steps and we will lift you up on the horse," I said, but at the first step the outer left leg seam tore loose at the knee opening up a 12 inch exposure of very white skin.

Trainers and instructors try to anticipate and avoid every possible disaster. But this time we had no time and my idea came out of no where. We painted the exposed knee and I held the material in place, Charlie rolled the friction tape below and above the knee. This done, two grooms gingerly hoisted the poor girl into the saddle.

"Angel on horseback", Mary Bateman Angel.

Photo by Sargent

I hastily uttered a prayer that the forthcoming individual workout would not contain the command to dismount and mount, and she entered the ring on time - but just barely!

Did she win? I have no idea, but no one ever observed that this tardy and patched-together finalist was anything but perfectly attired.

The riders had always been cautioned to check their riding habits and to come to the show one hour ahead of their class to change from their slacks into the jods in the extra stall fitted out as a dressing room. I thought it was a neat and foolproof arrangement. Wrong!

And again, on a later year at the Royal we experienced another near sartorial dilemma. I have received permission to use the riders name because she was one of my wonderful assistants, named Mary Bateman. She is now Mary Bateman Angel and she and her husband Randee are in the Thoroughbred business and they are our dearest friends. Mary's trouble began in the make-up ring. She had inadvertently donned Randi Stuart's jods, which were also a tight fit but appeared to be able to withstand actual riding.

Suddenly Mary felt the jodhpurs loosen and to her horror she realized that the middle stitching had given way from the belt in the front all the way around to the belt in the back. It is probably the only time that jods in an instant turned into a pair of chaps. Mary leaped from her horse handing the reins to an astonished passer by and together we ran back down the ramp.

Mary was competing in the equitation championship having won her older age group so this was no tiny youngster we're talking about. I told Mary to go into the dressing room and, thanking God that our stable colors were black and red, I yanked some black bunting from a stall front, shook out the dust and yelled, "drop your pants!"

To a startled groom I yelled, "Bring me two blanket pins!" And thus equipped, I went to help Mary. We fashioned a diaper from the bunting, secured it with the blanket pins and pulled the pants back into place. Mary retrieved her mount from the startled lady who was still holding her horse. Evidently our desperate plan was effective because no one ever knew that the riding habit hid a black bunting diaper.

Sometimes it seems to take weeks before a trainer-instructor "solves" a problem. My problem was with a very beautiful and fragile fifteen-year-old girl whose beauty made up for her lack of strong body strength. At the time the individual workout of riding without stirrups seemed to crop up in every championship. Although I had purchased a beautiful dappled grey gelding for the beautiful rider. I did not anticipate that this duo might ever reach a figure working championship. But we had to be prepared.

In growing frustration because of the poor child's weak thigh muscles, l realized that something had to be done since the endless practicing was wearing out an otherwise cheerful horse.

It was after what I considered careful pondering that I came up with the idea that the pretty child must perform some exercise that did not involve her horse. So I suggested to her that she practice posting atop the large postal collection box near her home. The following Saturday I asked the rider how our plan worked. "Ooh, Mrs. Crabtree," wailed the scarlet faced girl, "I was doing what you said to do when a station wagon full of boys came down our street." "Stop right there," I said, "It was a lousy idea."

It must be obvious by now that the best ideas are not always the result of timely planning.

7
Caretakers

Just as much as the contribution that our wonderful owners made to our lives is the devotion of the grooms who cared for their horses.

Precision, responsibility, and deep love for their charges marked so many of our caretakers. Imagine, today, putting together a crew of 26 grooms! This we did the year Crabtree Farms showed 58 head at the Kentucky State Fair.

Earning the respect of our industry was L.T. Armstrong, first to be honored at the Lexington Junior League Horse Show. L.T. came to work for us when he was 16 years old and he is still working on Crabtree Farm in 1997. Leasing our stable are Mike and Nancy Spencer who value L.T. Armstrong as a man who loves his job.

Mike Spencer came to us as another raw recruit at the age of fifteen. With the exception of two years at Redwing Stables for Judy and Roy Werner, he had been with Crabtree Farms or the Charles and Helen Crabtree Stables. Mike and Nancy own Gold Leaf Farm. They lease our stable for training operations that consistently turns out winners at the important shows.

What a joy it is for Charlie and me to still have these talented graduates of our past keeping alive the professionalism and talent that make our lives still interesting.

I have mentioned John Washington prominently in the Legal Tender story. He came to us, also inexperienced in our profession and only ill health and death 20 years later took him away from his beloved horses.

The list of World's Champions that the three men rubbed is mind boggling. Why were these horses champions? Yes, we always did our best to develop our horses with hard work and understanding, but that would have never been enough without these three dedicated men.

Tommy Biederman and L.T. Armstrong.

Heavenly Flower and Mike Spencer.

8
The 10th Anniversary
(S & B December, 1994)

I was amazed to discover while cataloguing material for a forthcoming book, to find that this particular column was begun in *Saddle & Bridle* in 1985.

Several years before that I had written a column for *Saddle & Bridle* entitled "Line Up, Please". That column was discontinued in order to give me time to write the original "Saddle Seat Equitation".

However, this time I will continue with this column. If I had sufficient sight, I would still be riding and judging, but this condition gives one more time for serious thinking and I am grateful that writing is such a compelling part of my life.

When I invented the Crabtree adjustable stirrup saddle several years ago I had a fine agreement with Whitman Saddlery that the Crabtree saddle would be sold by Bobby Beach through his National Bridle Shop. Then the new Whitman generation made their own translation of the agreement. I suppose that imitation really is the most sincere form of flattery. Now, again, in the true holiday spirit I give to Whitman and all others my latest invention - rubber stirrup leathers!

When I told my literal-minded husband what I was going to do he hit the ceiling. "Somebody will think you are serious," he prophesied. But in true wifely fashion I went ahead. It was offered absolutely gratis. I even wrote their sales copy - "Rubber stirrup leathers are great. Just pull the left one down, insert the left foot in the stirrups and you will be tossed lightly into the saddle without any effort on your part. However the greatest advantage is in posting - one merely sits still in the saddle at the trot and the feet go up and down!"

Why is it that husbands are always right? I actually got a couple of calls from horse owners wanting to order.

I am proud that my Whitman saddle has given such pleasure

and success to so many riders (from eight and under to the World's Grand Championship).

To get back to serious business, I would like to thank the many people who have taken time to write to me. I hope that they will continue to enjoy the column for many years. My biggest wish is for all who ride — "May your horses be true and your ribbons be blue."

Merry Christmas!

"The New Grooms Carol"
(To the tune of "Deck The Halls")

Deck the legs with sheets of cotton
Tra-la-la, la-la, la-la-la-la
Is there something I've forgotten?
Surely not, la-la, tra-la-la-la
Don we now the jersey leg-wraps
round and round, up, then down-one, two, three
Oh! My gosh! Here's the leg brace
I'll be fired, just been hired. Woe is me!
I'll just put a trifle on his stifle
And the rest I'll rub upon his knee.

"Eight and Under Carol"
(To the tune of "Jingle Bells")

Up and down, up and down, trotting all the way
O' what fun it is to ride
In my first horse show today
I see Mom, I see Dad, teacher's by his side
I may not win, but that's no sin 'cause I just love to ride!

"Kentucky Christmas Carol"
(To the tune of "O'Little Town of Bethlehem")

O' little town of Lexington
Your horse show's in July
The Big Red Mile makes league girls smile
But all the trainers cry.

Then comes the tractor scraping
To make the footing right
But heed the fears of yesteryears
It rains on Monday night!

"Horseman's Lament"
(To the tune of Irving Berlin's ballad "Remember")

Remember the night at Tattersalls
I bought you? Remember?
You racked way too high - up to the sky
"WALK TROT!", thought I. Remember?
I took off your mane, we shod to trot
We practiced, I thought you'd learned a lot,
I entered the ring all hot to trot
But you forgot to remember.

"Prayer"

God bless our faithful animals
On this the Christmas Day
And keep in mind the humankind
who helped us on the way.

The barren mares, the geldings old
Remember them each day
The dogs, the cats and all our pets
God bless them all, we pray.

Adolph Zell.

Jeff Priebe.

9
Here's To The Boys!

It is so nice to be able to write about two riders who made a lasting impression on me at the recent Rock Creek Riding Club Horse Show. In fact, I was very impressed with the overall quality of the riders in equitation and it does seem to me that there is a growing tendency of the riders to relax their upper bodies and not to cramp back into an S curve as was so apparent in the two or three preceeding seasons. The quality of the figure work was more precise than formerly.

Perhaps the reason that I was attracted to this equitation rider is because he, yes, a boy rider and a good one ... because he sat in the middle of his horse and was balanced to go any direction at any time and to stay in command the entire time. I first saw Adolph Zell the last time I judged the Morgan Grand National a few years ago and as I recall I tied him first. Anyone who has seen Adolph ride his hot equitation mount the last couple of years will have to give him a lot of credit for sticking with this horse who is an expert in committing the worst sin a horse can have and that is rearing and whirling to balk. I am sure the Byers would not have let Adolph proceed on this particular horse if he had been a very high-rearing horse, but as treacherous as rearing is, it can be tolerated if the horse rears just enough to whirl. This is nothing to recommend for any equitation horse, so if any of you "backyard" youngsters hope that your rearing horse will quit the habit - forget it - because the horse never will. I firmly believe that Adolph's correct position and balance in the saddle are the keys to his success in improving this difficult horse. I am making a point of this particular rider because he should be the pattern for all of those riders who have been sitting reared back in the saddle with straight arms right down the reins to the horse's mouth. Adolph is seated in such a way that his horse cannot get ahead of him - a fault of the riders who over-arch the backbone to where the upper torso weight becomes a dominant factor and realigns the body to be forward in the hips and buttocks and behind the movement of the horse in the upper torso. This does not mean that Adolph sits forward in his saddle. No, he sits well back where he should, but he keeps his entire body balanced over his feet so that he is in the perfect position to let the stride of the horse dictate the posting. Riders who lean back from the gravity center are constantly riding behind their horse - his motion and his direction.

As I have said so many times before, the hands and seat must be independent. They work together but never one at the expense of the other. If you have ever read any books about equitation in hunt seat, stock seat you name it - by the top instructors, that old phrase "the hands must be independent of the seat" will appear. The good rider may get by with faulty position on an automatic "teenaged", horse who can do the individual workouts if they are left in his feed box before the class. Not to say anything derogatory about the perfectly prepared mount, but equitation is a learning experience and if an automatic horse will roll into a left circle lead with the slightest touch of the heel, help the rider find the intersection and then stands there patiently until the rider catches up and finally gives the aid to canter, then we can see that the rider is truly riding behind the horse - both mentally and physically. Good riders make immediate corrections, great riders know what the horse is going to do and avoid the mistakes.

Perfection results from a myriad of little things and every good rider must ride mentally before the fact (only to the point where he knows what the horse will tend to do) and be there with the horse in concert. Just read the rule book and it will tell you how to make a simple canter change. Come to a halt, take one stride at the walk and proceed on the next lead. This is TIMING and this is what Adolph has. He does not give his horse time to "decide" what to do, his horse is moving into position for the change while he halts and takes the step. ALL riders should do this. I wonder, at times, why judges will tie riders who halt at the intersection and then stand there for what seems like a Kentucky Minute (and that's long, folks!) to pick up the second canter lead in a figure eight. Only a saint of a horse would stand there while the rider peeks over the leading shoulder, draws the outside heel back, then finally aids the horse and then, after all that, decides that guiding is next because the rail seems to be getting in the way!

Adolph knew which way his horse liked to whirl and he executed his figure eight facing away from the rail so that on the lead passing the outgate, the lure of the gate and horse's tendency to whirl the opposite way negated each other. Now that is thinking and everyone can do it if they will sit in the slightly forward erect position and move from one gait into the opposite in cadence with the horse's strides. That is the only way that one can ride a green horse and the only way you should ride a horse that has his doctor's degree in figure work. How many times have my riders heard me say that riding is 10% muscle and 90% brains? Well, Adolph, here's to you. You get 100%.

Jeff Priebe made everyone sit up and take notice of his juvenile stake ride on "Time To Go". I have always liked this horse as have many others, but he made shows at Rock Creek that gave everyone something to chase after. The horse was collected, animated, speedy and downright exciting and it looked as if you had cloned Adolph Zell in that saddle. You could not come out with two better riders. The two young men were sensational and Jeff was the proof of the pudding that Adolph served up in his brilliant figure work. Perfect examples as to what equitation should be and the rides that proved that GOOD equitation is truly riding a horse at his best whether it be in an equitation class or a performance class.

10
Red Faces In The Show Ring
(S & B March, 1993)

In reliving so many of the interesting experiences we have had showing horses, I have come to the realization that the biggest jokes always seemed to be on me. Charlie feels that my proclivity for adventure comes from the attitude that anything is possible if you want it enough.

Vicki Gillenwater had a new walk-trot horse, Street Music, which she had purchased from Blythewood - a very useful kind of horse and just right for her. We had made a show or two and she was in the top half of the ribbons in tough going. One night after the show at Louisville, I was working the horse and decided to see if he would buckle up and get a little fancier. Was I surprised! In his rhythm, I bumped him pretty hard on the curb and here he went, a big-time trot, I recall Tom Moore and Jean McLean Davis asking me what horse I was riding.

It was too late to teach the new technique to Vicki at the show, but she came up to Simpsonville once before the American Royal and really got the hang of the new rein work. I could hardly wait until the Royal because Vicki and the gelding were a treat to behold.

The juvenile three-gaited class was held in the afternoon session and so we were perched on the front row where I could talk directly into my rider's ear. The class entered the ring and my pair were going the old trot but I thought that I would remind Vicki the next time around. Charlie was glaring daggers at me because he knew what I was going to do - but I did use discretion as one of the judges was stationed right across from us. The next pass I calmly said, "Nip" to Vicki with no results. The next trip I said it a little sharper. As the class went on the admonition to "Nip" changed to "Bump" - this time in a tone of voice that a baseball umpire might use. Still no results. I noticed that I was beginning to get odd looks from the two women seated next to me, and just as they moved to the row behind me I completely lost my cool and said to Vicki,

"JERK!" I heard one of the ladies say to her companion, "Now she called her a jerk". Unfortunately Charlie heard the remark so he beat a hasty retreat up the steps to the refreshment stand. I will never know what Vicki was thinking because she could remember none of this when the class was over. Showing can be stressful and apparently cause deafness in some riders! Somewhere in Missouri are two women who were ready to call the Child Protection League. We have had many a laugh over this and had I been seated closer at the UPHA Convention in January, I would have called "Jerk" to Vicki as she went up to get her Hackney Pleasure Pony award.

When Josephine Abercrombie had the outstanding string of show horses it was almost unheard of for her to lose a class. "Shorty" Beghtol from Industry, Ill., was the tops with Shetlands which was a big division in the early 50s and he had sold Josephine the best pair of ponies in the country, coal black and perfectly matched. I drew the assignment to show them the first time at the great Chicago International and I knew that I was not in there to get second or third. I happened to have a gorgeous suit with matching small hat which boasted a black feather that curled rakishly under my chin. The top of the suit was a saffron yellow and the skirt was the black and dark green Black Watch plaid. It really was a stunning outfit and perfect with the black ponies. Shorty was a nervous wreck as it was the maiden voyage for the ponies and he had not taught them to back in the line-up, as required then in ladies pairs.

I was happily aware that everyone was looking at the gorgeous pair of ponies and the smartly attired driver. Well, when things start to go wrong there is no stopping the tide. My first hint that all was not well was when I looked up in the boxes and observed Mrs. H. Leslie Atlas in a suit exactly like mine and she was crimson with exasperation. Nothing like owning Radio Station WGN and seeing a horse trainer wearing a duplicate outfit! I would not dwell on this mishap, because to my horror, I felt my lovely little hat breaking loose from the bobby pins on the left side of my head. The hat, turning upside down, was sailing along in the air with the black feather wound around my neck. What a sight I must have been - my hat still firmly attached to the right side of my head (I couldn't be lucky and have it fall off) and it looked like a collection plate at a church service. To further the problem was the judge - a very popular pony judge from the East who liked nothing better than to see a Saddle Horse trainer come apart in a pony class. She was liberally fortified with Seagrams and kept us going forever. I reasoned that my pride was less important than the ponies' performance, so we made it to the line-up with hat still askew. The only thing that saved me from utter despair was the fact that the judge was laughing so hard when she got to us that she forgot to call for the ponies to back. Shorty was so nervous that I don't believe that he saw my sartorial disaster and we proudly drove up to accept the blue ribbon, Shorty all smiles, and Helen with her feet firmly planted on the hat in the bottom of the viceroy.

I'm sure that Mrs. Atlas went home and burned her outfit, but I continued to wear mine with much pride secure in the knowledge that one of the wealthiest women in Chicago had confirmed my idea of what to wear while driving the black pair of Shetlands, Fame and Fortune.

11
Doing it Right: Victory at Louisville
(S & B October, 1987)

What a propitious time to be writing about the amateur and five-gaited riding! I am still in a fever of excitement over Randi Stuart Wightman's rides on Admiral's Mark in the Gelding Stake (which she won) and the World's Grand Championship Five-Gaited, in which she was a thrilling reserve. After three years of the head-to-head matches between Sky Watch and Imperator, one wondered if the Gaited Championship might be a "ho-hum" one horse class. Never say never - not only was the 1987 World's Championship Horse Show the best show in memory - the gaited Championship was an incredibly close contest between two horses and two superior riders. What made it memorable was that the rider of the Gelding Stake was a lady amateur (which had been accomplished only three times before) and the World's Grand Champion Reserve rider was this same lady-amateur, Randi Stuart Wightman who exited the ring to a thunderous roar from the crowd and a standing ovation. This was not to in any way criticize the judges, (Bill Munford hires experienced and able judges), but I believe that it was the crowd's tribute to a great horse and a great rider. And taking second to the five-times winner of the Mare Stake, Our Golden Duchess and her popular and gifted rider, Merrill Murray is no disgrace in anyone's book.

What made this Championship one to be forever remembered was the moral triumph that accrued to a perfect rider on a perfect horse by a perfect lady. To those who have been so mistakenly adamant in the idea that a woman will never be tied in the "The Grand Championship" at Louisville, step aside. They came within one vote of doing it this year. I am supposed to be writing an instructive column about equitation and amateur riding, so I will get immediately to the point. A superior horse can be just that when ridden in perfect form and with great intelligence. Randi Stuart was one of the all time great equitation riders. Her record proves

Randi Stuart Wightman and Admiral's Mark.

that, but what the general public may not know is that Randi Wightman is just as good a rider as an adult as she was an equitation and juvenile rider. I have stated so many times that riding is 90% brains and 10% muscle. At Louisville we saw 100% brains and 10% muscle. It takes 110% to win the stake there.

Randi started her riding career briefly in Tulsa and shortly moved to Crabtree Farms. She was 12 at the time and had been told that she would never learn to ride by an academy teacher in Tulsa. Her three-gaited mare was not suitable for a young rider and we bought the grand three-gaited gelding, King Again, from Ellis Waggoner. Her first show was at Lawrenceburg and another trainer said, "Helen, I never thought I would see a Crabtree rider ride all hunched over the horse like that." I told them to wait until next week. That was at the Shelby County Horse Show and I put Randi and King Again in the over-two class just for ring experience. Frank Bradshaw had champion Penny Stonewall in there and she made one of her few very bad shows. Guess who was lucky enough to win? King Again. I know Randi was ecstatic over her classes but no more so than with her very first blue ribbon in a three-gaited class. Her rise was meteoric after that and she stood out all during her juvenile and equitation years with wins on these greats: Storm Cloud, I've Decided, Sensational Princess and the two immortal champions, Legal Tender and Yorktown, and many other winners.

In her later years as an amateur she moved over to Redd Crabtree's tutelage and there teamed up with the lovely mare Cactus Flower - but the great one there was the unequalled mare Summer Melody, considered by many the best five-gaited horse of her time. Randi made her last ride on her at the Houston Pin Oak Show where the mare contracted a virus and died. I do believe that Randi never did give up the idea of a try at the Stake at Louisville. She continued to show but not with the same stock, as her attentions were now on being Mrs. Fred Wightman and mother of two children (who also are beginning to show).

At the Asheville Horse Show this spring, Redd asked Randi if she would like to win the stake at Louisville. Of course she said yes and that is when he told her that Mary Gaylord had decided to sell her gelding Admiral's Mark. The rest is history. Aside from pride in Randi and her trainer, I just want to point out that I know the public's appreciation of Admiral's Mark and Randi Wightman was not just based on the proof that a rider does not have to be an acrobatic maniac to win a big class at Louisville - the rider does not have to challenge certain horses and riders and a class can be won with exquisite form and horsemanship. Such riding is the epitome of what we have all been teaching our equitation riders over the years. My heart is with Mary Gaylord for her years of success with Mark and so is it with his trainer, Redd Crabtree who made those wonderful combinations work.

I have asked Randi's permission to use a part of her letter that I received a few days ago. "I want to thank you for all you taught me and showed me how to use, especially of myself, the determination, desire, grit and general cussedness(!) that's required for a lady to make a statement in the only arena in which it counts, as far as horse shows go."

Here's to all the great young equitation riders who are learning the basic skills and horse knowledge who can look forward to the day that they too, can have that great thrill. It is a long road but every step is its own reward. The rest we leave up to God and the judges.

12
A Great Win - A Great Loss
(S & B June, 1994)

It was great news for the equitation riders and instructors when it was announced that the Good Hands would continue to be held at the New York National. Getting from New York to the American Royal in Kansas City was tough going for everyone, but the thrill of winning in New York - the "Big Apple" was unique for me. So obviously mind shattering to win one of the finals, that I remember with embarrassment walking along in front of Rockefeller Center after Eddie, one of my riders, had won both the Medal and the Good Hands. I must have seen a John Wayne movie just before because I found myself thinking these ridiculous words - "I own this old town!" It is hard to imagine that I would admit such a stupid thought, but it has remained so fresh in my mind, not because it was an enormous honor for any instructor, but because of the fateful events that followed several years later.

My first double winner remains a very special rider in my memory. In 1965 we had gone to Massachusetts to the Eastern States show and while there we had met a strikingly handsome, young man whose mother asked if we would take their horse home with us after the New York National and accept her son as a new student. The young man was Edward Lumia, from Croton-on-Hudson, N.Y. His father had just died and Eddie needed to find some diversion from his recent loss and a change of scenery to help him through the crisis. We agreed to bring his mare back to Simpsonville where Eddie would come to ride during the Christmas holidays. Fortunately Redd's "bachelor pad" was available. When Redd had left to operate the Tampa Yacht Club Stable, we had made his place a dormitory for our out-of-state riders. Then when it became too small, we built a large dormitory. We added a swimming pool and the former small dorm became known as the pool house and it was the perfect place for Eddie and other boys who followed.

I have been unable to find who had instructed Eddie or who sold him his mare, but do remember that they were at Jack McGrane's stable a very short time before our taking the mare home from the Garden. The mare was attractive enough, sound and had a long neck. There was no reason that she could not set her head and respond to the bridle but she made a career of resisting any attempt to get her to wear the bridle right. When Eddie arrived at the farm he told me that was the reason they were able to purchase her. Every trainer gets one of these treasures once in a while and they are tough. Fortunately, Charlie had spent the last 25 years collecting and making curb bits. Every time we would use a different bit I would think I had solved the problem, but after one day the mare would tighten and refuse to set herself.

Eddie was pleased that first holiday because we had a new combination for every day. I told him that we would continue the experiments. Eddie was a natural rider and he quickly learned the excellent use of the leg aids and body weight. It was so frustrating for me because he was such an outstanding figure on a horse and he had the patience of a saint. He watched all of the other lessons, soaking up those fine points that were too advanced for his problem horse. We did make some progress but the mare was infuriating. There was no physical reason for her to freeze up on the bit, but I had a rider who was just as determined as I was. So the holiday ended and I set to work. I was able to teach the mare all of the required workouts but the progress in setting her head went slowly. I knew that the mare had to accept the rein work and that it must be kindly, even though I wanted to yank her mouth in frustration. It was apparent that severe bitting rigs had caused the problem and only time and patience would convince her to accept the curb bit (or the snaffle, too) and cure the problem. Eddie was the perfect student. He never lost his temper and was pleased with every small hint of progress.

In earlier times the big shows offered boy's equitation. Joe Greathouse was undefeated in those classes for several years, but when Eddie was at our stable those classes had been discontinued. There was a formidable group of riders that season - Andrea Walton, Randi Stuart, Janet Henry and a dozen more top riders from other stables. I saw Eddie time after time come out of the ring with pastel ribbons or none at all. He never complained, seeming to realize that he was making progress with the horse. Finally at the

Illinois State Fair the mare relaxed enough to make it possible for Eddie to win both the Medal and the "Good Hands". Those were the only finals, the UPHA beginning in 1972. I think all who knew Eddie Lumia were happy for him as he was universally liked and admired. Our next show was Louisville and I felt that Eddie had won the class (age group) outstandingly. The judge was a horse trainer with no equitation background and left Eddie out of the ribbons. I have never felt prouder than I did when Eddie came out of the ring and told me that he got the mare to set her head better than ever before.

When school started I redoubled my efforts with the mare and it did seem that she was coming our way. But with her vile temperament one could never be sure of her. That fall, at New York, all of our riders did well but all who knew Eddie and that his steep path to the top was a near impossible feat rushed to congratulate him when he won the "Good Hands" that morning and returned the next day to take the Medal. No instructor has favorites and it is up to the judges to determine who wins, but I had tears of joy in my eyes to see a modest and persevering rider make it to the top. He had only the one season and I have always felt that those wins exemplified what equitation was all about.

We all bid Eddie a heartfelt good-bye never realizing that it was a final farewell. The Korean War was on and Mrs. Lumia needed the comfort of her son, as dealing with her husband's death had been devastating for her. Eddie enrolled at a New York University and Charlie and I enjoyed our frequent telephone visits. One winter night Eddie joined a young married couple to attend a movie. Returning home, the driver lost control of the car on the icy road. It crashed into a tree, throwing Eddie out and he suffered a broken back, paralyzing him from the waist down.

For three years we would communicate with the desperate young man who would never ride again. Each time I would try to convince Eddie to become an instructor. How great he would have been. His knowledge was complete and he had the patience and personality to be an excellent teacher. But for three years nothing came of the idea as Eddie drifted, unable to believe that anyone permanently confined a a wheel chair would be taken seriously.

Then one day I received a call from Florida. It was Eddie, the enthusiastic, vibrant Eddie we love. He told me that he had a special van that he could drive and that he had decided to go back east to teach riding. A trainer had agreed to set him up with horses for instructing. He was so excited, anxious to get back in the sport that he loved. We invited him to come see us on his way and plans were all set. We were so happy for that wonderful young man and knew that he could make a great contribution to riding. I cautioned him to take his time and drive carefully as he had mountains to cross in Tennessee.

The next day Charlie and I were taking Mrs. Sinclair to see some show prospects at Mountjoy's stable. I was sitting in the back seat of the car and after several miles I had an overwhelming feeling that I should return home. It soon became evident to Charlie that there was nothing to do but turn around. I had been home less than ten minutes when the phone rang and a lady identified herself as Mrs. Lumia's sister. I replied that we were so excited about Eddie's coming for a visit. She replied, "Mrs. Crabtree, he WAS coming." Stunned, I asked why she said "was", not "he is". Then she told me the horrifying news that Eddie's van had gone over the side of a mountain and Eddie was killed.

That was almost 30 years ago. Every time I see a young man riding in equitation my heart breaks once more. The list of present day equitation instructors is awesome, but I can never overcome the certainty that the sport is missing the contributions of one of the finest human beings I ever knew.

13
A Giant Of The Industry
(S & B June, 1995)

Last week while organizing some lesson tapes that are intended for production next spring, I was delighted to discover a tape of a speech I had made for what was intended to be a friendly "roast" of Alvin Ruxer-philanthropist, entrepreneur and undoubtedly one of the most influential forces in the history of the American Saddlebred Horse.

His dear wife, a victim of Alzheimers disease was not with us that night. The talks were hilarious and thoroughly enjoyed by all of the thoughtful group of trainers and friends, including what was an embarrassing campaign speech by an aspiring candidate for the governorship of Kentucky, topped off by Donna Moore's remark that in all of her dealings with Ruxer Farms she had never gotten the best of a deal with Alvin.

Then came my turn, someone who could be counted on for irreverent but zany humor. When I stood to speak, I could not bring myself to joke about a relationship with a family who had so indelibly influenced the lives and careers of the Crabtrees. The transcribed tape in its entirety may reveal in some way the great respect that we had for a giant of our industry - the impact of Ruxer Farms.

We had an owner that was a little hard to handle, mostly because he was inebriated, and we kept a pretty watchful eye on him. However he got loose from us and his wife at one session of a sale that was held in St. Louis and when the smoke had cleared he had bought this enormous walk-trot gelding for his daughter. Charlie tried, we all tried, and he improved some, but it was obvious that this horse was just too much for a 12-year-old child, so we disposed of him. The next thing we knew, we heard that this horse had been bought by some farmer down in Jasper, Ind. And I said, "Well I hope he's a great big, strong man because it's going to take somebody like that to

Alvin Ruxer at his roast in the fall of 1990.

ride that horse." Well it was a big, strong man in every sense of the word. It was Alvin Ruxer and the name of the horse was Atomic Bomb, his first show horse and probably he will tell you that it was the beginning of his interest that developed into an empire as we all know it, and a most successful addition and help to everyone in this horse business.

In the 50s we moved to Arkansas and Charlie was in the generator business with his brother, a business closely akin, and in fact they sold and did business with the Jasper Engine Company which was Alvin's company. One night, just at dusk, Charlie was driving into this little town of Strawberry, Ark., and started across a suspension bridge and as the wheels got on the bridge the other end of the bridge flew up. Well it scared him to death, but there was nothing to do but keep going. So when he got in there he asked the dealer, "How do I get back to Little Rock, I've got to get back there?" The man looked at the truck and said, "With that truck? You can't." Charlie said, "Well Alvin Ruxer's trucks get through there all the time." And the man said, "Oh are you a friend of Alvin's? You can get over that bridge."

In 1954 we moved to Rock Creek, in fact it was Derby Day, a terrible time. The following Sunday morning, our first day at Rock Creek, we awakened, looked down and who was waiting for us but L.S. Dickey and his son. Mr. Dickey was known throughout the horse world as an absolute miracle worker — all the miracles in his favor. So we didn't want to get hooked up with Mr. Dickey and Charlie said, "Let's not go down, maybe they'll go away." I said, "You know Mr. Dickey, he's not going to go away." So we went down and after he suggested that it would be a good thing for all of us to go into business together we tried to change the subject and Charlie said, "Are you acquainted with a Mr. Ruxer over in Jasper, Indiana?" "Oh," he replied. Finest fellow you ever met. I mean he's the cream of the crop, there's just nobody better than Alvin and Hilda Ruxer." Well, I'm telling you that nearly scared us to death, because we had thought so much of the Ruxers up to then but we received such a glowing recommendation from this mountebank, we didn't know what to think. But we soon found out of course.

We visited the Ruxers many times, and as anyone who is here knows, and almost everyone here has visited the Ruxers, they have to be the world's greatest host and hostess, the kindest people.

They love gossip. They would never gossip, but they loved to hear it. They were off in the country and didn't hear much. We were down at Rock Creek working so hard we never heard anything, but what little tidbits we could pick up they always wanted to hear. I remember Hilda sitting at the end of the table, her eyes just sparkling, glistening, and every once in a while she would say, "Now Alvin, now Alvin," and Alvin's sitting there leaning over his plate, his eyes and his glasses sparkling, saying, "Yeah, yeah." But you know you had to be careful up there because if you liked anything and admired it they would give it to you. Kind of like the South Africans. I just want to tell Alvin that he gave us a bug fryer and we still haven't figured out how to use that thing.

We had a young stud that we were right proud of, three-year-old by Valley View Supreme. Mr. Ruxer came by, he always came by to see colts Charlie was working. Charlie said, "Let me show you this stud colt we're so proud of." Alvin took one look and said, "What are you keeping that ugly thing a stud for?" Well there wasn't too much of an answer for that, so Charlie took the horse back to the barn. A few years later, after having watched with interest that Bob Lewis had done very, very well on the West Coast with this horse and that he had sired some very, very nice horses out there, we were at Ruxers going down the hallway and as we went past one stall Charlie stopped and said, "This horse looks familiar Alvin, who's that?" Alvin kind of scuffed his toe in the pavement, looked up with that sly grin he had and said, "That's Makers Mark." Charlie said, "Oh, that old, ugly stud colt we had." Alvin said, "Well you know Charlie, horses can change."

I always remember we were Ruxer watchers at Rock Creek because they had such unbounded enthusiasm they made you enjoy everything, even if it was a boring class. We were watching one night and here was Alvin with his elbows up on the rail in front of him, his head thrust forward watching every move. Two little boys were sitting behind us and we overheard one of them say, "Hey what's that fellow doing out there, *leaning forward like that. He looks like a hawk." And his friend said, "No, he's an owner. They all look like that."*

Barbados Exit was our introduction to Bobby Ruxer. We saw him show him, and then we bought him and he was a wonderful horse for all of us. It was the beginning of the public's awarness that it just wasn't a pair of Ruxers, it was a triumvirate of wonderful, wonderful people.

We moved up here to our new place and built a barn a couple of years ago. One day the doorbell rang and here was Alvin. Charlie worked a horse every year for Alvin for years. We never knew when he was coming. He'd hop in and if the horse hadn't been worked why he'd watch him work and if he had he'd say, "That's fine, that's fine." Well we never knew when he was coming and this day unfortunately Charlie wasn't there and we were so anxious to show him our new barn. We were so proud of it and had put so much thought and effort into it. So Alvin and his friend walked through. "Oh nice barn, Helen, nice, nice." I couldn't believe it, I kept waiting for the ax to fall, I knew we had done something wrong. "No, it's a lovely barn, it's a lovely barn As we went out he turned and looked back and said, "You've got a low spot in your yard. That's gonna cause you trouble right there." And Alvin, I want to tell you that we're on the third tree and none of them have lived yet.

We all have indelible impressions of people who have been important in our lives. If I were a good enough artist I could draw you this picture, maybe I can tell you this picture. It was at Rock Creek and the show was just getting ready to start. The mounted patrol was at the gate and here went Alvin and Hilda. Alvin with big strides, his head thrust forward - didn't want to miss a thing - Hilda taking those little skip steps to keep up with him. They would watch the most boring part of a horse show and stay interested in it. Their interest never waned and they infected more people with that interest. But what they did for me that moment was to put that indelible picture that I will always remember - of the Hawk and the wind beneath his wings.

Lady Carrigan with Garland Bradshaw, up.

14
Garland Bradshaw
(S & B October, 1995)

Of the many famous and fascinating trainers we have met over these years, none was more entertaining than Garland Bradshaw.

Not as tall as his brother Frank, Garland was moderately short, somewhat bowlegged, and burley chested. His most compelling features were his twinkling eyes, blue as the sky and never still, they saw everything.

It was a pleasant surprise to the Crabtrees to find this legendary trainer was such a kind and thoughtful person who not only welcomed us to Kentucky, but was extremely generous in sharing his wealth of knowledge with us to help in any way he could.

Quite often we would look up to see the Pontiac car turn in the driveway at Rock Creek. Out would hop Bradshaw, saying, "When I had the fourth student (horse) in a row act like he didn't know anything, I figured it was me and I just quit before I made things worse."

Right there Garland taught the valuable lesson of accepting responsibility for the trainer's part in horse training.

Then he would sit down and "talk horse" to a family anxious to be better. Garland's merry eyes danced with every emotion and his rather squeaky, trembly voice cracked with enthusiasm as his partially palsied hands moved with every inflection of his voice.

The list of Bradshaw's great champions is awesome, but my stories deal with the more personal aspect of the people and horses I've known. Show records are dull and useful only for statistical purposes.

However it is impossible to think of Garland Bradshaw without remembering his first great world's grand champion Nellie Pigeon. One incident in particular is horse show lore and Charles Crabtree was standing on the rail to observe the occurrence.

It was at the Chicago International Horse Show. The judges were two professors whom all trainers dreaded to face. They were very honest, unbiased gentlemen, but had an academic approach to their judging. For instance, they would test the severity of the bits in a ladies class, they would pull on a horse's tail to see if the hair was all natural. Years later Joan Farris, Andrea Walton's mother, had this wonderful saying that I thought completely characterized the judging of Professor Don Kayes and Professor Trowbridge. That marvelous saying was, "If you can't be good, be technical." So when the two judges approached Bradshaw and the nervous mare Nellie Pigeon in the lineup and asked Bradshaw to back the mare, he nearly exploded with indignation. Purple faced he squeaked, "Back-up?! I've been a year getting her to go forward."

Garland was not unaware of the impact of his clever sayings and it is very possible this same remark was repeated on other occasions, but it is a great story and so characteristic of the quick-witted man.

In recalling Garland Bradshaw, one must immediately think of his great world grand champion five-gaited mare, Lady Carrigan. Winner in 1954, 1955, 1957, and 1958 for three different owners, the startling bay beauty must be recognized as one of the most beautiful American Saddlebreds of all time. A dark, lustrous bay, the mare was cameo-fine, wild, willful, explosive and blessed with the ability to execute five gaits to perfection.

Although her championships were at Louisville, her most unforgettable performance was in the five-gaited championship at the Lexington Junior League Show on the big Red Mile.

The class had been worked and then the horses came to line up and have the saddles removed for the judges' evaluation of conformation and beauty. While the rest of us had been busy showing our own horses, we were aware that Lady Carrigan was making a spectacular show. Bradshaw lined the mare up at the far end of the ring. Just as the judges began their tour of inspection, Garland snatched the reins over the mare's head and dashed down the infield side of the ring, leading the glorious mare in one of the most thrilling exhibitions in show horse history.

The mare followed, going what is termed a "barnyard trot", her legs moving higher with every stride. Her eyes were white-rimmed with excitement, her nostrils flared as she gave out a wild snort and her chiffon-like tail waved high in the air.

The rest of us in the line-up could only stare in amazement at the spectacular performance.

I do not think that Garland Bradshaw had planned the solo exhibition. That mare had been so great in the class, that her inspired rider could not end the event at a standstill. It was an impulse so powerful that he had to show the spectators how great the excited mare could be.

Had anyone but Bradshaw and Lady Carrigan dared to leave the line-up, the ringmaster would have called them back to the line, but the bay mare was so astonishing, that judges and ring officials could only marvel at what they were seeing.

Those spectators who saw that glorious mare trotting behind Bradshaw can recall every step the mare took.

Even today, I look at that infield fence, just past the flag pole, and I see once again that ecstatic trainer and the wild and fabulous mare.

A job as assistant to Garland Bradshaw was coveted by every aspiring young trainer. Their devotion to the master horseman went beyond ordinary admiration and one might say that those fortunate young men were almost a cult.

He was a hard taskmaster never sparing himself nor the boys who worked for him. The hours were long, the work bordering drudgery. Garland was a farmer and if hay was down and rain threatened, everyone went to the fields. The Bradshaw stable was modest, having no arena, but making use of an enclosed area at the very front of the stable no more than 120 feet in length. The success of that enterprise depended entirely on the masterful approach to horse training of one of the great trainers of all time.

The following well known names put in their apprenticeship with Garland Bradshaw - Dave Clark, Jack Nevitt, Harold Poil, Carter Cox, Jack Noble, Mitch Clark, Jim Koller, Lee Shipman, Bill Becker, and Warren Bugg. Many of these trainers show Bradshaw's style of riding. He did not post the trot, but he did not stiffen his body and bounce as some do. As he rose to the top of each stride he would fling his short legs out to the side of the horse and for that one moment there would be no weight on the horse's back. He appeared to hold the reins in his finger tips and the palsy he lived with would cause a fluttering effect of the reins. One of his disciples copied Bradshaw's mannerisms to such an extreme that one wondered if he was going to stay on the horse's back, he bounced the trot and jiggled his hands convulsively. I often wondered if he knew that Bradshaw could not hold his hands still.

Of the trainers now showing who were Bradshaw boys, the influence of the master is evident. Mitchell Clark thinking his way through the complicated stallion Sky Watch, Carter Cox with his always thoughtful and deliberate approach to each horse as an individual, to Jim Koller whose fingers on the reins are so reminiscent of Garland Bradshaw who seemed to handle the reins like a master harpist plucking the strings to produce beautiful music.

Garland Bradshaw's contribution to the American Saddlebred defies words. His understanding of a horse's mind, his hard work, his great show ring presence, his tenacity as a competitor, and above all his willingness to share his great knowledge make him one of a kind in our industry. His influence is as strong today as it was when he was showing, and every one of us in this profession are the better for it.

15

William P. Harsh
(S & B February, 1996)

To a majority of young equitation riders today, the name Bill Harsh is only a name on a trophy presented to the winner of the American Royal Equitation Championship. That is why I am writing about William P. Harsh of Overland Park, Kansas.

It was 24 years ago that one of my riders Kathie Gallagher, (daughter of Mrs. F.D. Sinclair, and sister of Mary Lou Gallagher Doudican) won the trophy in the show championship. Upon noting the inscription on the trophy, given by William P. Harsh in memory of his father, George Harsh, I mentioned to Kathie that William Harsh must be a very nice man. Whereupon, we found where Mr. and Mrs. Harsh were seated. Introducing Kathie and myself, I explained that we were very impressed by his obvious reverence for his father, and Kathie thanked him for the lovely trophy. Mr. Harsh introduced us to Mrs. Harsh and the Hall family and praised Kathie on her ride and went on to say that he had never before been thanked for a trophy.

That was the beginning of a friendship that survived almost 25 years until Bill Harsh died a year ago. That is why every year the announcer says, the class was first won by Kathie Gallagher in 1974, the first year for the equitation championship at the Royal.

Bill would still laugh at the time they clapped and smiled as I ran out of the ring with the winner. I held up my right hand, denoting that our riders won first through fifth. I'm sure this feat has been duplicated as more and more riders want to ride at the American Royal. With the addition of the UPHA Finals and the AHSA Medal, all accomplished because of Bill Harsh's intense interest in young riders and his conviction that the future and very existence of the American Saddlebred horse was rooted in young riders and equitation.

As the only officer of the famous Hallmark Company who was not a family member of the Hall family, Bill was an incredible man.

William P. Harsh

Mrs. Margaret Harsh presenting replica of American Royal Equitaiton Trophy.

I have never known anyone who cared about his fellow man as much as Bill. He loved the American Royal, he loved all of the trainers and workers who brought their horses to that show year after year.

Why would anyone want to show at the Royal when most show seasons were ended and the weather was generally uncomfortable? The answer comes down to that one man, Bill Harsh. Every morning one could expect to see him visiting every stable, no matter how small, to see if there was anything he could do to make the week in Kansas City more enjoyable. Harsh was not a show manager, he was only a member of the large organization that put on "The Royal." But what endeared him to everyone was his sincere interest in us all and the fact that every morning we knew that Bill Harsh would come past every stable to inquire, "is everything all right? Is there anything we (not "I"!) can do for you?"

Did you know that Bill Harsh never owned or showed Saddle Horses? He rode with the Mission Valley Hunt! Bill loved horses. A love dating back to his third birthday when he received his first pony. His chief form of relaxation and pleasure always involved horses and he liked all breeds. In addition to his involvement with the American Royal, Mr. Harsh could often be found riding his horse Cracker Jack at the Saddle and Sirloin Club or with the Mission Valley Hunt Club.

It became a tradition for my winner of the championship and me to be taken on a tour of the fabulous Hallmark headquarters. We met the talented artists turning out their marvelous designs. Rick Ruddish, who drew the enchanting animals, offered to illustrate a child's book of riding if I would write it. His premature death came before I could write such a book.

Bill was extremely proud of the Hallmark accomplishments and would point out with pride the original Grandma Moses card. Yes, it was Hallmark who discovered Grandma Moses. A visit to Mr. Hall's office was awe-inspiring. I will always remember looking at the cast of Churchill's hand on Mr. Hall's desk.

Bill Harsh was always generous with his time and shared the Hallmark experience with so many of us. In 1983 it was a complete and unusual coincidence that he presented Charles Crabtree, then president of the UPHA with Honorary Citizenship of Kansas City, and Charles Crabtree, as UPHA president, presented Bill

Harsh with the Outstanding Achievement Award at the convention the following January.

Only the finest lady deserved to be the wife of Bill Harsh and that is exactly the role Margaret Harsh held so many years. These few words are hardly adequate to describe the place Bill and Margaret Harsh played in the lives of so many owners and trainers.

16

George Gwinn
(S & B March, 1996)

Of all the successful Saddle Horse salesmen, no one has ever equaled the quintessential southern gentleman that is George Gwinn, master of Gwinn Island Stock Farm in Danville, Ky. Although long retired and still living in his elegant home, Gwinn's influence lives on in the descendants of the great horses he bought and sold.

Surely his most lasting influence on our industry is in the many horsemen who apprenticed with their idol. Some of the many are George Nash, Dave Clark, Kenny Walker and the most famous of all Jim Koller, whose winning ride on Onion in the 1994 World's Championships surely must have made Gwinn swell up with pride.

Our experience with Mr. Gwinn began two days after we moved to Rock Creek Riding Club. Gwinn called and welcomed the young couple to Kentucky, offering his help in any capacity and embellishing his invitation to come to his stable with a glowing description of a bay five-gaited gelding.

It was strictly coincidental that Shine Ogan had told me about a chestnut mare from Adam's Stable in Odebolt, Iowa, who had just won the three-gaited stake in the Des Moines Spring Show. So when we went to Gwinn's the first thing I saw as we got out of our car was a big white horse van from Odebolt and coming down the ramp was a chestnut three-gaited mare. She had to be the mare Ogan had described so enthusiastically. I turned to Gwinn and said, "I'd like to buy that mare and if she checks out sound I'll give you $4,000." "Oh, Mrs. Crabtree that mare is tired from the long trip I could not show her to you." "I am aware of that," I responded, "but I would like my offer to stand until I have had the chance to come back in one week and see the mare."

Gwinn accepted the offer and we made a date for my return in one week. I was buying the mare with our own money, but I had her in mind for Joe Greathouse, a fine young rider at Rock Creek. Now I had one week to convince Joe's father to buy the mare.

Fairview's Blanchita and Joe Greathouse.

I called Mr. Greathouse and told him about my offer of $4,000 and that I wanted him to consider the mare for Joe at $5,000. That began one of the longest weeks of my life. I have never met anyone who wanted to buy a horse but who wanted even more to make my life absolutely miserable in an attempt to convince him to say yes. If I had not such a strong initial impression of the mare and having returned to check her for soundness, I might have given up trying to close the deal with such an obstinate man. In my mind the mare was ideal for Joe and I was willing to fight it out to see that pair together.

Finally Mr. Greathouse agreed to go to Danville to see the mare, but he wanted to take his own veterinarian. His choice was a veterinarian located on Broadway in Louisville whose practice consisted mainly of dogs and cats.

When the three of us arrived at the farm Gwinn led the mare out and posed her. The vet said, "My, isn't she beautiful! She's O.K." Hooray, I thought, the deal is set. Then came the confrontation between George Gwinn and Hunt Greathouse. Greathouse insisted on seeing the mare's papers and asked that Gwinn sign them over to him. Gwinn replied the papers would be transferred immediately upon his receipt of a check. Greathouse demurred and said, "If I give you this check, how can I be sure you'll sign the papers?" At that I turned and walked away mentally throwing up my hands in defeat and watched from afar Gwinn and Greathouse entering the office to finalize the deal.

It was a wonderful combination and Joe rode Fairview's Blanchita almost without defeat including wins at Lexington, Louisville and all the big shows at that time.

Gwinn called a few months later and asked us to come to see some nice horses. One of the Rock Creek horses was temporarily laid up so I asked Gwinn if he had anything to lease for the remainder of the show season. "Yessiree," he enthused, "I have just the mare. We intend to breed her next spring and she is a very pretty little mare." This was just what we hoped to lease.

When we arrived, we entered the office and were treated to his southern hospitality ice cold branch water and the best bourbon. When all were sufficiently glowing, the dapper host opened the office screen door and a horse appeared like magic. The horse had taken only a few strides, when Charlie said, "George, that is the same bay gelding." Unruffled, George said, "Well not entirely because he had improved so much!"

Then I walked down the aisle to watch a pretty little three-gaited mare being saddled. Sensing that this was the "lease" mare I watched with a critical eye. Was this mare sound? Why was she waiting to be a broodmare? As the trainer led her from the stall he turned her sharply to the left and the mare took a suspicious stride. However, that can happen to any horse, so I kept quiet and we put our young rider on the mare.

Gwinn suggested that we all go outside the barn where we could better view the mare. "No, don't go down the cinder path, get over on the grass." Gwinn told the rider. The cinder path was hard but the ankle-deep lush bluegrass was soft as a feather bed. Now Gwinn had a wonderful Collie dog who knew the difference between a trot and a rack better than some judges I have seen. The rider gave the little mare the signal to trot and she started off at a half trot half amble. That smart dog knew that it was not a real trot nor was it a real rack at which he always barked excitedly, so he looked up in his master's face and began to whine. Everyone laughed. Gwinn told the rider that she could return to the stable and we told him that if he intended showing the mare to anyone else he had better lock up the dog.

George Gwinn would never misrepresent a horse, but if one were foolish enough or too ignorant to evaluate an animal he would not interfere with their conclusions. In addition to the dog and the fine young horseman who teamed their trade at Gwinn's farm, his most valued player in the scheme of things there was his right-hand assistant George Winfree.

Winfree was a very small man — you had the feeling looking at his guileless grin and twinkling eyes that one was just seeing a grown up boy. Not so. Winfree and Gwinn choreographed the same tactics for every visitor. At some moment Winfree would quietly come up and say, "Slip away with me and I will show you the best horse, because Mr. Gwinn would like to keep him."

History does not keep record how many horses were sold with this ploy but the old student trainers always smile and say that, "Mr. Gwinn never did anything by chance." But of all the things that were amazing about George Gwinn was his psychology of selling unlike anyone I have ever known. Gwinn did not point out a horse's obvious attributes. Instead, he would deliberately point to a horse's worst qualities and say to the poor trainer whose customer had already fallen under Gwinn's spell, "Isn't that a beautiful neck?", and the trainer was stuck.

All of the many people who have ever known George Gwinn consider him the finest Saddle Horse dealer of all time. Even at his advanced age, I am sure that George Gwinn will be wearing a necktie.

17
Mrs. Sinclair

It was very difficult in writing this book to mention those outstanding people over the years. There were so many of them that we owe so much to that I have hesitated in talking about them for fear that I would leave someone out. If I have it is with my humblest apologies. This book would not ever be large enough to hold the number of people that meant so much to us in our lives. I think I would be remiss, however, not to make a particular reference to a particular owner and that is Katherine Sinclair.

We all know her as Mrs. F.D.Sinclair but when we all started she was Mrs. Gallagher and she had two daughters who rode. Kathie the older daughter and Mary Lou. Mary Lou is still showing with the Crabtrees. Her married name is Doudican and she has two children. Katherine Sinclair (not to be confused with Kathie) is still such an active and wonderful owner.

She likes good horses and has such a tremendous talent for them. She had a background of showing long before we knew her and we were so happy for her to join our organization. She wanted to drive harness horses and to say she did that or owned them would be the understatement of the century. The horses she bought that either she drove or Charlie drove (or both), set records that I am sure will never be equaled again. The nicest thing about Katherine was that she never complained. She always loved to show. She knew enough to know when she had a good show and when she had a bad show but she never complained about the judging or about how her horse worked. She just left all that to us, the trainers. With the girls-Mary Lou and the wonderful Lad O'Shea among others, and Kathie, with the Tempest which Charlie trained, it has been a family affair for many years.

After Katherine had to stop driving because of an operation on the palm of her hand there were times when Radiance was still showing and she would ask me to drive her. Oh I hated to do that.

I loved driving that wonderful mare but every time I drove her somebody beat me. I drove three times for Katherine and I was second every time. The first time was with Supreme Airs. This was a very doubtful tie. I mean Garland Bradshaw was infuriated along with some other people, but it was a close tie. So we can discount that. The other two times I just plain did not drive well enough and Sallie Wheeler had the wonderful harness mare, Tashi Ling at that time and it was always nip and tuck between those two mares who was going to win. When Sallie was not showing her mare, Katherine would ask Sallie to drive the mare instead of me which suited me fine. I was always busy anyway and could never dress up in the pretty clothes because I was in riding clothes getting people in and out of the ring and showing. So it was a favor to me and also I have to add that Sallie was such a gracious person that she always said, "I think I am cheating you out of driving this wonderful mare." Then she would turn up with an Hermes scarf (which any girl who reads this book will know is a wonderful gift).

When the time came for Katherine to retire Supreme Airs who showed for her and Charlie for nine years, it was at Madison Square Garden that she made her last show. Charlie was so nervous that he was practically in masculine tears before the class. I went in the arena and climbed to the highest seats to try and take any tension away from him. What a thing to have the 43rd blue ribbon on the line and know that if he won the class it would be an undefeated season, not only for this mare but three others, including Captivation.

He did win the class and when he left the ring there were tears running down his face from relief, pride and gratitude to a lady who was willing to have the Fine Harness horses that Katherine had and the good ones. She took chances. She did not just go out to buy the established champions. She went by our recommendation and let Charlie develop them into the great champions that they were.

Now considering this when Supreme Airs was relegated to the broodmare ranks we thought that perhaps Mrs. Sinclair would have a retirement ceremony for her. We had had retirement ceremonies before and certainly knew how to go about it. She said nothing about it so one day we asked, "Are you going to have a ceremony at Louisville next year for Supreme Airs?" she said "No, I am going to send Mr. and Mrs. Charles Crabtree to Hawaii for ten days as my guest in recognition for all of the wonderful times they have given me. Supreme Airs will be retired to a wonderful life and get her just desserts but I want you people to know how much joy you have brought to this family." I think that merits mentioning. Not the fact that she did not give a retirement ceremony, but that she wanted to do something nice for two people who had given her family so much pleasure. Now if all the owners were like that wouldn't life be wonderful.

Mrs. Sinclair still has horses with the Crabtrees. This is the third generation. She had horses with Charles and Helen, then with son Redd, and now with grandson Casey. Now that's loyalty!

18
"Big Mama" and Laurie
(S & B June, 1996)

One other memorable trip was to San Francisco.

Laurie Bechtel is the daughter and granddaughter of the men of Bechtel Oil, one of the most powerful corporations in world-wide oil productions.

Grandfather Bechtel was a true patriarch and had decided that Laurie could come to Kentucky for one year of showing Saddle Horses. Sister Shana was established as a fine Stock Seat rider on the west coast where the competition is very deep and the instructors are the best.

Laurie was a tall, lovable young girl whom everyone immediately adopted and welcomed into our group.

Obviously, her horse had to be tall, so we selected for her a grand moving three-gaited mare from Garland Bradshaw. Her name, befitting her size, was "Big Mama".

There was one feature of this mare that bugged me, and that was her ears. They sat on her head right, were not too long, but they flared very wide. I had a friend whose daughter had an unfortunate facial feature, so the wise parents resorted to plastic surgery and the result was wonderful. The child gained self confidence and was a changed person.

Why could we not perform plastic surgery on Big Mama's ears? Just narrowing them would be sufficient. I had closely examined the ears to find that the seemingly extra width was outside of the outer vein.

We were acquainted with a vet who was an expert at trimming Boxer dogs' ears. He also did work with horses. So I asked him to consider the ear job.

It went remarkably well and within ten days I could put a full show bridle on Big Mama. We had given her around-the-clock care but the stout-hearted mare never acted like anything had been done. The ears were beautiful and Mama must have been proud of them, too, as she never put an ear back in the show ring or at home.

"Big Mama" with a new look.

Charles, Helen, Leila and Bob.

The "Dancing Crabtrees". Guess who we just saw?

I knew that the mare's appearance had improved 50 percent. What I did not know was that no outsider ever knew what I had done. But they all complimented me on improving the mare's way of going. Improve a Garland Bradshaw "student"? No way!! But never try to tell me that a great deal of performance is NOT beauty.

Laurie had a wonderful Kentucky summer and no girl was ever more popular than she.

We were all sad when the season was over and Laurie returned to the West Coast, where Big Mama was sold to Helen Wallerstein, a middle-aged horse enthusiast who fell in love with the mare and I was astounded that this little woman who was barely five feet tall would like the 17 hand mare. But Helen bought her and enjoyed winning seasons with the mare whose remodeled ears had so improved her way of going.

That winter the Bechtels sent two plane tickets and three days of reservations at the San Francisco Landmark, the Fairmont Hotel.

Their chauffeur met us at the airport and returned to the hotel that evening to take us to the Bechtel's beautiful home on the bay. Both girls were there with their mother. Steve their father and grandfather Bechtel were in Saudi Arabia.

What charming people were Mrs. Bechtel and Shana. It was a tearful reunion with Laurie as her Kentucky days were over.

For two days the chauffeur drove us everywhere in the fabulous city. We have been fortunate to have visited many foreign cities but none can compare with fascinating San Francisco.

The Robert Lewises had been dear friends from years back, so we stayed over to visit with them. The first evening we went to a Mexican Restaurant to dine and dance.

Charlie and I were whirling around the dance floor when we collided with another couple. As we hastily apologized we realized that the gentleman was from Shelby County, Kentucky, and his young partner was definitely not his wife. They made a hasty retreat and we continued to have a wonderful evening with our friends Bob and Leila.

The following night we enjoyed a Chinese restaurant that was definitely worth the pushing and pulling to negotiate the extremely steep sidewalk that lead to the restaurant. We have had many a laugh over that San Francisco hill!

When one considers the fact that Charlie and I had been treated to one of the most memorable trips of our lives by a family whose daughter had ridden only one season with us — one must conclude that these were not only wonderful people, but were a family expressing appreciation for a summer with a girl that will always remain in our memories.

19

The Little Goat Who Thought He Was A Dog
(S & B January, 1995)

We were going to get a goat at Rock Creek Riding Club in Louisville, Ky., where my husband, Charles and I were the managers. It would be the fulfillment of a lifelong dream for me. Most childish dreams disappear in time, but this one had stayed with me throughout my life. I had wanted a goat since seeing a pet goat (complete with harness and cart) when I was a very young child. Everything that I really wanted I had gotten, and now the goat, at last.

We had a very nervous five-gaited mare and the president of the club, also president of the Stockyards Bank, was bringing a young goat to the club that very night. The goat had been orphaned at birth and a local family had raised him on a bottle. But no one wanted the grown goat when the owners moved away from Kentucky. So, I was not only getting a real live goat, but I was saving him from being butchered at the stockyards.

When he jumped down from the station wagon someone said, "What a dandy goat!" Since his former owner had called him "Jim" I said that we would call him "Dandy Jim" as in the vernacular, he was a "Jim Dandy Goat" '

He was a Toggenburg goat, a handsome little fellow, sandy brown coat, white legs and two stripes running up from his suede-like white muzzle to join the two dainty horns that sloped back from his forehead. He had soft, delicate ears and an immaculate little goatee on his chin. His most amazing features were his large topaz yellow eyes flecked with bronze.

We put him in an empty stall in the horse barn to get accustomed to what was to be his home. I could not get the little fellow out of my mind. He had been neutered that morning and I was sure he had to be uncomfortable. So long after the rest of the family was asleep, I tiptoed down the stairs where we lived at the club, across the porch and down the driveway into the stable. When I opened his stall door Dandy came up to me - so glad to see a friend

Sketches by Polly Holabird.

after his harrowing day. Not only did I go to see Dandy, but I had two aspirin tablets that I thrust down his trusting throat. Then he leaned his trembling shoulder against my side. Drawing my robe closely around me, I sat down in the stall and he laid down with his head in my lap. Without knowing why, I rubbed his forehead and slowly he stopped trembling. I wanted him to know that he was in a safe place and that he had at least one true friend. Only then could I leave the lonely animal and return to my bed.

The next morning we tried to get the mare to accept the goat, but it soon became evident that the plan would not work, as the mare was an absolute shrew and would do her best to kill the goat. Therefore I was not surprised when the mare's owner, Mr. Green, made me a gift of the goat.

Our family pets included two dogs and a cat. The beautiful scotch collie was "Cap" ' His constant shadow was a demure, little female of assorted lineage. People who knew dog breeding thought they were seeing a French Papillion, the "butterfly" dog because of her large upstanding ears crowned by long hairs extending from the tips, thus the name "Buttercup". However the stocky body, long, shiny reddish coat and very short legs gave lie to any hint of planned breeding. A sweet, gentle temperament gave "Buttercup" a special place in our hearts. "Butch", the Siamese cat, was the intellectual of the group and my constant companion, day and night. We feared an integration problem with the goat, but happily Dandy Jim was immediately taken in by the other three animals.

How those four animals would entertain us! Cap would crouch in front of Dandy, rump high, tail wagging furiously, front legs and head flat to the ground, his eyes sparkling at the prospect of a wonderful game of tag. Buttercup would wait for the action to start and Butch would crouch on the porch steps, waiting to join the game. All were still until Dandy did his favorite thing - rearing on his hind legs, curving his back to twist the neck to the side and "dive bomb" the collie. Then the chase was on! Cap wildly racing in circles, Dandy going as fast as his stiff, little goat legs would permit. Buttercup following as fast as she could go. Butch, with typical feline shrewdness would wait until the pace slowed. Then he would leap from the steps and out run everyone. If any of the three would dare to bump into Butch, he would dash for the hole in the screened porch and sneer at the bullies while he stomped his rigid walk, tail straight up, the end snapping forward at every stride. Anyone who has ever owned a Siamese cat will know that "Siamese Stomp"!

The two dogs and the goat became inseparable. We called them the three musketeers. Not very original, but in light of the fact that Dandy had no recollection of his heritage, he must have thought that he really was a dog with horns and odd cloven feet.

I taught my riders from a wooden-slat park bench beside the outdoor riding ring, using a megaphone to amplify my voice. When I started for the ring I would be followed by Dandy Jim, Cap, Buttercup and Butch. I must have looked like the "Pied Piper". The two dogs at my feet, the cat sitting beside me. Dandy would put his head on my knee, waiting for me to lower the megaphone so he could rub his forehead on the inside of it. Thus I found that his favorite caress was not a pat on the neck but a rub on his bone-hard forehead.

On returning to the stables after lessons, the parade would follow. As we neared the barn, Cap, Buttercup and Dandy would dash after the rabbits that came out beside the barn to feast on the tender clover. Butch would just sit there watching what was always a fruitless chase. He knew that the rabbits would escape to safety through the thick hedge at the edge of the property.

Animals know when a person does not like them, and this was certainly the case with Dandy Jim and his former owner, Mr Green. A big, shiny black Cadillac was the man's pride and joy and every time it pulled into the parking area, Dandy would be fascinated. What a wonderful climb! Realizing this we kept a watchful eye on the goat. One unforgettable day Dandy sneaked away from his three playmates. When one of the riders gave a strangled cry, "Mrs. Crabtreeeeee!" I looked in horror to see Dandy tip-toeing around the narrow water ledge that encircled the topsides of the car. Mr. Green, who still detested the goat saw what was happening and raced across the drive, flailing his arms and yelling, "Get off my car!" Startled, Dandy soared into a big dive and landed with all four of his sharp, cloven hooves on the front of the car and slid the length of the long, shiny hood, leaving a perfect and awful set of tracks etched into the beloved Cadillac.

Rock Creek Club was located across the street from beautiful Cherokee Park, a city facility that had sport fields of all kinds and a lovely golf course. One morning we heard a frantic clattering of hooves on the driveway, and here came the two dogs and the goat racing back to the club. They ran behind the stables and flopped down in the shade. Very shortly after that a police car drove in and an officer asked Charlie if he had two dogs and a goat - that golfers were complaining that the animals were tearing up the greens. Charlie pointed out the three panting culprits and said, "There mine are. It must have been two other dogs and a goat!" Luckily the policeman had a wry sense of humor and told Charlie that he was sure he knew better than to let his animals tear up the golf greens!

We had a jolly, cook who came to work one day laughing so hard that the tears were streaming down her cheeks. On the bus to work that morning she heard that Dandy had gone up to one of the neighboring houses and had reared up to look in the top glass window of the front door. In doing so he inadvertently put one hoof on the doorbell. The maid opened the door, saw the goat with the pointed horns and little beard and immediately fainted. She was sure that Satan had come for her! What we referred to as "dive bombing" was a purely typical movement of all goats.

But it was the only true goat action that Dandy Jim ever displayed. We would occasionally see him staring at the side of a highly polished car. Was he seeing his reflection or being fascinated by the moving images faintly reflected?

We had to conclude that he really did think he was a dog being constantly with them and to our knowledge he had encountered only humans and dogs since birth. But this was soon to be changed when we took Dandy Jim to the Dayton, Ohio Horse Show. I snapped a lead shank into his collar and took him for a stroll around the stable area. Imagine my delight when I discovered a fellow trainer walking his pet goat, a very large, black Nubian goat who measured at least five inches higher than our little Toggenburg. The black goat was very ugly. He had a large V-shaped head with long pendulous ears, a huge, hard forehead sloping into a Roman nose to complete his formidable appearance. Dandy seemed fascinated by this odd looking animal. Then he reared on his hind legs to engage the stranger in his favorite "dive bomber" game. BLAM! The Nubian had reared and crashed head-on with a very surprised and frightened little goat who scrambled to his feet and ran around behind me to peek at the big, black, oversized "dog" that had just knocked him down on his behind.

The poor trainer! He was very apologetic, but I explained that our little goat actually thought that the Nubian was a dog, never having seen a goat. To lend credence to my remark, Dandy spied a shaggy, brown cocker spaniel and rushed up to make friends with something he was accustomed to. Those two played together all that week, steering clear of the Nubian villain.

In January of the following year we left Rock Creek to establish our own business in Simpsonville, Ky. Our home and stable were facing two roads, one being the main east-west Kentucky highway. There was no way that we could control Dandy to keep him away from the dangerous traffic, so we moved to the country without my beloved goat. How I dreaded leaving my dear Dandy. As I drove away for the last time, I slowed to make the turn into the street. I looked back and those wonderful young riders, knowing that my leaving was heart breaking, were gathered around Dandy Jim, stuffing him with the carrots that were supposed to be for their horses. Neither Dandy nor I could know that it was a final farewell. A man who had a small farm near Fort Knox with a few sheep that we hoped would "adopt" a goat was coming that afternoon to take Dandy to his new home in rural Kentucky.

Our business grew rapidly and what with training horses, teaching, showing and judging, I had no time to miss Dandy Jim. In due time Dandy's three buddies, Cap, Buttercup and Butch died. We buried them side by side as they had always been.

Several years later we took some local owners to a show just west of Fort Knox. An elderly gentleman approached me and asked my name. When he heard it, his face broke into a smile and he told me he was the man who had taken Dandy Jim to his farm. "We thought that 'Jim', that's what we called him, would like the sheep. But he didn't cotton to them. All he would do was pal around with 'Shep' our old dog."

I told him about Dandy's love for Cap and Buttercup. The farmer said, "Oh, he loved our old dog. He went everywhere with Shep, even slept with him on the back porch." He then said the goat had disappeared and was gone for about two years. "Nobody ever saw Jim," he added. "We looked everywhere - even went to Fort Knox, but he just vanished."

"My wife had passed away," he said, "and I was mighty lonesome. Every evening I'd go set in the swing on the front porch an' watch the sun go down. I was all alone." He told me that one evening he was sitting there and he heard a clippity clop sound on the road and Dandy had come home. "He looked bad. Something had happened and the end of one horn was gone and he had a big scar over one eye. Jim seemed real glad to see me and he jumped right up on the swing and put his head on my knee for me to rub his forehead."

"Every summer night me and Jim would set there an' watch the sun go down. Then the frogs would start singin' and the lightnin' bugs would wink over by the marsh pasture across the road. Jim lived to be real old. We never missed a nice evening when we could set on the porch swing. In the late summer we would watch for fallin' stars."

Then he went on to say, "It really got to me when Jim died, but he gave me a lot of pleasure and company. I always wanted to tell you that Jim had a good life and I buried him right next to old Shep here on the farm."

Tears rushed up from my memory, welling in my eyes. Those four animals were a very special part of my life especially Dandy Jim. As I turned away, the man put a hand on my sleeve and said, "But, Mrs. Crabtree, there was always somethin' odd about Jim. He would be there in the swing with me, but just let a dog bark off in the distance and he would jump down and go over to the steps and just stand there and listen ... just stand and listen..."

Sketch by Polly Halabird

Butch.

20
"Butch" Phi Beta Kitty

"Okay, we'll take him, but we're not going to call him one of those sissy names like Ting-a-Ling that people always name a Siamese cat. We'll call him Butch", said Charlie, and that is how we became the owners of a pet that would become a part of our lives for the next seventeen years.

We were operating a Saddle Horse stable in Little Rock, Arkansas. One night after enjoying a lovely meal at some new friend's home, the hostess asked if we knew of anyone who would like to have a Siamese kitten. When we saw the litter, there was one male who seemed to dominate his brothers and sisters, so "Butch" was not an inappropriate name for this kitten. Much to my surprise, when I picked him up, he did not struggle to get away, but snuggled into my arms and started to purr. From that first moment I knew that he was not only Mister Cat, but that he was a veritable cream puff who knew how to capture a heart.

Although the litter was registered, Butch did not have the slinky body and slender face of the breed. His head was beautiful, wide cheeked with a short nose. His color was seal point, head, legs, and tail a stunning dark brown. And unlike the show cats I had seen on TV, his body was almost pure cream colored. His eyes were a pale sky blue adding to the appeal. He was beautiful, and he displayed his remarkable wisdom by reaching up to give me a loving kiss on my neck. This cat was determined to go home with us and from that moment on he was truly my cat.

The next morning I bought a cat harness envisioning myself parading around the horse shows with my beautiful cat preceding me at the end of a fancy leash. In short order, Butch shattered my grandiose dream. At the first tug on the leash, he turned into a screaming bundle of fur. Flipping over onto his back he grabbed the lead with his front paws trying his best to chew it in two. Not to be bested by a cat, I dragged him along on his back for a moment until a passing motorist honked his horn and shook his fist. That was all I needed - to be branded as a cruel cat dragger! Right there I learned a lesson that applied over the years. No one was going to convince this cat to do anything that he did not like. I was not going to be outsmarted by a cat. His air of being in charge was the trait that charmed us. So I decided that I would be the boss, but in order to get my way, I would have to resort to the wifely trick of making that cat think what I wanted was his own idea. And that was the foundation of our relationship for his entire lifetime.

Butch went with me every morning to the stables. Cap, our collie was a wonderful companion and watch dog, so he and Butch became good buddies. Imagine our surprise when Cap went racing and barking one night to challenge squirrels at the back door and Butch went right along yowling fiercely. I had read that in ancient days Siamese cats were used as, "watch cats" at their Emperor's palace.

Lying on our bed one night scantily clad as the house was not air-conditioned, we were reading the Sunday papers when, without warning, Butch raced into the room, up on the bed and made a playful swipe at Charlie. Charlie shouted at Butch and the cat made a desperate leap at the bedside window where the venetian blind was lowered! The slats sagged as the cat scrambled for a foothold and he actually wove himself in and out of the slats until his head was at the top of the window frame. Walt Disney at his best never concocted a more hilarious picture. Charlie, now in a dressing robe, had to get a stool to reach the thoroughly frightened feline.

As time went by, Butch matured into a gorgeous animal. Generally acting more like a dog than a cat, he was my constant companion, following me to the stable to watch us train the horses, back to the house for lunch, then back to the stable for the rest of the day. The afternoon was nap time for Butch.

Ordinarily, most pets will avoid those people who dislike them. Not so with Butch. I had received a call from an old boyfriend who was a dedicated bird hunter. Those two facts alone were enough to put Charlie in a bad mood when Harry and his fellow hunter came to call after a day of fruitless hunting, failing to even see a quail. This mellowed Charlie somewhat and our guests settled on a sofa with drinks in hand. Flanking the sofa were two end tables holding the then fashionable planter lamps. (Copper bowls filled with dirt for the ivy; the lamp bulb perched at the end of a copper shaft about eight inches above the bowl. A fabric covered shade completing the arrangement.) The conversation was proceeding better than I had hoped when into the room came Butch who made an impressive leap and landed in Harry's lap. A visit from a skunk could not have been more unwelcome. With flaring nostrils and a backward thrust of his body, the poor fellow tried heroically to ignore the beast. Suppressing a smirk, Charlie clapped his hands and shouted at the cat. Butch reacted with a frantic jump and landed amidst the ivy in the lamp. Struggling upward, throwing ivy and dirt everywhere, he became completely hung up inside the lampshade. There was nothing to do but put the lamp on the floor and remove the shade. Butch was finally free but not yet at the end of his shameful performance. He dashed out of the room, veering off course momentarily to defiantly leap into an open corner cupboard, knocking a silver pitcher to the floor. Needless to say, we apologized and our guests made a rather quick exit. The calamitous visit was at an end. I finally got my breath and Charlie and I sank to the floor helpless with laughter. For days afterwards he would break into sudden laughter which I tried to ignore. That is one family memory forever etched in our minds.

A wonderful eleven year old boy had become a member of our family. Our life was rounded out. He took the name of Charles Crabtree, later to be known in the Saddlebred world as Redd.

Our stable in Little Rock had reached capacity by December. We decided to have a Christmas party for our owners - young and old. So there were two kinds of eggnog, plain and the adult drink liberally laced with bourbon whiskey. After the guests left we cleaned up the lounge at the stable. The punch bowl was set out in the aisleway still holding about a pint of spiked eggnog. When we reached for the bowl, it was empty and we could not find Butch or Cap. As we headed for home we stopped in our tracks. There was Butch racing around in circles, slamming to a halt and leaping straight in the air. Barishnykov should be able to do the Grande Jettes like that. Our cat was smashed to the gills. We finally chased him down and put him in the laundry room to sober up. Cap never came home that evening. The next morning he appeared in the barn aisleway walking very cautiously. His lower eyelids were crimson and he could not face the sunlight, obviously suffering from a terrific hangover.

Little Rock was not a good location for training show horses and we were pleased to accept a private position in Collierville, Tennessee to build and operate a show stable for Mr. and Mrs. J.W. Wrape and their daughters who had been chauffeured to Arkansas every weekend for instruction.

On our final night we were invited to dinner at the home of the friends who had given us our cat. Butch, apparently protesting the signs of leaving could not be found. Finally we discovered him 30 feet up a pine tree in the back yard. We tried everything we knew, including telephone pole harness, but we could not get him down. I was terrified, but the men assured me that he would finally figure out how to clamber down. To everyone's relief he was at the car door to meet us when we returned - ready to move to Tennessee.

The next day, Charlie and Redd left with the van loaded with our horses and equipment. I was to follow with our personal effects loaded almost to the car roof of a station wagon and Cap and Butch. I had only to lock the house door, get the dog and cat into the big wooden-sided station wagon and catch the van to follow it in to Collierville. The logistics had been carefully planned as I was not sure that I remembered how to get through Memphis and out to the farm.

As I started to close the house door the phone rang and it was Charlie's father who had come down to help us move. Charlie had driven the van past the train station where Mr. Crabtree was taking the train back home to St. Louis. Mr. Crabtree had left his good shoes in the house and I had just minutes to get them there before the train left, so I jumped into the car and raced down Mablevale Pike, leaving the dog and cat behind. Flooring the accelerator, I was making the turn before the main highway when the right front door came open and my purse flew out, exploding in a pasture, scattering paper currency everywhere. I slammed on the brakes and dived into the pasture frantically gathering up my money. Several passing motorists saw me and I nearly died of embarrassment. Rushing on, I was able to get the shoes delivered just as the train was pulling out of the station.

Time was racing and so was I to go back for the dog and cat. I had filled a pie tin with sand and dirt for the cat's convenience. I put the cat atop our clothes in the back, loaded the dog in beside me on the driver's seat and carefully placed the pie tin on the floor.

The moment I moved the car, the dog stepped down, scattering the dirt all over the floor. No time to stop now, so off we went. I drove as fast as that car would go trying desperately to catch the van. It was not long before the cat let loose a terrible howl. There we were, passing a car loaded with children who were in a state of excitement at seeing a cat racing around on top of our clothes while the dignified collie sat erect beside the wild driver. As soon as possible I pulled to the side of the road and frantically swept some loose dirt in the pie pan. By this time the children were screaming and pointing to what must have looked to their parents as a bewitched woman scraping up dirt for gold on the side of the road. Butch would have nothing to do with the pan, so I threw out the dirt, hopped back in the car and raced down the road, overtaking that same family.

I was no more than a mile down the road when Butch really shrieked an unholy howl and I was certain this time that the cat really did want to use my great idea for a feline toilet. Once again I jumped out to fill the pie tin with roadside dirt. Here came the same car with mother trying to control the children who by that time were in a hysterical scramble to see, once again, the crazy lady who persisted in filling a pie pan on the side of the highway. I was beyond the range of normal reactions by this time and starred back at the car to see the father hunched over the steering wheel in a vain attempt to ignore the road show that I seemed insistent on performing for his family.

By now I had faint hope that the pan was going to be useful and I also got the feeling that the darned cat was more interested in singing than in going to the bathroom. Once more I overtook the now familiar car and looking straight ahead I passed the confused people again. I could hardly believe my eyes when I spied the van just entering the bridge in Memphis. The rest of the trip was slow, orderly and uneventful. Actually, in light of the fact that the Crabtrees had arrived all together at our new location was a sort of anticlimax.

Not until four years later when I chauffeured that same cat to Louisville and the Rock Creek Riding Club did I discover that anytime I drove over 60 miles an hour, the cat would howl bloody murder and it was not his bladder that bothered him — it was his ears!

Collierville was three miles south of Gregnon Farm, near the

Mississippi line. The "downtown" area consisted of three sides of an open square, rimmed with stores sitting on the edge of wooden sidewalks with overhanging roofs. In the center of the square was a genuine antebellum gazebo, large enough to seat band members who entertained all who came to town on Saturday nights. The fourth side of the square consisted of the railroad tracks and a large concrete loading platform where blacks would parade to their own musical accompaniment in the famous Cake Walk contests. The name was genuine as the best strutters were awarded a cake as a prize.

Gracious old homes were situated within a short distance from "the square". We rented the upper floor of a house owned by two lovely maiden ladies, the Misses Dosia and Anna Hinton - genteel, refined elderly ladies straight out of a William Faulkner work. Happily they liked cats even permitting their fat, orange colored cat to move upstairs as a companion to Butch. This settled a problem for us as the Wrapes owned a cat-killing Doberman. Handily, the city high school was directly across the street and the Baptist Church next door. Construction was almost finished on the stable and plans in the works for our beautiful little home in an apple orchard about two hundred yards from the main mansion. Now this was the South that I had envisioned when we decided to move to Little Rock. Butch and his friend had it made in the shade and Redd was very happy in his new school.

The barn was completed and the two older girls had horses and sufficient instruction for us to enter the upcoming Pin Oak Horse Show in Houston, Texas. My parents were coming down from Illinois to be with Redd and also to watch over the cats. Imagine our grief when Butch could not be found the day before we were to leave for Texas. I was terrified he would be mistaken for edible wild game by the same locals who loved possum pie. So I immediately made several posters with a drawing of a Siamese and the warning, DO NOT SHOOT - THIS IS A CAT. REWARD - SEE MRS. CRABTREE OR THE HINTONS. The school principal even released the student body at noon to search for the missing animal. Luckily the local paper was out shortly after we left so an ad was placed there.

It was with a heavy heart that we bid Redd and my parents good-bye. They promised to continue the search and for three miserable days there was no sign of Butch. Finally we retired to the hotel to find a message to call home. My hand shook so much that Charlie had to dial the number. Mother said that they had Butch. A lady from Tupulo, Mississippi about 12 miles away heard something like a cat mewing under her front porch. The folks went to see if it really was Butch. Redd crawled under the porch and the animal started to purr when he called his name. The poor cat had apparently fallen into a pit at a filling station where crankcase oil was gathered. He was blind and a solid mass of oil. Fate has always been kind to me and if my parents had not been there to tend to the pitiful creature he would have died. For several days they bathed him in watered detergent. His sight returned and Mother worked day and night with the detergent to rid his poor body of his coat of oil. He was a willing patient, so happy to be home. When we returned on Sunday I found my precious cat alive - but not well. It was obvious that he would lose every hair. Would it come back? Had it not been for Mother's ministrations and Redd's inspiration to call the cat by name, he would have perished beneath the porch. Surely someone had stolen the cat away and he had escaped only to fall in the oil. Happily, the coat grew back, even more beautiful than it was before the "oil spill". Emotionally I lived through the Valdeze Oil disaster years later when I saw the awful fate of those poor trapped sea creatures.

Butch seemed to be growing up. No more wild tricks happened and cricket and field mouse hunting in the orchard and long "cat naps" in the afternoons were mellowing him. In the evenings we would watch television. Redd was busy with school activities, a real sports fan old enough to drive the car and form his own evening entertainment. Cap had taken up with a pretty little, red female whose five adorable puppies we easily found homes for. After a trip to the vet and no more possibility of puppies, Cap and Buttercup as she was later named were constant companions, so Butch joined our human family and actually became a real housecat. Television in the early 50's was not very good, but it was the main entertainment in our house. Butch would sit in my lap, wide awake and actually watch the programs.

One evening we had invited Mr. and Mrs. Wrape to our home to watch the election returns of the famous Truman-Dewey race. Mrs. Wrape had a severe case of aleurephobia (fear of cats) so we decided to lock Butch in the bathroom out of sight. Yes, out of sight but not out of sound! Since we had to know exactly where he was we could not put him out of doors. It was a long and exciting election night and Butch had apparently fallen asleep on the bath mat. When our guests had left we hastened to get Butch only to find that the devious cat had figured out that the doorknob was the key to his escape. Unfortunately in trying to work the doorknob, he had pressed the lock and we had to take the door off the hinges to let him out.

Butch had always been a very healthy cat and it was hard to believe that he was sick. When we took him to the vet he had a very severe cold bordering on pneumonia. For six days we left him at the vet's facility. Every day I would call and they had controlled the fever and cough but he appeared to make no progress. He had cried so much that he lost his voice. The vet called and told me that they believed that they had actually cured the cat but the group had come to the conclusion that poor Butch was in danger of dying of homesickness. When I arrived they carried out a very weak cat. Ill as he was, he did manage to purr the moment I picked him up. Almost lifeless in my arms he managed to raise his head and give me a kiss on the neck. His voice was gone and he was terribly weak but the vets apparently were right because Butch put his front paws gently around my neck as if to make sure that he would go back home with us.

I held him in a soft sweater in my lap and when it was bedtime I put cat and sweater in beside me in my twin bed. While Charlie was as worried as I about Butch, he said, "Helen, you're surely not putting that cat in bed with you. You may wake up in the morning with a dead cat". I said, "well if he doesn't make it at least he will die knowing that he was loved all of his life". Obviously the vets had been right and love was the healer. In characteristic Butch fashion, he made a rapid recovery and all of our lives returned to normal .

On the fifth day of May in 1954 our family along with cat and two dogs moved to Louisville, Kentucky to operate the beautiful old private riding club soon to be known nationwide as the famous Rock Creek Club. The facility was in very bad physical shape and extensive renovations were being made on the club house where we would occupy the upstairs apartment. It would be ready for us in ten days. In the interim we were graciously given quarters in a member's guest house. This worked well until Butch killed our hostess' favorite robin. What a calamity. We were saved further embarrassment by the cat's disappearance. I was inconsolable. After several sleepless nights, one early morning just at dawn, I thought I heard the inimitable "meow" that meant "where are you?". Yes, Butch was, back and we took him immediately to the club and put him in the barn loft. His disappearance was never discussed and remained a mystery. The next day he was gone again! I do believe that the cat enjoyed driving me crazy, because he reappeared the day we moved into the apartment and never left again.

A goat, Dandy Jim, joined Butch and the two dogs. Now our group of pets numbered four. Life at the club was wonderful for all but after four years it was time to move to our own farm which we had developed in Simpsonville, Kentucky. Sadly, the location of our farm next to a busy highway forced us to give Dandy Jim to a farmer in Western Kentucky. After the move life changed for all the Crabtrees and our pets. We hired a wonderful cook who delighted in preparing meals for the young owners who came to stay with us during show season. Martha took good care of all of us and we were so glad that she liked dogs and cats, as that was extremely important. Many times the three of us would be away from home, either showing the beautiful American Saddlebreds or judging them.

Butch had settled in as "top cat". Catching mice was the work of many barn cats with whom Butch would not fraternize. We had a snob for a pet! Although Butch was admired by everyone, he was my cat. When I packed my bags to leave for a show, Butch would keep getting into my suitcases. I would lift him out and when I returned with more clothes there he would be again. This is not uncommon in cats, but if I, alone, left the farm he would make Charlie's life miserable with his crying. Butch had an extensive vocabulary. The most raucous was the piercing yowl that meant, "Where are you?", as he ran up and down the stairs looking for me. Butch also changed our furniture to anything that was attractive and "claw-proof". When we built on a new sitting room I boldly purchased a very expensive chair and ottoman upholstered in a magnificent snowflake patterned cotton. Anticipating the inevitable, we installed twin louvered doors. One day I was going up the stairs and noticed that the doors were open. Butch was right on my heels, but he saw the new chair sitting in unguarded glory. Quick as a flash he darted back down the stairs and watching me, he proceeded to claw the lovely ottoman. Then he scampered back to the stairs at my heels. To this day I still know that the cat was laughing at me under that meek little smirk on his face.

It is a common fault of all cat lovers to think that their pet is special, but Butch developed a habit that I have never heard of. We were dedicated TV watchers, being too tired to do anything else. Every night I would sit in my lounge chair and Butch would position himself in my lap with his back leaning on my stomach while I held him secure with my arm. He was a sight, watching TV, hind feet comfortably relaxed sticking in the air. One night I happened to reach for his tail and started to tickle his nose with the tip. Instantly he grabbed the tail with both front paws, like a squirrel holding an acorn and avidly licked and chewed the tip, accompanying this incredible action with grunts and low growls of complete ecstasy. He finally learned that I would give him his tail if he gave me a rough tongue kiss under my chin. "That's disgusting", Charlie would say, but he was as intrigued that Butch had really learned a trick on command. We must have been a sight - me holding the cat around his middle, staring at TV, while the cat groomed the end of his tail.

When Redd left to start his own business, Charlie moved downstairs to Redd's bedroom where he could maintain watch over the barns. Butch, now my soul roommate, was in his glory. We had a game we played for the rest of his life - he would leap up on the end of my bed as I lay there reading a book. I would pretend to ignore him until he would pat my face gently and give me a kiss on the chin.

The sad day came when Cap, almost blind and totally deaf, passed away. Poor Buttercup. We had heard of what happened next but thought it was a sentimental myth, but it was sadly true. Buttercup lay on Cap's grave in the back yard, refusing all offers of food or water. Within three days, she too died and was buried next to Cap.

Seventeen years had passed since Butch came to brighten our lives. He was very feeble but still wanting to be with us every minute. We could not force ourselves to face the inevitable, but one evening the cook called me aside to say that Butch was now completely blind and helpless. Knowing that pets do not live forever is no preparation for the grief one feels when pets die at the end of their lives. It was long after office hours when we called Dr. Kresin. He told us to bring Butch to his home and there he would administer the shot that would give our friend eternal peace.

Since we were ticketed to fly to Oklahoma for a show the next morning the decision was never in doubt. We had to take the cat that night. Dr. Kresin told me to hold Butch in my arms and that, I would never know when it happened but that he would be gone by the time we got home. The dreaded event was over and I never did know the moment that Butch left us.

In 1964 I had been named the Horsewoman of the Year by the American Horse Shows Association. The trophy was a lovely bronze statue - a copy of Italy's most famous equestrian statuary. It arrived in a gorgeous green tooled leather trophy box which was lined in ruby red satin amid velvet. Friends thought that I was joking when I said that the case would serve as a casket for Butch. Now the time was here and I placed that dear pet on the red satin and locked the case. Charlie and I were in the backyard, tears running down our cheeks, burying the cat who had held our hearts for those many years. He was placed alongside the two dogs.

Horse trainers have a very strenuous life and you will notice that we always have dogs and cats around the stables. Outsiders assume that we keep them to eradicate the rodents. That is the lesser reason for their being there. Our pets are always there for us. If a horse performance lets us down and self-esteem is low, we are still the greatest thing on earth to our pets. They restore us and give us love that keeps us going. I thank God for Dandy, Cap, Buttercup and Butch. They live on in our memories forever, never to be forgotten.

Redd and Helen Crabtree. Our first Kentucky show — Springfield, Ky.

21
The Bull Rings Of Kentucky
(S & B September, 1992)

When the Crabtrees moved to Rock Creek in Louisville in 1954, our family was making many changes. We had adopted Redd and we were all coming from Memphis to the place where most horse trainers dream of being - Kentucky. Although Charlie had lived his first ten years in the flatlands of western Kentucky, I was a Yankee born in tablelike Illinois moving to flat Little Rock and then to even flatter Memphis, so every little bend in the road, any hint of a forested hill or a gurgling pasture stream was a delight and a surprise.

As all things change, so did we discover that the county fair horse shows in those days were a radical departure from those we were accustomed to in our "life before Louisville".

Kentucky county fairs were big deals in the early 50s and the great majority of them held the greatest surprise of all - the show rings were not the areas of race tracks in front of grandstands, but were proudly referred to as "bull rings" and indeed they were - absolutely round, with a grassy knoll in the center where the spectators sat in cherished wooden chaired boxes, the announcer perched in a gazebo and the proletariat wound up in the world's most uncomfortable stands of solid bleachers. The stands main redeeming feature was that there were roofs overhead that unfortunately cut off the errant summer breezes but they did offer haven from the thunderstorms that are a part of Kentucky's summer heritage.

Our first show was at Springfield, Ky., and to van there was a balancing act as the only road, while blacktopped, was very narrow, twisting and winding - albeit beautifully scenic.

When we arrived we were stabled in age-old horse barns (many of which still serve the purpose) - an admitted improvement over the tents of the Midwest and South. What we came to discover was the unusual sloping of the rings. Although the Thoroughbred was the hallmark of the state, I feel certain that the Hatfields and the McCoys owned road horses and they were the ones who graded the rings at such a sharp angle. At that time Standardbred exhibitors held great positions of power on the fair boards and they were the main architects of the grading of the rings. Now we gasp at the speed and excitement of the racking classes, so did all of the country folk who attended their county fairs for what appeared to the outsider as the annual bloodletting.

The roadsters sped around the circles at incredible speeds and the faster they went the louder the screams from the crowd and the wilder the drivers. It was not uncommon at all to see whips not only hitting the rear ends of a driver's own horse, but wrapped around the neck of a competing driver. It was rumored that many of the drivers carried pistols. The winding drive up to the barns was cut through some low rises and the first morning we were sitting in front of the barn and beheld what appeared to be a horse whizzing up the drive. When it pulled up at the loading dock we discovered that the apparition was a road horse cross tied down to the low sides of a dump truck! By this time I was convinced that anything could happen at a county fair in Kentucky and when it became apparent that the dump truck was incompatible with the loading dock, I turned to Redd and said, "Want to bet ten dollars on how they unload him?" Redd answered with astonishment to his otherwise sensible mother and said, "Mom, they wouldn't" - but they did! After surveying the situation the driver untied the cross ties, reached for the lever and dumped the horse out of the truck.

Then up the drive came what was to be a familiar sight - a very large and a very old, barefoot, snowy haired and full bearded man wearing blue bib overalls and nothing more; a fact only realized upon his turning as his great white beard covered his chest and his long hair covered his back and shoulders. We found that his name was Ben Wilson and that he was a revered horse show lover who walked with only the aid of a long sapling pole from show to show. He was devoted to Frank Bradshaw and if you were competing with Frank, that long pole could appear over the wooden fence during a class with unexpected results. Nothing was ever done about this - it was simply one of the facets of the bull ring. Our first showing problem was in passing as by the time one rode down the slope and back up to the rail you discovered the same horse in front of you. The next problem was in finding the out gate after racking and cantering around an endless circle.

The folks who gathered there from the small towns and farms

know their horses and they let the exhibitors know if they pleased them and they also made their thoughts loudly known to the judge.

After watching the final class of the evening, not the five-gaited but the roadster class "speed only to count", I returned to our stable still dizzy from the equine gladiators. I was told to go to the secretary's room where I would be given the evening's winnings. Just as I approached the small building I saw a driver still in his silks rush into the office and without a word spoken, grab another driver and turned him around to meet a big fist which immediately knocked out several front teeth. Before I could get my breath, the assailant said "Oh, pardon me, I thought you were someone else" (who obviously wore the same color scheme).

I have to write for those readers who never saw our Kentucky County Fairs 40 years ago, that couth has prevailed and no nicer or more gentlemanly group of exhibitors and spectators can be found anywhere. In looking back, I cannot help feeling a bit nostaligic about those horse shows. Feelings ran high and so did the excitement, but you knew that if you made a good show those Kentuckians would let you know that you had made a winning ride.

The Harrodsburg, Ky. Bull Ring - 40 Years Ago

Of all the bull rings we rode in when we first came to Kentucky, the most interesting was the one at Harrodsburg. While the beautiful ring at Shelbyville had the usual grassy center and a majestic elm tree so tall and outreaching that the riders felt as if they were showing in a forest, the ring footing was only somewhat slanted. Not so at Harrodsburg. In fact the slant was so acute the riders who were accustomed to turning their horses into the rail for the canter were in real trouble as the high outside foot would be leading. We found that the only place to keep the proper lead was to ride the canter close to the center where the ring flattened out. What was most unusual to us was that when the horses entered the ring, trainers and grooms also rushed into the ring and stood by the grass area and coached the riders - not only that, but since the center at Harrodsburg was fairly elevated and there was a large gazebo for the announcer, many an "adjustment" was made in the back where the gazebo hid the horses from the judge. There have been instances where a horse with a particular poor gait would stay in hiding until a change of gait would be called.

The ring was clay and when it rained (which it always seemed to do at Harrodsburg) the footing became impossible and the water gushed down toward the center part. I know that we won classes at Harrodsburg, but the most vivid memories are of the wildly funny things that happened there.

We had a youngster at Rock Creek, Billy B. Girdler, who rode in the shadow of his very successful sister, Lynne, which perhaps is why Billy was more of a "showman" than a rider. We had bought him a full bred Hackney walk-trot pony who would change gaits when he heard the announcer. Billy B. was too busy waving at friends, yelling at the coterie of waiters who came to see the show because Billy had rounded them all up to applaud him. How he loved to show, but practice sessions were zilch as far as he was concerned. One night the ring was in such terrible shape after a torrential rain that the tractor was brought in and scraped about six inches of mud down to the center of the ring - forming a swamp of thin watery clay - a veritable moat. Billy was beginning to lose his enthusiasm for the show ring and we were using every psychological trick we knew to keep a rider going who never won a ribbon.

Everyone in our stable went to work to encourage the six-year-old rider and we really had him revved up for his class. I told Billy to go in first and make a grand entrance and ride hard. At the time the boys wore top hats with the formal habits (the top hat bit really appealed to Billy), so when the gate opened, Slick Chick, his pony, was in full stride as he approached the gate. What we did not anticipate was that a motorcycle exhibit was right beside the gate and as Billy charged up to enter, the stuntmen started their motorcycles. Billy made his brilliant entrance more than we had intended. Slick Chick slammed on the brakes and planted his feet at the gate. Not so Billy B., who sailed right over the pony's neck like an arrow and slid on his belly in the gooey swamp that had been shoved into the center of the ring. The mud was so deep and sloppy that Billy disappeared, a quivering wake indicating where the body was, as the top hat stayed on top of the mud, mute evidence that there was a horseless rider somewhere. It was a good five minutes before the spectators quit screaming with laughter as Billy B. came to the surface, spitting mud, a chocolate covered rider who struggled back to get his top hat to wave to the admiring crowd. That should have been a portent of Billy Girdler's future as he grew to be hailed as the coming great producer of movies in Hollywood only halted by his tragic death in a helicopter crash while scouting movie locations in Central America. It was a sad day for us all and every time I see our good friend, Avis Girdler, I can still see Billy covered with mud, saving the day with a triumphant wave of his top hat. Billy B. had been a hit even beyond his wonderfully imaginative mind and he made the most of it.

I had an under-two mare in a large class that included Frank Connors riding Small Wonder - world's champion 15 hand mare. My mount was as pretty as horses can be but the almighty had forgotten to give her a heart. She was torture to show because an atomic bomb would not have awakened her. I had clucked myself spitless, spurred to no lasting effect and had even taken a page from Garland Bradshaw's book and had a small nail in the handle of my whip, and we were still in low gear when Frank Connor, whose mare was acting up, yelled a loud and frustrated "Whoa"! I never knew what his mare did, but mine slammed to a halt and I went half way up her neck. The next time I showed her (and the last!) we were trotting when she heard a soft-drink vendor in the stands shout "Cokes" and she threw out the anchor again. She was on the truck to Indiana the next morning.

Our judge that year was a good horseman from the far west who probably thought that county fair meant a small insignificant show. Poor fellow, he was over his head and to add to his troubles he stood in one spot right beside the worn pathway from the stands to the center ring boxes and every horse that went by jumped over the down trodden path. The night before stake night exhibitors all asked to meet with the show officials to discuss the judging problem. Recently we have all been saddened by the loss of Jim B. Robertson, but remembering all of his triumphs, most of our keen memory is Jim's remark at that meeting. He, like the rest of us had his fill of the judging and also his fill of Jim Beam. Before any discussion could begin, Jim growled, "Well, why did they have to go and get a "Furriner" to judge the show?" That put everyone in a laughing mood and the meeting ended even before it began.

22

R.C. Flannery
(S & B August, 1993)

The American Royal was the first big show that I judged. It was for equitation, but because Garland Bradshaw was showing there and brother Frank was one of the main judges, I was asked to take over in Frank's place when Garland had an entry in the ring. This was very exciting for me as it was the first time that I got to know Frank, personally. He and many other "big names" were just legends to me at that time. Herbert McLain, whom I knew from our Gregnon days in Memphis and David Neil (husband of Betty and father of a little girl named Ann - now well known as Mrs. Sam Stafford) were the main judges.

It was a fine show and all of the officials, including the great ringmaster, Bob Snyder, would be driven to the show together. After a couple of days, Herb would have a cab waiting and his wife, Vivian would say, "Helen we have a cab, wouldn't you like to ride back with us?" So I would be back at the Muehlbach Hotel waiting for Snyder to join me to have a chocolate soda. Oh, I was really living it up!

It so happened that the roadster classes were very heavy at the Royal, and that is one reason that David Neil was one of the judges. No better road horse driver lived than David, and none more daring. One of the regular extra entrants in the Missouri shows was R.C. McCarthy, a rather hulking figure in a bike as his broad shoulders and craggy, deep lined, angular face with large yellowish teeth gave a formidable appearance to anyone who did not know that there was no nicer person on earth than "Mac". His horse was a good county fair horse in Missouri but was overshadowed in showing at the Royal.

Frank and David seemed to be having the best time judging and it was then that I discovered that Frank Bradshaw, who appeared so solemn when riding, was a real clown when he got together with someone who enjoyed life, like David Neil did. All week, I would hustle to join the McLains in the cab after the sessions. Herb was a very quiet and genteel man and Vivian was the epitome of the soft spoken little southern lady. I wondered why we never saw them until show time, but decided that they were not the sort to sit around the lobby and tell horse stories. Just before stake night began, Frank and David revealed that David had written a letter addressed to McLain that implied that it was from the "fierce" looking McCarthy threatening the judge with unspecified dire predictions if his horse did not win a class. That was when I found out that Bradshaw and Neil together were unbeatable practical jokers. David, with his devilish square grin and Frank, red faced and head tucked into his shoulders, looked like the Devil wouldn't hold them. Poor McLains — prisoners in their room all because of David's note and too polite to reveal their plight.

Another wild character in the road horse division was R.C. "Doc" Flannery - a brash Irishman who didn't have a nerve in his body and the tougher the competition, the wilder he drove. I can see him yet, tan Stetson blown straight up in front, left foot braced against the buggy axle and the man, screaming like a banshee, taking incredible chances that could have spelled disaster for him and his fellow competitors. As Doc grew older and his horses waned, he got wilder and wilder until the other drivers decided it was time to put a stop to Flannery's dangerous driving.

I had had enough of Flannery on the southern Illinois Circuit known as "Little Egypt" where Flannery generally showed in front of good friend judges. When he turned up in the three-gaited with a big-footed, white-legged purebred Hackney horse and tied over my good mare and another good one shown by a young lad named Don Harris, it was just too much.

One night at the Lexington show the roadster drivers got together and decided to put a stop to Doc's wild and dangerous ways. It was the wagon class and Doc was prepared to cut loose when they were called to "turn" 'em on". Since horses were then stabled at ends of the track, exit spaces were left open next to the rails. David Neil had waited during the road gait for Flannery to pull along side, then David cut inside and when the horses headed into the first turn, David held his ground, turning at the last moment and sending Flannery flying out of the exit gate. The steward must have been forewarned because when the maddest Irishman in the world got his horse stopped and attempted to re-enter the ring, time was called and the steward informed Flannery that he had left the ring without permission and could not come back in the class - which not only eliminated him from that class but voided any chance he had to come back in the wagon championship. Talk about vicarious enjoyment!! All of us who had suffered the indignity of getting our walk-trot horses tied under "Top Hat" the heavy footed Hackney, all of the roadster drivers who had pulled up to keep from a disastrous crash and even the spectators, mainly those of faint heart who covered their eyes every time Doc Flannery answered the call to "turn 'em on" cheered to see Flannery bested — and it was by a cool headed devilish minded David Neil who taught Flannery a lesson in ring etiquette.

Doc retired shortly after that, having a last try with the famous race horse "Greyhound" who was not a good show horse. Several years later I was staying with Pat and Chat Nichols during a horse buying trip and they asked if I would like to visit Doc and his lovely bride, Frances, of Muscatine, Ia. - a very elegant and beautiful widow. They were just moved into a new home and it was a different Doc that greeted us at the door. A heavenly chorus and cymbals would have completed the picture as the reformed reprobate entertained us royally. We drank hot tea, Doc with his pinkie finger curled just so. I was still trying to acclimate myself to this dramatically changed wild road horse driver when his wife suggested that I might like to see the rest of the new home. Doc was graciousness itself - pointing out every feature and explaining that everything was of the finest material. Then we came to a room and he stopped and told me that the workmen had finished out a fireplace with veneer and he said to me, "Helen, that was when the shit hit the fan!" Then I knew that I was indeed visiting with the inimitable Doc Flannery.

23

Hang In There
(S & B August, 1994)

Judging was always one of my favorite parts of the horse business. That was where I got to see a lot of grand horses that I would have missed unless they had shown on our circuit. It also introduced me to a very wide variety of exhibitors. So I might as well tell the story of my first encounter with an irate mother. I am happy to report that such an experience happened only three times during almost 50 years of judging.

At my very first AHSA recognized show, the American Royal, I was hired to judge equitation only and did experience what all untried judges worry about encountering. The class in question was an open under 13 equitation in which the rider counted 50% and the mount was to be given the other 50%. Over 40 riders swarmed into the crowded ring, 20% of them thinking it was a race. The variety of mounts and riding styles discernable was mind boggling. There was an outstanding small western tacked pony ridden by a tiny little girl who energetically posted every step the pony trotted - and some at the canter. For her sheer bravery and having an outstanding mount, I did finally tie the child in the ribbons. Of course the audience applauded wildly for the tiny tot when she rode up for her eighth place ribbon. What a way to launch a judging career! As I exited the ring to return to the judge's box, I was almost knocked down by a very drunk woman whose clothes matched those of the tiny rider. "Oh no!", I thought. I felt sorry for that cute little rider who had to belong to this fishwife. I had never been in a real fist fight in my life, but I had always heard that the best defense was an offense, and acted accordingly when the word "crook" wafted my way on a cloud of alcoholic breath. Convenient for me, the woman's western get-up sported a silver and leather bola and I grabbed it and took up the slack. In a voice quivering with rage and annoyance I informed her that " I am not a crook!" (And all of the time you thought that President Nixon made that one up!) When the woman struggled to get her breath, I told her that if she did not hush I would call the security guards and have her ejected from the building. Mustering as much dignity as I could dredge up I returned to my seat. Immense crowds probably obscured the ugly performance and nothing was ever mentioned about my effort to choke an exhibitor!

Fifteen years passed without incident until I went to the big South Miami indoor horse show. There were several good riders there, dominated by one very attractive and talented rider mounted on a nice mare. She actually won five classes with this tiring horse and made an inhumane effort to ride this poor spent mare in the equitation championship. It is a credit to the American Saddlebred that the mare was able to carry the girl to a reserve championship. Imagine my surprise when an attractive lady approached me to ask why her daughter had not won the championship. Realizing that no answer would mollify this agitated mother, I countered with a question of my own. "Do you think that I am a bad judge? Because, if that is so then you need to take those five blue ribbons back to the judge's stand. Perhaps it would be advisable to enter a sensible number of classes or get an additional horse." Christian Barham had taught me the fallacy of showing a horse, or rider too often and I was happy to pass on his wisdom.

As a judge, I would never accept the offer of a program when I reported to the show office. All I wanted was a time sheet and schedule of the classes in the upcoming session in order to review them in the rule book. I think every judge does this, but if they do not, they should.

I had been judging a lot of Morgan shows in the 70s. This was when the "new look" was becoming the dominant subject for discussion and wide variances of type and opinion were inevitable. If there is such a thing as a "dream show" for a judge, it is one in which every trainer has at least one outstanding winner and everyone is happy with their horses and the judging.

Most of the time a judge is so busy evaluating the horses that the owners and trainers go unnoticed. This was not the case in a large Morgan show in New York State. A family of three, a father and two sons, were prominent trainers. I knew the father well and the sons by sight. As much as I would have liked to tie one of the son's horses, it just could not be. Time after time his entry would leave the ring with a second place ribbon. The trainer had become more and more obvious as the show progressed. Finally it was all over and the steward advised me that I was wanted for a discussion. It was the entire family. I was disappointed in the father as we were good friends and he knew that I was a qualified and honest judge. But one son had stirred up his brother and father. I listened politely to their harangue until they said, "You're just like other trainers we know!" I thanked them profusely and then they explained that I was prejudiced and that was when I came apart! "Prejudiced?" I cried, "I could give you lessons in prejudice! The way I overcame prejudice as a woman trainer was to improve my stock, and I suggest you do the same." The steward was wonderful, and suppressing a smile, he announced that the interview was over. The young man was an excellent trainer and continued on to the top of the ladder. He is judging now. I wish him luck and tolerance.

24
Judging Memories
(S & B December, 1988)

With the passing of the American Royal Horse Show this year, my judging career is over. It was difficult to send in my membership renewal to AHSA and not fill in the judging requests. My span of judging covers over 50 years and I can hardly believe that it has been such a very long time. Some of the experiences have been hilarious and I want to share some of them with you.

Judging is a very serious business and I am sure all who judge agree with me. Perhaps what keeps one judging is the uniqueness of every show and every class and the inevitable amusing incidents that crop up.

One year I was judging the Devon Show, all Saddle Horse classes and equitation. That was back in the dear departed days of one-judge shows. All was well except for the new footing in the ring which had just been put in - a full eight inches of sand! An expert from one of the New York race tracks had supervised the addition and had his special little ruler to show me that the ring was exactly eight inches deep. It was a very difficult footing for the Saddle Horses - which I pointed out, even venturing to say that whereas runners made one trip on that surface, Saddle Horses could make many laps over the everchanging depth. The only funny part was that I bought the winner of the junior gaited class after the show. I had a need for a nice little gaited mare with a good mouth and one who loved to rack. The new owner had had polio and there was considerable loss of grip in both hands. I could hardly wait for the new mare to get to Simpsonville. I knew that she was easy to rack because she was practically the only entry in that sandy gaited class who could handle the heavy footing. As it turned out the mare was perfect in every respect except for the fact that the new owner had a terrible time getting the mare to rack - and she was no picnic for me to train. Apparently she was only happy to rack in eight inches of sand!

At that same show, Honey Craven was manager. We judges noticed that the Hackney judge was late getting to the show the first night and was busily chewing some very strong chewing gum. The next night he was also rather late and explained that he had had a flat tire. The third night Honey came to me and said, "Helen, stick close by, since you have a judging card for Hackneys I may need to call on you." Very shortly he came back and asked me to get ready to take over the judging of all of the Hackney horses and ponies. I asked if the judge had failed to appear and he said that he had gotten there but that he had run into the officials stand. I immediately asked if he had wrecked his car and Honey replied, "No, Helen, he was walking!" I did get a singular thrill, however, because there were a lot of top Hackneys there - Canadian and American - and the great horse, Mr. Pepper, was making his last season at the shows. What an exciting horse to watch. He had been a walk-trot pony for Brian Henderson and later was put in harness in the horse classes. He will always vie for the top when I recall great horses that I have had the privilege of judging. And he is rated as one of the great Hackney horses of all time.

As chairman on the AHSA equitation committee, I worked hard to get one of the individual tests removed from the rule book - the test that called for riders to ride a strange horse supplied by the committee. Well, they really used the right adjective because one of my riders had to deal with this workout at New York in the Good Hands Finals. I was well aware of the test and I had had my rider practice hunt seat. She really looked grand and I approached the show with confidence. Sure enough, three riders were called for a third workout and Sarah was the third to ride. Just as I had expected at a New York show, the strange horse was a hunter. The first two girls to ride were either scared or angry because they really gave this horse a fit in his mouth. He was fair for the first rider, annoyed with the second and downright hateful by the time Sarah got him. He rooted his head down to his knees and took off at the fastest cantered figure-eight in NHS history. So much for trying to figure all the angles! However, it was apparent to all that the "strange horse" workout was not viable and it was removed from the list.

I always seemed to run into odd situations when any show from south Florida asked me to officiate. My first time was as equitation judge alongside Lee Roby who was judging horses. Lee Roby was one of the most humorous and entertaining people I have ever known. It was before the time when everyone had furs and I had borrowed a mink stole to fit the occasion. The first class I had was a beginners academy class and it was a mess. When I finally sorted out all of the survivors and went back to the judges' stand, Lee said, "My God, Helen, you're lucky to get out alive and that will teach you not to wear a skunk and scare the horses to death."

I was judging the Baton Rouge Horse Show with "Sarge" Hessler and Jeff Harston and Lee Roby was showing. He always had top horses and no better showman ever lived. The show is in the fall of the year, and for this last show of the season, Lee changed a gaited gelding called "Warren Miller" to the fine harness division. The class began and to this day "Warren Miller" hasn't trotted a step. By the time of the lineup Roby was crimson with rage and we three judges had all we could do to keep our faces straight. The final class of the night was a gaited class and Lee hit the ring with a beautiful light chestnut stud. Oh, how he could burn the track at the trot. When we called for the slow gait, Roby spent quite a while circling up for position and when we said rack, THAT horse never racked a step. And I know that he never again was asked to, because when we got the line-up, Sarge said, "Lee you better run back and get Warren Miller." Roby said, "I'll never put a saddle on this - horse again. And he never did.

25

Mothers and Motivation
(S & B November, 1988)

Andrea Walton was one of our top riders during the 60s and 70s. She was one of the very first equitation riders to be winning in equitation, five-gaited ponies and five and three-gaited Saddle Horses. She had many accomplishments and many things to be proud of. However, none of this could have happened if it had not been for the devotion of her mother to the sport. Joan Farris, Andrea's mother, was a good horse woman herself and perhaps this is why she was able to indulge Andrea in practice by bringing her to Simpsonville every Friday night and starting back to home in LaPorte, Ind., every Sunday afternoon. You could set your clock by their arrival at 10:45 every Friday nite and their departure on Sunday afternoon at 3:15. That is dedication with a capital D. But it was not done just so Andy could win blue ribbons - no, Joan Farris knew that she was giving a talented daughter an opportunity to achieve her very best - her personal best. None of the Walton girls, and there were three, all of whom rode, were ever pushed to win. They were left to the sessions with the Crabtrees as their trainers, and we were free to teach, train and make show entries at our own discretion. I can recall only one instance where she "explained away" the older daughters tears on leaving the ring at their first show. I was horrified and asked her why the girl was crying, throwing in the added admonition that Crabtree riders were not bad sports. Joan explained that the daughter cried when she was nervous. I replied that she could cry when she won. Nothing more was ever said and no one ever had three better sisters to teach than Allison, Andrea and Barbe Walton.

Joan was one of those wonderful parents who knew enough about riding to appreciate the little triumphs that did not necessarily mean blue ribbons, but knew the family joy of mastering a skill, inconsequential as it might seem. What a joy! To know and acknowledge the fact that great riders are those who have all of the basic skills and then learn the tiny subtleties that make champions out of just good riders. She was one parent who could be truly objective about her girls.

Only now it occurs to me that she really had her eggs in three baskets and that made her heroics a bit easier! Joan always had a "just right" comment for every situation. Of all of her interesting remarks, my favorite was the saying, "If you can't be good, be technical". I might have forgotten this wonderful saying if I had not been recently watching the political debates. What a pity that Joan Farris could not have lived to hear what is going on today! Those presidential hopefuls' advisors could take a lesson from many an equitation instructor who pats the rider on the knee as he enters the ring and says "Have fun"!

Since I will probably have judged my last horse show by the time this column comes out, I feel free to reflect on some of the amusing things that have happened to me during the five decades that I have been judging.

First of all a judge must be qualified to judge. Only time will tell whether a trainer is a good judge. I have known super talented men who could train a horse and yet were not good judges and still others who were mediocre trainers and were splendid judges. While a judge is not out in the ring to please the crowd, the judge can conduct classes in such a fashion that the placings are apparent to anyone. I will tell you of a fix I found myself in years ago while judging a small show in Georgia, concerning a fine harness class. Well, several good stables showed up at this affair and I had some high class horses to judge. However as is often the case in shows of small area, there can be a local hero that the citizens would kill for. Here came an old chestnut stallion who thought he was the best thing in the ring - and his equally aged driver drove him with all of the pride in Dixie. How the crowd loved that pair! There was no way in the world that the stud could win - he was low in the back, turkey necked, spindled shanked and the only reason he didn't knock off both knees was that the old veteran could trot "above level". At least three horses were better than he, but that local crowd didn't think so. I knew how I had the horses tied when I asked them to line up, but I was also wondering how God was going to let me get out of that ring alive when the results were announced. This was during the 60s and AHSA rules permitted the judge to ask for the horses to back. Somebody "up there" must have been looking after me because the local driver chose to park his horse on the pitcher's mound! The horse was in front of the mound and the buggy and driver were back of it. Salvation was at hand! I asked each entry to "Back your horse, please" and the old veteran hung his hind shoes on the pitcher's mound and would still be there if several good friends had not leaped into the ring and lifted the buggy forward off the mound. That may be known as taking advantage of the breaks, but the horse received the ribbon he deserved, the driver was a hero for surviving the experience and the local friends and well-wishers were satisfied. I have often thought of that night and wondered how one might ride a rail out of town in a dress!

I was judging in south Miami when the Paso Fino horses came to the states to enter their first show ring competition. Twenty-six of the little horses showed up, most coming from the Central American states and a few from Georgia and Washington D.C. Riders, trainers, owners, show officials and I met to determine how the classes should be conducted and what gaits were to be called for. Finally it was agreed that three progressions of speed for the paso (the gait) would be called for - the Paso Fino, the Paso Largo and the Paso Grande. Now, mind you, these horses were making the maiden voyage for the breed and all sorts of surprises were in store for us all. Some horses had English saddles with riders attired in the customary saddle suits. Some tack was totally Spanish as well as the attire. Some must have whipped up their outfits on the nearest sewing machine. What a spectacle! Everything was going smoothly. Even the hunter-jumper classes halted in an adjoining ring so that all could see this new breed of horse. Then trouble - no one in the center of the ring knew the Spanish word for "reverse" and we all flailed away with outstretched arms and pointing fingers until we got the entire bunch reversed. The winner was a beautiful little grey stud (obviously part Arabian) ridden by a most autocratic Spaniard in authentic tack and regalia. When his number was announced, the rest of the riders all yelled and screamed and raced over to the winner. Imagine our relief when it became apparent that the rush was to congratulate the winner! It was obvious that it was their first show. They hadn't been at it long enough to get jealous! However, one rider was waiting for me at the gate and he wasn't holding a bunch of roses, so I braced for whatever was coming. My two years of college French were little help with his broken English but I finally deduced that the rider felt that he had not gotten his just reward. Of course, I remembered his performance which consisted of one medium speed at all times. He retorted, when I mentioned this and that the rules had been established before the class, that he did not agree. This did not ameliorate matters whatsoever so finally I told him, "Sir, your Paso was not Grande enough for me." End of discussion.

26

The Humor of Texas
(S & B February, 1993)

Last Sunday, while I was waiting to watch the David Brinkley Hour on TV, I heard a pastor on a preceding program speaking about thanking God for giving mortals a sense of humor. As I listened, I became aware of the fact that humor is such a necessary ingredient of a horse trainer's makeup. Without it we would have done in all of our relatives, owners and every horse in the stable. One thing horsemen agree on is that our business is like no other and we may cut our throats in frustration but none of us will ever die of boredom - we will die laughing!

Many of my most entertaining happenings occurred at the Pin Oak Horse Show in Houston, Tx. Let me tell you of one that happened in the early 50s. Mr. Abercrombie, who with his wife, daughter Josephine, and friend, Mr. Meyer, produced the fabulous Pin Oak show and did everything to assure its progress. In an unprecedented gesture, Mr. Abercrombie called me at our home in Little Rock to urge us to bring our young riders and horses to the show. He offered to pay for the horse hauling and to send their private plane for us and our owners. I felt that the horse hauling bordered on favoritism (Although I'm sure Mr. Abercrombie was unaware of the possible jealous repercussions). We did, however, accept the plane ride in their VERY posh plane. Among the riders we took was a new girl from Shreveport, La., Helen Bragg White, for whom I had bought the cocky little walk-trot gelding, Radiant Aire, from Dick Duncan at his Woodburn Stables in southwestern Kentucky. Dick Duncan is the most fastidious man I have ever known, and that includes the entire western hemisphere. One could not find a speck of dust on Duncan, his stable or his horses. He always dressed in navy blue jodhpurs, immaculate shirt with tie and on his small feet the shiny black laced boots. However, his hallmark was his very discreet Stetson hat, triple creased to bring it down to a very tasteful proportion for this slender Southern gentleman. His horse was just as impressive as Duncan and I was thrilled that we were getting the clientele who could buy the best.

So off to Pin Oak we flew. The ring was new then and did not have the permanent bandstand in the center with its brilliant blue roof and gorgeous red climbing roses. We showed in a ring contained by the canvas walls that so many college football fields used at that time. Helen showed in the juvenile three-gaited class. The show ring happened to adjoin a "free act" as extra entertainment was called in those days. So, practicing right next to the show ring was a gentleman and his Liberty horses. These are the horses that go through their pirouettes, etc. at the command of the maestro's big bull whip - a very noisy whip that really revved up the horses in the show ring. I was so pleased with my new horse and rider. Every time the whip cracked, Radiant Aire would buckle up more and try to trot out of his shoes. Helen appeared to be having a good time too, since she would look at me every time she passed and flash what I thought was a triumphant smile. I smiled back and gave the V-for-victory sign. By the time the horses lined up the new team had been spectacular. I ran into the ring to head the horse for the winning picture (we didn't do victory passes then). Helen seemed as thrilled as I with tears streaming down her cheeks. Just as we exited the ring I asked Helen what she was saying as she passed me at the gate. A very disgruntled man who was beside me during the class snorted - "She wasn't smiling, she was asking you to let her get out of the ring!" Two years ago, I was delighted to see Helen Bragg. She had come over to Baltimore from Washington just to see me get an award and to renew our friendship - and every time she smiled, I would see that same facial movement that could be a smile or a grimace.

One time, much later, we had a horse that would come out of the stall every morning like he was tiptoing on eggs. Anyone seeing him would think that we were the meanest trainers alive for exercising such a pitiful looking animal. After a couple of minutes at a walk, the horse would relax, let his back down and return to normalcy. It was Yankee Robinson, and I was working him for Redd who came later to the show. Knowing what a sight the horse would be, I sneaked out of the back of the barn and started down what was supposed to be a private lane to Josephine Abercrombie's brick stable. Luck was not with me, as I had hardly entered the lane, only to be met by a handsome young trainer on his horse. (He was stabled in Josephine's barn.) As he drew near I could see the look of compassion on his face - I'm probably right in sensing that he not only pitied the horse but pitied the poor dumbell riding what was an apparent lame horse. I stopped and he stopped; finally he got up his nerve to say to me "Lady, did you know that your horse is lame?" As kindly as I could, I answered that the horse always did that and that I was trying to hide until he relaxed. I thought the young man was going to die of embarrassment - but we all got to know the trainers from far away as Pin Oak attracted top stock from every part of the USA. That young man is now one of the very successful trainers in our business, but he still turns red when (once a year) I remind him of our memorable first meeting.

It is a shame there is not another show anywhere that can compete with that Houston horse show. It was first class, A-One, top drawer and any other combination of words to describe the very best. Our stable missed only one show at the old grounds and that was because I was judging there that year. Roy Register from California and a nice trainer who meant well but had judged very little if at all made up the panel of three - call judge, second judge and referee. Classes were filled as everyone could enter everything and show in whatever one chose. So the program always showed more entries than actually were in the ring. Whenever I judged with Roy we agreed right down the line. When I judged with the other man, he would walk up as the horses lined up and ask me who I liked. I thought he was being nice to the lady judge (we were rare enough then to merit extra consideration for our sex). When I told him how I had tied the class, he would mark his card and say "That's the way I have them." After a few classes, Roy and I agreed that the man was not really judging. I told Roy that I would test him the next class. It was a junior fine harness event and as we approached one another, I beat him to the punch and asked him "Who do you like?" Art Simmons had a very strong stable that year and I was not surprised when he said "I like Art Simmons." I replied "So do I, but Art isn't in this class!" I never read any account of that poor fellow judging after that. I am sure he must have been asked to judge but being aware of his own timidity as a judge he wisely refused. He was a good trainer and respected by everyone and he showed a lot of class by not judging any more.

27

Dual In Houston, Texas
(S & B August, 1995)

Lynn Weatherman called me a few weeks ago to discuss a rare find of an 80-page memoir written by Mrs. J.R. "Lib" Sharp. One of the sentences referred to the stake at the old Pin Oak Horse Show in which the two main judges, Roy Register and Helen Crabtree had tied King Lee, shown by Art Simmons over her beautiful gaited World's Grand Champion, Daydream. Her less then unbiassed conclusion was that the defeat was one of the worst judged in the history of the breed. Fortunately, Lynn called me and I recounted the incident which was gait by gait, indelibly imprinted on my memory.

Recently, I mentioned this to Redd and he said, "You know, Mom, unless people saw King Lee at Pin Oak or the American Royal when he was fresh and rested, they had no idea how great he and Art Simmons really were. There was no way to beat King Lee at these shows."

It was in the late 60's and Art had a big and powerful stable, headed by the great doing, handsome gaited gelding, King Lee.

I loved judging that show because Roy Register was one of the finest Saddle Horse judges I knew, completely knowledgeable and eminently fair.

That was in the wonderful days of call judge, second judge and referee to break ties. It was also when the judging was based 60% performance and 40% conformation.

Daydream, masterfully shown by her trainer, Lee Roby, had won the mare stake and Art Simmons rode King Lee to the victory in the stallion-gelding stake. So it was no surprise to judge the two horses in the championship. Happily, Roy and I judged the class. I say "happily" for me as we both had the same judging standards and had agreed down the line for the entire show, a match-up that did not exist with the third judge.

Pin Oak was the first big show of the summer. Horses were at their best and victories at the prestigious show were very important.

Lee Roby and Daydream.

Tanbark was the footing in all of the major shows. The Texas humidity and occasional hard rains could deepen the footing as time went on and such was the case that year. Preliminary classes had normal footing, but by stake night the sodden tanbark was quite deep.

Prize money was excellent at Houston, and all classes were well filled, including the five-gaited championship. Nine horses charged into the ring with not a bad one in the bunch. But it became obvious that there was a terrific dual developing. The elegant Daydream given a true stake ride by her famous trainer, Lee Roby and the wild going handsome King Lee with Art making the ride of his life.

In order to understand Lib Sharp's feelings, one must be aware that her horses were the core of her life and the unparalleled mutual admiration of Sharp and Roby made every class a potential for great elation or utter despair. Green Hill Stables was Lib Sharp and a great majority of the time Green Hill horses won. Lib Sharp was not accustomed to losing and her devotion to her horses and her trainer made every contest doubly important.

Then add the gorgeous and ill-fated Joan Robinson and her sensational gray champion, Beloved Belinda, a prized part of the Roby entourage and it is easy to see why everyone at the stable had only one gear - all out to win. Vitriolic Ash Robinson, Joan's father, the highly ambitious owner was the catalyst that ignited the uncharitable idea that Green Hill horses were invincible.

The class ran its course. Both Daydream and King Lee were magnificent and by the call to the line up and strip they were evenly matched.

It was during our tour of the line up that the incredible happened. Keep in mind that conformation was 40%. King Lee was a beautiful chestnut gelding, masculine, bold and exciting. Daydream was every artists' idea of a breathtakingly beautiful mare, one considered to be the most spectacular ideal of the breed.

Art, never one to miss an opportunity, hastened to a point directly in front of the announcers booth that was situated 20 feet above the end of the ring.

Roby, feeling an advantage in close comparison stripped the mare second in line to King Lee. As we started our inspection, King Lee raised up, stretched his neck, pricked his ears and stared up at the announcer. It was one of the greatest displays of beauty and brilliance that ever happened in the show ring (only The Phoenix at the American Royal years later could remind one of King Lee and his startling magnificence at Pin Oak).

As we moved to the next horse in line we saw Roby moving Daydream down the line. One could almost feel Roby's rage and frustration with his beautiful mare turned into a defiant disaster. "Whap! went the whip around her front legs as she repeatedly refused to park out. Finally Roby was at the end of the line-up, red faced, furious and desperate to get his mare right.

As for Daydream, she had become completely sullen, refusing to park out, neck stretched into a horizontal line in resisting her trainer's frantic pull on the curb rein. The mare was so angry that her ears were flat on her head and her eyes were squinted shut in complete defiance. One had the feeling that if Roby stopped pulling on the reins that Daydream would have sat down in the sodden tanbark.

I looked at Roy and before I could say the words, he was nodding his head that we had a two-horse workout facing us.

King Lee was a big handsome show horse, and his feet were wide. Daydream was a dainty built mare and her compact feet were small and went down through the thoroughly dug-up tanbark, whereas King Lee managed to stay on the top of the heavy footing.

We did not have a long workout as no judge ever wants to harm any of the horses. It soon became evident that the gallant mare could not match performance with the bold striding gelding who handled the deep going with ease.

Then it was over. The crowd had gone wild during the workout and thunderous applause greeted the announcement that King Lee had won. Equally generous was the applause for the spent mare and her wonderful rider.

When I returned home, Charlie was sitting in the television room. "Who won the stake?" he asked. I told him, King Lee. "Who was second?" Daydream, I said. "You're crazy," he shot back and I walked on to my room.

Several days later he told me that he had heard trainers who were at Pin Oak say it was the right decision.

Two years's later Mrs. Sharp called me to see if we would take her granddaughter, Rosemary. "Now, Helen," she said, "I know we had our problems at Pin Oak." "No, Lib, you were the one having problems."

... and Rosemary came to Kentucky.

There are many reasons for remembering horse shows - triumph, defeat, joy, despair and just plain fun.

Such a show was the Youngstown, Ohio Horse Show.

Rosemary Sharp had arrived at the farm along with her homebred, three-gaited mount, Snooty McGee. He was sired by Greenhill's own stallion, Gold Note. As much as Mrs. Sharp and trainer Lee Roby wanted this stud to be a successful sire, he was a failure. He was very handsome with a typical classic Genius Bourbon King sculptured head, large eyes, sharp ears atop a highly carried arched neck. His body full and rather long-backed was set on four short legs that were devoid of show horse high action. He was a true breeder and his progeny were all low-slung pretty horses with very little motion. We called them "Book Ends."

When Rosemary and Snooty arrived we found that we had a gorgeous young girl whose riding interest loomed larger in grandmother Lib Sharp's mind than it did in Rosemary's liking the sport. Here was the impossible match of beautiful girl, beautiful horse and total lack of interest in horse shows. It became evident to me that the girl had no enthusiasm in learning and that the horse shared her disinterest. Knowing that, the pair had no chance to win in any division. All well represented by Randi Stuart, Andrea Walton, the Barmeier sisters, the Lowary sisters and other equally expert riders on world class horses, I came to the only logical conclusion that Rosemary and Snooty McGee should concentrate on practicing the one thing at which they excelled - lining up! And this we did at every practice. The parked horse and rider were gorgeous!

Youngstown, Ohio had a big show on the local fairgrounds which we attended each year because of our many Ohio clients. This particular summer broke all heat records and matinee classes were almost unbearable. The race track that served as the show ring had also been used for miniature auto racing and the footing was as hard as Fourth and Broadway. The show dragged on with many interruptions. The poor riders were desperately trying to remain neat and cool as the juvenile three-gaited class could be called for at any moment. In an attempt to work out our problem, I had the six riders in the class sit on the tack trunks to wait. Unnoticed by me was a groom who tossed out a bucket of water down the aisle separating the two groups of waiting riders. Without warning, Rosemary decided to change sides. As she skipped across the watery clay path she slipped and slid full length on her side in the sloppy mud. Poor girl, she was terrified of what I might say, and the other riders were heroic in attempts not to laugh. The new navy riding habit was plastered in a film of red clay!

What to do? Quickly a groom helped the poor girl up, and we decided to have her stand out in the broiling sun to dry. Luckily, the class delay lasted another half hour and we all gathered around Rosemary to brush off the mud coated habit.

The class was called and our six entrants entered the ring! Charlie Houston of Chicago was the very able judge. It was apparent that one of our girls was winning the class and Rosemary was dutifully going through the gaits, but was in no way a contender for a ribbon. But wait! We had not played our trump card! Came to the line up and Rosemary parked Snooty at the end of the line as directed. She straightened the hems of her coat, sat there like a beautiful angel and lifted Snooty's head. Wonder of wonders, an airplane drifted above the very tall grandstand and Snooty was almost on tip toes craning his neck to stare at the plane.

Houston had surely tied the class, but as he approached the last beautiful picture of brilliant horse and lovely rider, he stopped in his tracks and looked at his card - up and down the card he hunted for the number. Finally he wrote on the card and handed it to the ringmaster.

First, second and third winners were called out in the large class. Then the "missing number" of Snooty McGee was called for fourth place! Rosemary was astounded but a natural born performer proudly walked the horse up for her ribbon and cantered out of the ring as instructed by me. I had no wish to embarrass the judge who had honestly chosen this beautiful horse and rider. She never did let Houston see that flat footed helpless trot again for which I am forever thankful. Never did a well rehearsed demonstration of the one and only accomplishment of a horse reap better rewards.

I had been successful in convincing Rosemary's grandmother to replace Snooty with a more suitable mount and had arranged for a beautiful bay mare to be brought back to the barn following that class. But where was Rosemary? She was nowhere to be found. It was quite apparent to me that showing horses was definitely not in Rosemary's future. So I called Andrea Walton who was second in line for a new horse and had her try the lovely mare. That mare's name was Georgia Denmark, who became one of the great equitation horses of that era, carrying Andy to the heights in equitation and paved the way for Andrea Walton (DeVogel) to thrill audiences in later years with home bred gaited sensation Rage Of The Stage.

One never knows on what thin threads of fate careers hang. One girl dropped from the show scene another took her place and has been a dominate force on our industry to this day.

Art Simmons and Colonel Boyle.

28
Colonel Boyle and Art Simmons
(S & B July, 1995)

It is impossible to separate the horse, Colonel Boyle, and his trainer, Arthur Simmons. Both were unique individuals and each left indelible marks on the American Saddlebred industry.

Mr. Ike Lanier owned Grassland Farm, a highly respected Saddlebred breeding establishment in Danville, Ky. Our son, Redd, had just graduated from Eastern High School in Jefferson County and our family had moved to the then unknown area named Simpsonville, Ky. We wanted Redd to have a college education, and Ike Lanier's kind interest in Redd and our family made the enrollment of Redd in Centre College in Danville a reality by giving the young man a job at Grassland Farm to supplement his tuition costs.

One weekend Redd came home in a high state of excitement to tell us about the magnificent stud foal at Grassland. "He is like nothing you have ever seen before, but they gave him the worst name in the world - they named him Colonel Boyle!" Somewhat mollified by my explanation that Grassland was located in Boyle County, Redd raved on about the super colt and spent every moment away from college at the farm.

Had grades been given at Grassland Farm, Redd would have made Phi Beta Kappa. But like so many students of his era, his excellence in high school did not develop the study skills that a tough college like Centre demanded. After that one year Redd left Centre, took night classes at the University of Louisville (including my suggested course in public speaking) and the fabulous colt with the ugly name was forgotten.

In the meantime Arthur Simmons was making history at his very popular and successful stable in Mexico, Mo. Many champions emerged there, but the greatest of all had to be the electrifying fine harness world champion, Colonel Boyle. He was a big horse with a great big way of moving and his "park trot" was about 50% faster than the other horses and every trainer took off in hot pursuit. What a sight Art was, holding the reins high and wide, leaning at every turn and simply swamping the competition. Art was a consummate showman and he had the giant Colonel Boyle who completed the excitement. Crowds went crazy to cheer on the exciting horse and driver.

In those days, the rules specified and described the "park trot" as a high, brilliant and collected gait. In Colonel Boyle's case, his cadence and restraint were observed, but the reach of his stride forced the smaller, light footed horses to go beyond collection in many entries. Many of the casual audiences already had the idea that fine harness was akin to roadster classes, so the faster the "park trot" became, the louder the applause.

Anyone who ever saw Art Simmons show saddle classes recalls Art, shoulders hunched, hands held high and wide. He always posted the right diagonal and before the class ended, his back number would be perched almost atop his right shoulder. Records will reveal the huge wins of Art and Colonel Boyle, but my delight is not in listing dull show records, but rather in recounting the individual foibles of trainers and horses that make each memorable.

One show, in particular, is vivid in my remembrance, because I was the sole judge and in an important attempt to rule the fine harness horse back to the true "park trot" sprang forth the following narrative.

The show was at Omaha, Neb., and attracted leading stables. All of the Missouri trainers were there and a very successful string trained by the outstanding team of Donna and Tom Moore. Now, I have always considered "Fine Harness" a literal term and everything about the horse, tack, buggy and elegant precision extremely important. The Moores were outstanding in their adherence to perfection, so that their beautiful mare, Tiara, was the ideal picture. Art, on the other hand, ran his huge stable on volume, as well as human and equine ability, but late in the show season the wear and tear of so many horses and so many shows often resulted in less than perfect turning out of his entries.

Colonel Boyle and Tiara met in the stake. Tom wisely kept his mare at a true park trot and the mare glistened in her brilliant perfection. Colonel Boyle, on the other hand, was a bit shopworn in finish, albeit the crowd pleasing bold, big moving stud was more dynamic. Art and Colonel Boyle charged around the ring to thunderous applause for the local boy who made it big in Mexico, Mo.

At that time conformation was 40%, not the disgraceful 25% of the present day. When the horses lined up I knew that I had to call a two horse workout. When Art heard his number called for the extra work he was furious and hit Colonel Boyle who leaped to the rail at a road gait. I can still hear Sug Utz and the other Missouri trainers shouting "slow down, Art". And he did take the stud back to the park trot. Then it was apparent that the 60% performance outweighed the elegance of the mare whose trot was a bit shallow. Art won, a very popular tie.

As I left the ring at the end of the show I was met at the gate by a noticeably excited newspaper reporter (a Midwest version straight out of "Front Page"). "Mrs. Crabtree," he shouted, "what do you have to say about the fine harness stake?" I replied that the class and workout were self-explanatory. "I just talked to Art Simmons," the reporter said, pencil poised to write down what appeared to this poor young man as a blockbusting headline. "He said that it was a disgrace to work out with the mare." Perhaps I should have been more polite in my reply, but I told him that I was Art Simmons' best friend in that class, because without the workout, Colonel Boyle would have been second!

That winter I attended the annual meeting of the American Horse Shows Association and introduced the present day specification of "park trot", then "show your horse". However the current trend is to speed up the trot at the second command. All I can say is that many of us tried and failed to preserve the most elegant gait, the park trot.

Logan McDaniels with Janie and Joe Cotton.

29

Logan McDaniels
(S & B April, 1995)

In the winter of my tenth year, my father sold our farm and we moved to the small, nearby town of Jacksonville, Ill. My father purchased a home which was situated just within the city limits, and only a mile from the Morgan County Fairgrounds. I will always thank God for my parent's far vision to allow me to dream of being a trainer of American Saddlebreds. The dream was unrealistic in 1925 and my intense desire to ride would have gone unfulfilled without the aid and encouragement of a remarkable man.

Logan McDaniels was well known in the community and all who knew him held him in the highest regard. He was credited by many for the success of three prominent business men in Illinois. According to local townspeople, Logue had been the guiding hand in the young lives of these men. There was no man more respected in a town where Negroes numbered less than a dozen. The term "African American" had not evolved. I hope that Logue knew how well liked he was by all who knew him, not just as a fine man but also as a horseman. I truly believe that without his wise counsel and patience, my compulsion to ride and show Saddle Horses would never have reached beyond my being regarded as only another "horse crazy tomboy."

Logue would let me ride the young horses that he trained at the fairgrounds. I asked him if it was all right for me to be riding horses he was being paid to train. He explained that the owners knew what he was doing and it added to the horse's value to be "kid broke".

Actually, I would ride and he would teach me. He was a wonderful communicator and his way of explaining training and understanding three and five-gaited horses is surely reflected in my approach to training both horses and riders. "Miss Helen", he would say, "You have to out think a horse, you can't out-power him. You have to out-think him."

Those were wonderful days. After school I would run home, change into riding pants and run another mile to the fairgrounds. During vacation time I would go in the mornings. Time of day did not matter, only bad weather interrupted the schedule. This kindly arrangement went on even after I started training at home. But I always conferred with Logue about those problem horses I fell heir to, because I would train for a dollar a day plus food and bedding.

My friendship with my teacher continued through college when I took over the riding department when Charlie and I married. Logue wanted to come to MacMurray College to work for us. Charlie told him that we would not be able to pay anyone at first, as we had to purchase ten head of horses, ten sets of tack and all the incidentals that go with the founding of such a program. "Just pay me when you can." - and that was the beginning of a contract that lasted his lifetime. Happily, within a month, we were able to manage his salary.

The first week, Charlie and I decided that we would "go it alone", without backing from his friend and former employer in St. Louis. Logue, noticed the worried look on Charlie's face and asked him what was worrying him. Replying to Charlie's explanation, Logue said, "Mr. Charlie, I have money saved up and you can have it." Imagine our gratitude! Fortunately, my father backed us on a bank loan and we were in business.

Ten months later, Valentine's Day 1943, Charlie left to enter the Army. Before I drove him to the St. Louis induction center, Logue made the statement that was a commitment greater than anyone could forget, he said, "Mr. Charlie, don't worry about Miss Helen, I will always be here for her and I will be here when you get back."

The first test was the following summer. A colt fell on me and it put me in the hospital for ten days. Fortunately, the hospital was near the college, and I got permission for Logue to work my nice three-year-old filly that I was gaiting — permission to work her on the hospital lawn so that I could watch from my room in the sun porch!

In 1944, I left the college to run the Missouri Stables in St. Louis. True to his word, Logue went with me and was head groom in the training barn. Very soon I was looking for an assistant. Perhaps my next step explains how grave the manpower shortage was during World War II. The best I could do was to hire a man whose qualifications for the job was his having driven a horse drawn milk delivery wagon. I had to settle for a person whose total equine experience was looking at the back end of a horse!

After a few months the training and teaching had grown tremendously. My bosses were two men who decided that Thursday morning was my "day off" and then asked me to come in at 6:30 that "day off" to teach one boss how to show his gaited horse! Logue would shake his head and tell me not to work so hard. Finally his wise counsel soaked in, and I rented Westwood Stables in Clayton Township on the western edge of St. Louis. Otis Brown, who trained hunters and some Saddle Horses there had received his Army notice, thus vacating a nice stable. Just my size, with living quarters above the stable.

Of course, Logue came along and made his quarters in the stable area. What a relief it was to be my own boss, no strings attached, and to look forward to training the ten horses that moved westward with me. Both Logue and I were glad to be away from my "slave driver" bosses and the prospects for peace, quiet and horses to train suited my situation beautifully. And Logue was a happy man, willing and able to handle the ten horses - what a difference 50 years makes!

My life was wonderful and peaceful after the enormous pressure and workload at the Missouri Stables. I felt very safe in my apartment. We had two watch dogs, "Joe Cotton", Logue's white collie and I had the full sister "Janie" that Logue had given us at the college.

In those days, no one in rural areas locked their doors, including mine. One morning as I dressed, I heard what sounded like a horse kicking in the stall. Moments later I heard someone dashing up my stairs. I whirled to see a drunken man who explained, "I have just shot your colored groom." Horrified, I rushed down to the stalls, only to see Logue sitting on a tack trunk, ashen and in terrible pain, clutching his abdomen. "Miss Helen," he groaned, "he dropped the bullets and when I handed them back he put them in the revolver and shot me." The drunken assailant went back to my apartment and called the police. Very soon they arrived to take Logue to the hospital. As I turned to get in my car, the phone rang and it was Otis Brown calling to warn me about the drunk. He and a woman had been at Otis' new barn. Cursing and brandishing his revolver, he had announced that he was going to take his horse from Otis and take him to "that woman trainer." He had fired a random shot which narrowly missed Otis' young son. Then he left.

Had Otis called me, or the police, to warn us about the wild gunman, we might have been able to avoid our tragedy, but Otis was afraid that I would misunderstand his warning. On what slender thread does fate hold our lives.

I spent every evening at the hospital. Logue, at 65 years, was not a young man, obviously, but his apparent recovery was encouraging enough that I went to Mexico, Mo., to try out a horse. On my return to the hospital I was shocked to hear that Logue had died. I could not believe it! No chance to comfort our dying friend. Blinded by tears, I gradually focused on an apparent celebration in the street. The nurse softly explained, "It's V.J. Day". The war was over for my husband, thank God, but I could not rejoice at that moment. All I could think about was that Charlie and I had lost our best friend.

A travesty of a trial was held, but the killer (an honorary deputy!) was set free because he had the privilege to carry a gun. When I went to the separation center to greet Charlie his first question was to ask about Logue. My letter had not reached him. And then I told him.

On what should have been a joyous reunion, we stood there frozen in our grief.

30

Getting A Start
(S & B July, 1994)

Over the years so many young trainers have asked Charlie and me how we got our start in our profession. Perhaps a revealing of our very humble beginnings may help. If not to help, at least they are good for a laugh.

The day after I graduated from college, I applied for and got the position as head of the riding department at MacMurray College in my hometown of Jacksonville, Ill. That was in 1939 and in 1942 I married Charlie Crabtree and we signed the contract to furnish the ten horses needed for the courses. We also had permission to train outside horses. That is when the fun started!

I already had two show horses and word got around that we were taking horses to train. Now this was at the end of the Great Depression and the public was still very money conscious and the farmers in central Illinois were cautious spenders, to say the least.

The wonderful black horseman, Logan McDaniels, came to work for us. We told him that we could not afford to pay help and that blessed men said that he had saved some money and that he would work for nothing until we could afford to pay him. Eventually, we were able to pay his salary, but to do so in the summer months between school terms we had to take anything that would generate income. The following account will explain the term "anything".

A lady called and said that she had a mare that she wanted Charlie to gait. Charlie said we would be delighted to train the mare before she revealed that the mare was not only spotted but that she had a suckling mule colt alongside. Now in retrospect we were about as desperate as any two people who considered themselves horse trainers could be. But it was income and we told the lady to bring them on. Surprisingly, the mare was very attractive and the bay mule colt was like a pet.

We got the mare shod and it was a pleasure to work her. She was a willing pupil and was learning to rack. There was only one complication, and that was the mule colt. The mare was an idiot if separated from her baby. So Charlie would let the baby out to run alongside his mother while he trained her. Needless to say, that mare got trained at dawn before the neighbors were awake. But it was income and in a short time other farmers had sent a couple of geldings to be broke.

Logan was a master at breaking horses - an invaluable help. We needed to start from ground zero with the horses that the owners said that they had ridden "a few times" - a term meaning that the horse had thrown them so hard that they had to get help - and Charlie was it. We learned a lifetime of horse psychology from Logan that has stayed with us over the years. We learned to use the horse's natural fear as an ally, which permits one to reward a horse with kindness instead of knocking them about to get their respect. Everything was going fine, we had an income, more horses were coming in for training and we were able to begin paying Logan for his invaluable help.

We had been annoyed by a young man who began hanging around the stables in the afternoons. The smell of the stables and all of the horses must have unhinged his mind because he arrived early one morning completely attired in western clothes - a real drugstore cowboy, wearing chaps, cowboy boots, ten gallon hat and the biggest pair of spurs anyone had ever seen. Proudly he asked, "Do you have any tough ones you need help with?" Charlie replied that he had a tough spotted mare that he could use some help with and Logan was already on the way to tack up the mare. There was no need for us to talk, because the three of us had the inspiration at the same time. With stall door firmly shut to keep the colt inside, the mare was led out for the "cowboy." The riding ring opened directly off the barn aisle and as soon as the fellow mounted the mare we quietly headed him in the direction behind the stall where the mule colt would hear his mother go by. We had cross ties in the aisle and with twinkling eyes had a barely concealed smile, Logan picked up one crosstie rope and Charlie took the other one and they snapped them together forming a rope barrier. As the cowboy passed the mare's stall, the colt let out a loud nicker and the mare put on the brakes. Her rider jammed the spurs into her side and the mare took off in a gallop around the ring. As they headed straight for the aisle the poor hapless rider fighting to stay aboard accidentally stuck the spurs into the mare's flanks. She put her head down and bolted into the aisleway. The mare went under the crossties like a bullet, but the rider was half on and half off - just the right height for the crossties to catch him and up in the air he went! He came down about the same time that the mare got back to her stall. No one said a word as the "horse breaker" grabbed his hat, dusting himself off in true John Wayne style and hobbled out of the barn, never to be seen again.

Charlie caught the mare and Logan silently unsnapped the rope barrier. Then, and only then did anyone make a sound. In chorus we all three hooted with laughter. I hope the cowboy was out of ear-shot as he had endured enough humiliation to banish forever his idea to help anyone do anything if they had a "bad one to train".

Success does not come overnight. But if you have talent, are willing to work very hard to improve any horse you may get and deal fairly with your customers and your help, you will have built a solid base of respect and recognition. With profound apologies to Kevin Costner, "If you build a solid base, they will come."

And that is how we got our start in the horse industry.

31

The Horse Dealer
(S & B November, 1995)

No recollection of past history of the American Saddlebred would be complete without mention of horse dealers. Before the dominance of the Tattersalls Sales, private "dealer barns" handled most of the sales of "riding horses."

When Charlie and I married in 1942 we had borrowed the huge sum of $2,500 to purchase five matched pairs of school horses and the tack. Imagine that! The sum was 2,500 not 25,000 and we did just that - in fact we got 11 horses, and thereby hangs this tale.

In St. Louis lived a horse dealer named Claude LaRue, coal black hair and fox thin face. The piercing black eyes should have warned us that here was a man dedicated to selling a bad horse to someone who should have known better, but who had fallen under the smooth-talking guile of a master psychologist.

LaRue had sold us a nice little gray mare, clinching the deal with the offer, free of charge, of a skinny bay gelding. With that, there was movement in a dark corner of the enormous old barn. LaRue, lead shank in hand, opened a stall door, and put the lead on an emaciated bay who followed him into the hallway.

"Here's a horse that fell on hard times and all he needs is groceries. He looks like he has been a real good riding horse and he would make a classy addition to your barn. Folks like you, who know how to treat a nice horse can get him back in order in no time." The gelding had an alert expression and was high headed and looked like the sort of animal that, fattened and well tended, could be a very useful horse. (Recently, I heard a TV commentator refer to a familiar name. It was about Eckerd Drug Stores' introduction of the sales gimmick of "buy one get one free.") I do not know how many years ago this idea was born, but I do know that Claude LaRue sealed a deal with Charles and me with the magnanimous offer of the free bay gelding. We really felt proud that we had outsmarted (!) a clever dealer to buy the little gray mare and get the gelding for nothing. Now, "nothing" is the key word here, as 50 years in this business has proven to us that when you pay "nothing" for a horse that is exactly what you get.

My father, a retired farmer, was delighted with our purchase and said that he would fatten the rack of bones in record time. We had dubbed the gelding, "Napoleon," as he was the bony-part of our lesson horses. I realize now that while we were clever at naming, smart buying was not our strong suit.

Our big purchase had been stabled in the historic U.S. Grant barn, now noted as Grant's Farm, owned by Anheuser-Busch and home base of the world famous Budweiser Clydesdales.

Every farmer in Illinois knew about "horse weeds." Equines loved the tall weeds that flourished in the area. I never did know just what those weeds were, but my father would arrive at the college stable every morning with armloads of the impressive plant. Many years later when we were all educated to recognize marijuana, "hemp" as it had been known, I had the strong feeling that horse weeds and marijuana looked very similar. However, equines had the advantage as Napoleon proved. Every day he gained weight. After three months of stuffing, the bones disappeared, a thick layer of fat over the healthy animal attested to the great recovery of what had been an animal almost starved to death.

Now was the time to start riding Napoleon. Although he flinched a bit when we drew up the girth "Nappy" as we then proudly called him, behaved himself when we bridled and saddled him. Oh, he really was a bright, attractive Saddle Horse, groomed to perfection sporting the Sears Roebuck tack that fitted our budget somewhat better than it fitted the horse.

Charlie held the horse while I confidently climbed aboard. He led the horse across the slick oiled street that separated the barn from the west riding ring. As soon as we entered the ring with its safe footing, Charlie turned the horse loose. Confidently, I gathered up the reins and urged the horse forward. WOW! that horse let out a bawling grunt and started to buck and he displayed the fact that he was an expert bucking horse. "Stop him!" Charlie yelled. "Get off!" Get off? I thought, I'm going to be bucked off! But I did manage to get back on the ground feet first, and handed the reins to Charlie. He hopped aboard and the frantic bucking resumed.

Strong as he was, Charlie could not get the gelding's head up and he, too, got off the back of a horse whose three gaits were walk, buck, and run.

Our rueful conclusion was that we had a horse that would never be trustworthy. Logue the groom, probably had it right when he guessed that the horse had been starved into submission and whenever he regained his strength, no one could ride him.

It was a good lesson for us, and a mistake that we would never repeat. Do not say "when" - the word is "if" when it comes to outsmarting a professional old-fashioned horse trader.

Fortunately, horse weeds were free and oats were 20 cents per bushel so we considered we had done a little better than break even on our great find which cost us "nothing."

We had taken Napoleon to a local auction leading him through and stating that he was not suitable for a child. As the new owner led Napoleon out of the sales ring, we heard him say "those kids got him too fat - what he needs is no oats and a lot of horse weeds."

Marijuana?? I never knew, my father had died before I ever heard of marijuana and I did not want to ask anyone we knew about horse weeds.

32

The Secret
(S & B June, 1993)

Did you ever have to live with an embarrassing secret for many years? Well, I have and only now can I write about it. It just proves that all of the foolish things connected with the horse business do not happen on horseback.

Immediately after my graduation from Illinois College I took the job of heading the Riding Department at MacMurray College, which was also located in my home town of Jacksonville, Ill. The college had just started their horsemanship program the year before and it was a natural thing for me to walk right in and take over the riding program from a very frustrated head of the Athletic Department who knew about as much about riding as I did about ice hockey. I enjoyed my time at MacMurray and developed at least two riders who would become highly respected professionals, Doris Greenwalt (Ryan) and Ruth Kauffman (Palmer). In May of my second year at the college, Charles Crabtree and I married and the following winter (Valentine's Day to be exact) he was called into the army, taking basic training in the Field Artillery and being sent post haste to Italy to slog his way up the boot of Italy in some of the most fierce fighting of the war.

My days were filled with teaching, but the nights were unbearable. When five o'clock came I was desolate - looking forward to a long night of loneliness and despair, as the Italian Campaign was incredibly tough and like any other "war widow" I could not banish the awful images that invade the minds of the helplessly fearful wives.

Then a call came from St. Louis, Mo., inviting me to come there for a meeting to discuss my taking over the management of the huge public facility, Missouri Stables. I was told that it was the largest public stable of its kind in the USA and I found that it was no exaggeration.

Missouri Stables was a huge facility, adjoining the famous St.

Louis Forest Park with its many miles of riding paths. My duties were to take over the entire management, overseeing the barns of personally owned pleasure horses, handling the 50 rental horses, private equitation lessons and the rejuvenation of the private school group program. All these facets of a successful stable had fallen into disrepute and the historic stable was rescued from destruction when purchased by a fine group of St. Louis sportsmen who realized that it could again be one of the best public stables in the country. This also included my training of show horses if I could work up the clientele. It was just what I needed - an enterprise so hard and demanding that I could only fall into bed at night, too exhausted to worry about the war and letting General Mark Clark run the Italian Campaign alone.

The arena, which also housed the business office and the booking office was a huge wooden structure, ingeniously designed to utilize an arching roof construction, with no upright supports. It was a clear span structure that had a show size ring and box seating for over 2,000 people. The annual St. Louis Spring Horse Show was held there every year, as well as two horse sales. It was an enormous undertaking but the salary offer was very generous (they knew what I was in for) and it would give me more opportunities to train horses, which has always been uppermost in my mind. So off to St. Louis I went.

During the demise of the stable due to improper management and carelessness, it had become a haven for every stable bum in the country. What was needed was to clean up the image of the place and get rid of the drifters so that it would once again be a facility where parents could bring their children for instruction and the private schools could send their groups for weekly instruction. It worked out very well - I wanted to work and they wanted respectability. Now it was my duty to organize the help and to get going.

Between the time that the stable was purchased and my arrival it was operated by an elderly Irishman whom the children adored and who was immensely pleased that he was in charge of his beloved stable. I knew how he felt and I spent a lot of worrisome moments figuring out how to tell him that I was the boss (a bitter pill for a man to swallow in those days). One of the barns had an end stall that gave a view of the entire arena, courtyard and the front of the rental barn. Someone had rigged up a tiny "office" by putting in south and west windows and had improvised a desk of sorts by laying several boards across the front end of the stall. There was room for only one chair and that is where I sat when Les came in for our discussion. He was a big man, mid 60s, white haired and florid faced. His blue eyes showed apprehension as he entered and my heart sank. I struggled mightily to explain to him that I wanted him to stay on as a valued manager of the rental activities, but that I would be the final say in every aspect of operating the facility. He appeared to be accepting my words, when a most embarrassing odor pervaded the tiny room. I immediately terminated my speech and he made a hasty retreat. What a humiliating thing to happen to the poor fellow - not only had he just been demoted but he had committed a most social error. I have never felt so sorry for anyone and as I sat there fanning the door with my foot, I noticed Les walking across the courtyard - rosy face redder than usual and a very enigmatic turn to the corner of his mouth. This puzzled me, but not for long as that same insidious smell arose again. Incredulously I leaped to my feet, knocking over the chair and looked down to discover my old and obviously flatuent Collie dog slinking out from under the "desk". My first thought was "thank heavens, the man knows that he was not the offender" and then came the awful realization that he did not know that the dog was under the desk. My puzzlement about the hint of a smile that I was surprised to see was no longer a puzzle. It was a grin and the red face only evidence of the man's effort to keep from laughing. He thought I was the guilty party! And I am sure he thought so until the day he died.

33

The Wayward Falsie
(S & B October, 1994)

When I left MacMuray to run Missouri Stables, Ruth Kaufman and Jane Grimes, her roommate, left MacMurray, transferring to Washington University in St. Louis. What a compliment for them to follow me to Missouri! Ruth was a very small young lady. Jane came to the stable and told me that the preceding evening they had been walking back to the dorm when they noticed a man following them. Emboldened by their silence he crowded into Ruth and attempted to fondle her. Not missing a stride, Ruth doubled up her fist and with a direct smash to his nose flattened him onto the sidewalk. She did not say a word and the two friends continued on their way. Dear Ruth, always a lady, but watch out for her left hook!

During the war many plants converted to the production of war products. Many workers could then afford to ride horses and we had night rentals. Not wanting our horses overworked or badly ridden, I offered to give free instruction to the group of 20 who came to the stable at ten o'clock at night when their shift changed at Continental Can Company.

Everyone was very patriotic in those fearful days and I welcomed the diversion in the lonely nights. They were a grand group - not good riders but very enthusiastic, so I came up with the "brilliant" idea of offering to coach 16 of the riders to form a drill team. Now my knowledge of proper procedure was only what I could remember of the simplest maneuvers of the Canadian Mounties Drill Team at the horse shows. I promised the group that they could be a feature at the St. Louis Spring Horse Show held at Missouri Stables since the Coliseum was filled with war materials.

The group practiced the simple routine. I bought a whistle and borrowed a white horse from one of the owners at the barn. Almost overcome with patriotism, everyone decided to wear bright blue cotton jodhpurs, thin white cotton shirts and wide, bright red sashes.

The group practiced the sitting trot as I wanted to be sure that we began and ended the drill with the original 16 riders.

The long awaited night finally came and the excited group made an impressive and patriotic entrance to loud applause. I dutifully sat on the white horse at the end of the ring, whistling away and very proud of my drill team. Midway through the drill, I heard what sounded like laughter. Quickly, I counted and found that all 16 were where they should be. But, to my horror, I saw what was amusing the audience. One of the girls was very slightly built (scrawny would be an honest description). In an effort to augment her flat bosom, she had apparently hung a pair of "falsies" around her neck under the thin shirt. The sitting trot had repositioned the guise and I watched in mounting embarrassment. I would not stop the group and by the end of the drill one falsie had risen to unexpected heights and was perched on the poor girl's shoulder like an epaulet! I felt so sorry for that rider, but the memory of my one and only drill team remains ever clear in my mind over these many years. To this day I can see those errant falsies every time we rise to honor America and the playing of the national anthem. It must be a sign of weakness of character, or perhaps it is an overwhelming sense of the ridiculous that has been a great part of my strength.

Already at the stable when I arrived was a charming elderly English couple, Mr. and Mrs. Ed Roseberry. In earlier days, Ed had been a noted exhibitor of prize Belgian draft horses. Mrs. Roseberry answered the phone and handled the booking of rentals. In an effort to give an aura of respectability and to let the public know that Missouri Stables was a high class operation, I instructed Mrs. Roseberry to say, "Good morning (afternoon - night), Missouri Stables. May I help you?"

A tiny lady in her 70s, Nora had a lilting voice that could charm the birds from the trees. Her eyes sparkled with good humor and she was so pleased at the rejuvenation of the place that she took great pride in answering the phone. One day I walked into the booking office to see Nora staring wild eyed at the clock on the wall. She had just answered "Good..." when she discovered that it was dead center at 12 o'clock. I hastily cut off the phone connection and told the flustered lady, "Don't worry, they will call back." In a moment she picked up the receiver, glanced at the clock which showed one minute past noon and said "Afternoon, Missouri Stables.

May I help you?" It is no wonder that Nora Roseberry was loved by all who came to the stables and she was a constant source of pleasure and pride to me.

I had many adventures in St. Louis — some great, some terribly sad. But I am thankful that the brightest mental pictures are still the wayward falsie and the memory of the dear, dear English lady who wanted to do everything just right.

34
Storm Cloud
(S & B April, 1988)

Every equitation teacher has at least one horse that was that teacher's gateway to success - a horse without price and a horse that will be remembered by riders and trainers alike as long as horse people get together and discuss the great horses of the past.

This is how I became the buyer and trainer of the great black gelding Storm Cloud. One afternoon at a show a group of trainers were sitting around discussing the subject of "the greatest horse I ever saw". This was in the year 1955 and many well known champions were named. When it came my turn, I said that the greatest horse I had ever seen was a big black five-gaited gelding that showed at the American Royal. The horse had absolutely captivated me. I did not remember where he placed in the class - it really didn't matter but the memory of that great moving horse with the presence of royalty was forever imprinted on my mind. (I did recall that the vets were called into the ring to look at the horse's eyes, but did not excuse him.)

A few years had passed and the Crabtrees were managing Rock Creek Club Stables in Louisville. The phone rang, and when I answered, a young woman named Hope Beatty from Iowa asked me if I remembered the discussion of great horses several years before? Remember? How could I forget! To my delight she said that my favorite horse was in a small town in Iowa, shown in three-gaited classes and cared for by two young girls and they had to sell the horse.

We had always shied away from consignments, but I asked the price of the horse and she said, "They want $1800 for the horse and $200 for the special high trailer that he required." I wired the money and sent for the horse. Tired and dirty as he was after the long ride, he backed out of the trailer like a champion — <u>and he never looked back from that moment on.</u>

Although the former owners had shown in equitation, it was at the local variety and the horse had never been schooled in figures.

Storm Cloud.

The moment I rode him, I knew who his new owner was going to be - Lynne Girdler of Louisville, an aggressive young redhead who had talent oozing from her pores. I told her father what I had given for the horse and said that I would sell him the horse for $2500 and I would keep the trailer. I told him, "Walter, you will buy many horses for Lynne but you will never spend your money more wisely than right now."

How prophetic were those words! Storm Cloud and his teenage rider were an immediate sensation in equitation, seldom losing a class. In fact, as invariably happens, the equitation schooling improved Storm Cloud's way of going so much that we entered him in a juvenile class, forgetting about the possible questioning of his sight. He was undefeated, winning first at Rock Creek and then taking the first leg of the Minton Memorial at Lexington. In the 1950s, the Minton Memorial was a three-time challenge class and was considered the world's championship of the juvenile three-gaited horses, as it is today. However, the Minton Memorial is retained only as a perpetual trophy in the class offered at the Kentucky State Fair. This was changed after Lynne and "Stormy" won the Minton Memorial three times - in 1957, 1958 and retiring the trophies at both Lexington and Louisville in 1959. No horse had ever done this before and the retirement of the trophy changed the nature of the win, but not the importance to any juvenile who is fortunate enough to ever win the prestigious class.

It was in 1957, Storm Cloud's first year in the Minton Memorial at Louisville, that a trainer protested during the class and the vet came into the ring to check the horse's eyesight. He found him entirely capable of seeing and there were no other incidents the rest of his life. Not only was the great horse's record impressive, but Lynne was winning equitation championships and the juvenile three-gaited at the same time at the same shows.

Storm Cloud never had a bad thought in his life. He learned equitation figures overnight, and every day he lived he just got better and better as a three-gaited horse. As many of the older horses are that get in their later years (Stormy was 12 when we got him in 1955) he had a favorite diagonal. In overcoming this I did a most unusual thing. Through experimental shoeing, we finally solved the problem by shoeing the horse with a different type shoe on every foot! Then both diagonal strides were the same.

Storm Cloud was foaled in Missouri in 1944. He was out of a great doing mare by Arletha's Easter Cloud and by the immortal sire, Stonewall King. Breeders search papers now to find Stonewall King breeding. This horse marked his progeny with such grit, presence and uncompromising show horse ability that we are still reaping his wonderful heritage. His colts were big, handsome horses. Not always the finest, they had the presence to make themselves magnetically attractive. We still look for that breeding to give present day show horses the spirit and courage that may not be so inherent in other families. The great fine harness mare, Supreme Airs was shown for nine years. My husband, Charles, began showing her as a three-year-old and in addition to her many world's championships she NEVER made a bad show and she always gave her very best.

I was judging the Columbia, Missouri, show when I saw a wild Stonewall King-bred gelding shown by R.S. Palmer. He did not win the class, but he was indelibly printed on my mind. That fall he showed at the American Royal and was a much improved horse. I bought him there for Linda Lowery and took all winter of working never faster than a slow gait or a jog trot. By Lexington time, the pair were ready and they made practically an exhibition to win the ladies gelding class and instant recognition as "one of those Stonewall King-bred show horses." There are so many more, but this is supposed to be a column dedicated to equitation training.

A Mr. Allen of North Kansas City bred Storm Cloud (who was registered as Duke of Wilmar, but his name was changed to Storm Cloud when he was trained in 1950). Lynne Girdler, his owner showed "Stormy" at Madison Square Garden in 1957. There were 78 entries in the AHSA Medal class that year and after separating the groups in the work on the rail, all 78 entries were brought back into the ring and lined up (corralled would be a better term). Then as each entry performed their workout they were excused from the ring. In retrospect, I suppose that I made a bad decision, but being so fearful of Stormy's being kicked in such a crowd, we elected to hide in the far corner away from the melee and ride last. By this time the only entry left in the ring was Lynne on Storm Cloud. Let this be a lesson - never say never. The horse who never made a mistake stopped his canter at the intersection of his figure eight whinnied and broke into a trot. By the next year after management and I had had a discussion, entries lined up outside the gate and came in individually for their work-outs. Lynne's victory was the first of many for me at "the Garden" but it will always be the sweetest. We were pioneering and to win with a top show rider and horse combination was very important. Such a sight is not unusual now, but in 1958, Lynne and Stormy were the sensation of the show.

Stormy was retired from open competition in 1961 at the Lexington Junior League Horse Show and Lee Roby said that night - "He's the greatest walk-trot horse in America." He was given to me to keep for the rest of his days. I studied my AHSA Rule Book and finding no ruling against my plan, I called the AHSA office to see if it was legal to show a retired show horse in equitation, since the horse did not count. They assured me this was so, and I asked them to put it in writing.

Now it was time for the Louisville show. Armed with a tape of Stormy's retirement at Lexington and the AHSA ruling of eligibility I went to steward Herman Miles and showed him my material and advised him that I was going to enter Sarah Nutting in the older age group that night. Anticipating some repercussions, I had made sure that not only was the entry legal, but that the steward would have such evidence in his hand when the inevitable would happen. Sarah did not have a horse of her own but she had been a wonderful help to the younger riders all summer and I felt that she had earned the right to ride Storm Cloud. She came to the stable and practiced at night. We shipped Stormy into the show grounds that afternoon. As we mounted up all of my other riders in the class I told them that Sarah was going to ride Stormy and if anyone had any objections to speak up. The riders all agreed that Sarah deserved her big chance and they went on up to the makeup ring. I kept Sarah back at the stalls until her class was called. Sure, it was a dramatic moment and one I savored, but more than that I did not want any commotion in the make-up ring to distract any of the other competitors. The beautiful rider and the spectacular horse made up yet another invincible pair and won their classes. Sarah qualified for the Good Hands at the show and went on to win the 1961 AHSA Finals in New York.

The following spring a tall shy 12-year-old young lady from Tulsa by the name of Randi Stuart came to the farm for lessons. After purchasing two horses, the Stuarts decided to move their horses to the Crabtrees. Randi progressed so fast on her first horse, King Again, that we arranged for her to take over Storm Cloud. By the spring of 1963, Randi and Storm Cloud were ready for the big time. They were practically without defeat in equitation the next two years. In 1963 Randi won the AHSA Medal Final, and the NHS "Good Hands" Final in 1964. This was Randi's last ride in equitation and it was Storm Cloud's final appearance in a show ring - a show ring that he had lit up for 18 straight years. I find myself writing this through a veil of tears, because no matter how great Storm Cloud was, no matter how he influenced the equitation picture forever, I have still wrenching memories of the wonderful horse who changed my life.

35
Glenview's Warlock
(S & B February - June, 1991)

The year 1990 was an outstanding year for many teachers and riders. It was also a triumph for several trainers. All in all it was a great year but it was a year to look back on to regret the passing of one of the great horses of our time.

I refer to the great Glenview's Warlock. Known everywhere saddle horses were shown as simply "Warlock", his story is one that covers over 20 years, ending only a few weeks ago, when the tearful end came. I say tearful because more than one trainer, teacher and rider had the privilege of riding Warlock. He was good to everyone who had him and there was something so different about his way of going and his supreme mentality that one never hears anyone claim to have "another Warlock."

His dam, shown as Sorceress, was herself an unusual mare winning at all of the big shows under saddle at three gaits, under Western tack as world's champion parade horse, and winning as an outstanding fine harness horse. Warlock did not arrive in this world as an accident. "Sorcy", his dam, was owned by Mrs. F.D. Sinclair, nee Gallagher, and her daughter Kathie showed her three-gaited and was in the Western attire when she was world champion parade horse. I had the great fun of showing the mare when Kathie could not get to the show and also won with her. In fact, as I recall, Sorceress was undefeated in parade classes. If the show did not have that division, Charlie Crabtree would show her in fine harness as would Mrs. Gallagher. A bold sound mare that could trot over the moon and never saw a class outlast her, she was a dream to have in the stable. Mrs. Gallagher had the grand champion harness mare, Supreme Airs, at the time and many a judge wondered which mare he had actually tied.

The mare never did wear out, but all concerned felt that she did not owe anyone anything and that she should have a chance to make her further mark on Saddlebred history as a broodmare. Sorceress was not a gorgeous mare, being by Private Contract, who

Glenview's Warlock in the Three-Gaited Stake at Rock Creek, 1973.

First time shown — Glenview's Warlock in Junior Three-Gaited at River Ridge, 1973.

The Sorceress the dam of Warlock.

was not noted for his beautiful offspring, as his colts tended to be a bit boxy headed. But the ebony mare was so consistent, bright and high stepping at all gaits and it was not until the later years of her show career that she bodied out and with the long mane and full tail became a very pretty horse.

In 1967 the Kentucky State Fair held a parade of stallions and there was one stallion in particular that appeared to be the ideal cross with the mare. That was Indiana Peavine, a gorgeous, glittering chestnut with tasteful white leg and face markings. He was exceptionally fine headed and seemed to have a good way of going as well as ideal temperament. Mrs. Gallagher agreed this was the right mate for Sorceress, so off to Happy Valley Farm the mare went in the late spring of 1968. As was usual for "Sorcy" she continued to do everything right and got in foal on the first breeding.

The following year she produced a beautiful stud colt, bright chestnut with large star and connecting stripe and four white stockings. Mrs. Gallagher was always ready with great names, so she dubbed this son of a sorceress, "Glenview's Warlock". No one would envision at the time what magic he would provide for so many riders.

Charles Crabtree broke and trained him and won the three-year-old National fine harness Futurity with the colt. He had gaited him but this division was not for him, so that was when Charlie decided to put him in harness. Although he won outstandingly, Charlie did not think that harness was his best division and that winter he trained the gelding as a walk-trot horse.

Only by a freak accident did I fall heir to the horse. Charlie was just recuperating from a spinal operation and when Warlock jumped when a workman dropped a wrench in an empty hot water heater, Charlie had been in the process of mounting the horse and the resultant fall forced him to forego riding for several weeks. Thankfully, he did not break his back, but it was a "break" for me and I inherited this wonderful prospect. Very shortly after this, we took Warlock to the River Ridge Horse Show and it was there that I trimmed him - and what a sight he was! I swear that when the trimming was finished that Warlock threw his head up in the air and snorted. What I think he said was, "Well, you finally got it right!" That afternoon I showed him in the junior three-gaited class. When we came into the make up ring everyone just stopped in their tracks. I actually thought something was wrong, not realizing just how wonderful the horse looked. He was a sensation and that has to stand out in my memory as one of my greatest thrills of all. Some horses can look good from the ground and feel clumsy in the saddle - not so with Warlock. Every time I rode him I felt sorry for Charlie and thanked my lucky stars. I had never ridden in a Rolls Royce car at that time but when I did I thought - this is the way Warlock feels to the rider. Trainers who saw the class have never forgotten it and neither have I. As I sit here writing about it my eyes fill with tears remembering that I was privileged to experience such a unique moment. Warlock affected people that way. One did not have to own him to love him. He was a once-in-a-lifetime horse and everyone knew it.

After the victory pass there was a line of trainers waiting at the gate as we trotted back to the stall - trying to beat the people back to the barn where I might have a chance to sell him to one of our stable owners. Jane Grueneberg grabbed my arm as I dismounted and asked me if her daughter Kristy could ride him. I said, "Isn't he too big for Kristy?" I shall always remember her exact words, "Helen, I didn't ask if he was too big I asked if Kristy could ride him." Of course I agreed and she said, "Well, now we own him" and he would stay with the Crabtrees. Mrs. Gallagher did not need a walk-trot horse at the time and, as she always has been and always will be a wonderful owner and the best sport in the world, she never regretted selling Warlock and was always his staunchest fan.

Warlock was a most unusual horse and had a host of friends and admirers all of his long life. In recounting the story of his dam, The Sorceress, I neglected to include an account of the birth of her first foal. When it was decided to breed Sorceress we called Alvin Ruxer to arrange her maiden breeding to Supreme Sultan. In a joking mood, I told Alvin that this was a "designer's" breeding and that we wanted a stud colt, black with a star and snip and some white behind, adding that if we did not get our order right that we would not pay the stud fee. It was a good joke and was promptly forgotten. When we decided to breed the mare to Indiana Peavine the next season, we sent her down to Happy Valley Farm in Rossville, Ga., to foal there. In due time the phone rang and it was Sam Brannon calling to report that "the black mare" had delivered her foal. It was not an easy time and Mrs. Hutchinson and Little

Bit aided Sam in getting the foal out. I said, "Sam, thanks so much and we really appreciate the good care you gave the mare, and, by the way what color is the foal?" He said that it was a black stud colt. I asked if there were any markings, and he replied that there was a star, snip and "some white on the hind ankles." I nearly dropped the phone and said, "Oh, no." Poor Sam thought it was a critical rejoinder but it was soon cleared up with my explanation of the "order" to Alvin Ruxer. We all still joke about that. As was her wont the mare produced a horse of history. Mrs. Sinclair named him Status Symbol! "Tubby" Bridgers bought him as a yearling and promoted him in a very positive manner. While he was not an outstanding show horse, he became very famous as a broodmare sire where the Sorceress influence was very much in evidence. Status Symbol broodmares are prized possessions.

I showed Warlock without defeat in junior stakes following his sensational debut at River Ridge — Rock Creek, Lexington Junior League, Cincinnati, Kentucky State Fair and completed that wonderful year with not only the junior stake at the American Royal, but the three-gaited grand championship. I suppose I should be thankful that of the countless number of horses that I showed over the years that I never had to ride while I was ill, but like many of the exhibitors at Kansas City, by stake night I had a raging case of what we all refer to as the "Kansas City Flu." I remember very little about the class as I was fighting so hard not to faint and fall off of Warlock. When we finally lined up, Dick Lavery, who was one of the judges, jokingly said to me as they came down the lineup "Helen you didn't have to work so hard to win this class." I must have been a pitiful sight, hanging onto the rail to keep on my feet and being absolutely drenched with perspiration. Somehow I managed to remount, get the trophy and make a very short victory pass. I did not know that it would be the last time I would show Warlock and I look back on that victory with mixed emotions.

Kristy Grueneberg showed Warlock all of the next season with great success. Kristy was little but mighty. She was one of the smartest riders I ever had and as the saying goes could "flat out ride a horse". What a pair they were, the beautiful petite girl and the magnificent gelding.

Not long after Louisville our son, Redd, called me in a nervous state to tell me that Mr. Grueneberg wanted to move Warlock to him to show in the open stakes with the World's Championship in mind. Redd was quite upset and said he had told Mr. Grueneberg that he would not take the horse. The rationale for moving the horse was that the owners held the popular belief that Warlock could win it all at Louisville but that judges would not tie a woman rider in the big stakes. And they probably would not have done so. It had never been done and the "men only" attitude in the big stakes at Louisville was a real thing in 1974. I told Redd that I understood the situation and that he must take the horse, adding "Redd, let's keep Warlock in the family!" In my lifetime of over 60 years of showing the unspoken prejudice was a real thing and I know that a capable lady rider has equal opportunities now. But it was many a year in coming.

Warlock was let down for the winter and was just back in the training barn for a short while when Redd flew west to judge the Indio, California show. The phone rang at our barn and we got the shocking account that Warlock had suffered a mishap in the stall and that the halter had broken and had hit him in the right eye destroying it. I put in an immediate call to Redd, but he had left for the airport and did not know of the tragic accident until he arrived in Louisville. A few years later I lost my right eye to cancer and I can honestly say that the grief I felt about Warlock was much harder to bear than my own loss. I still dream about that awful telephone call that I assumed meant the end of a glorious future for a glorious horse. Who could know what the future held?

The rest of the winter was spent in healing the eye and making preparations to show him the following season. According to the AHSA rule book at that time the phrase "must give an appearance of sight" seemed to justify the plan to have an artificial eye made to maintain the "appearance of sight." This was done very well by a firm here in Kentucky and Redd and the Gruenebergs assumed that everything was in order for the upcoming show season. It was late in the spring before the proper eye was fashioned, so the first show was at the Lexington Junior League Show. I had purposely stayed away from any connection with Warlock as I felt that my interest could be taken for intrusion, so it was not until I saw the horse at Lexington that we knew he was to be shown. This experience remains in my mind as one of my life's most difficult times, I did talk to Redd and he assured me that the horse show management informed him that the entry met class specifications. This was made very clear to the Gruenebergs, even assuring them that the AHSA had again approved Warlock's showing.

I could reason that there was an impass - the show management agreeing with the AHSA (whom they said again that they had contacted). Redd had even contacted those riders showing in his class and they all agreed that everything was all right. I suppose that I have a "Doubting Thomas" attitude towards show management especially when the manager told me that he had contacted the Association on Saturday. Because of my doubts and because I loved my son and that horse so much, I went to Redd and advised him not to show. My reasoning happened to be correct that the "appearance of sight" was certainly met with, but what bothered me was that under "artificial appliances" allowed, that there was no mention of ocular prosthesis. Ignoring my husband's advice to keep out of the situation, I did visit Redd at his hotel room and said that I thought that he would be barred from the class, or even worse, allowed to show and then have the placing over-ruled. My first mistake was not taking Charlie's advice, the second was waking Redd up in the middle of his afternoon nap and thirdly not realizing that my concern could be construed as interference. It is true that Redd was between a rock and a hard place since both management and AHSA had told the owners that the entry was in order. I did say to Redd that the "appearance of sight" was the basis for a favorable ruling but I suspected that someone would protest on the basis of artificial appliances. I was sick with regret at seeming to interfere, but it was being too protective on my part of the owners and Redd and not wanting them to be embarrased if a protest occurred - which it did. Redd was allowed to win the class and then the entry was rejected the next morning. I did not think that anything more than the sorrow of the horse's losing the eye could hurt me any more - but Lexington became a nightmare for me and its effects lingered for many years.

After Warlock was denied the opportunity to show in recognized shows following his appearance at Lexington, he stayed at Redd Crabtree's barn that winter. It was not without hope that the existing "eye rule" would be changed at the next rule change year. It became common knowledge that other horses were showing with the same problem by keeping everything sub rosa, so it seemed that there would be several owners in favor of allowing a false eye to be permitted in the recognized shows, as the horses in question were of high caliber and would be at the bigger shows.

I was not aware that Warlock was being worked with equitation in mind, but Danny Jenner was working for Redd at the time and he did what he could in the training areas in Redd's barn. The price put on the horse was commensurate with the probability that he could return as a stake horse. Thus it was that what became the "Warlock Rule" remained intact for many years, even after he reappeared in the ring as an equitation horse. Warlock was always a threat. The Gruenebergs finally took Warlock back to their farm near their home in Cincinnati. Kristy would ride him whenever she could and as far as I was concerned the horse was almost forgotten in the rush of the big group of horses that we were showing at the time.

In June of 1978, we took a large string of horses to the Cincinnati Horse Show, which was held in Lebanon, Ohio on the race track. It was a warm-up show for Lexington as the show ring was in front of the grandstand and if a horse could make those narrow turns there, then we knew that he would not have any difficulty negotiating the track at the Red Mile.

About midway of the show I contracted a severe case of poison ivy and went to consult a doctor. He advised me to keep out of the heat, not get excited or dirty. I told him that he had just described the horse business, but he reminded me that the grandstand at the show was air conditioned. So after our stable's last appearance that night I sat by myself in the cool grandstand. I cannot describe the emotion that overcame me when I looked at the ring and saw Kristy Grueneberg riding Warlock in an adult equitation class! After she had won the class, I jumped up to rush back to the barn. I crashed into the Gruenebergs who were leaving by the same exit. I was in tears, several people around were in tears and Kristy's parents were hardly able to speak. Mr. Grueneberg said to me, "Helen, why don't you buy him for equitation?" I answered that I would give my right arm for him, but that his reported asking price was not within equitation range. He said, "I'll sell him to you for what I gave for him," and I told him he had a deal. I had Shauna Schoonmaker in mind for him, but knew that we would buy him, if her mother would not agree to take him. By noon the next day Mrs. Schoonmaker arrived and we drove over to Harrison, Indiana where the horse had been hauled the night after his class. There was a small arena there and I remember making a figure eight on Warlock around a sawdust pile and a mower. Shauna and the horse were sensational together and we raced back to the show and told Mr. Gruenberg that we would take the horse. While we were at the farm, Jim B. Robertson contacted Mr. Grueneberg and offered him almost double the asking price. We were dumbfounded that there had been such a mix-up and I can honestly say that I went through that last night of the show concealing a broken heart. Warlock was ours and then he was not. We returned to Simpsonville on Sunday and I was a walking zombie for two days. On Tuesday morning the phone rang and it was Kristy Grueneberg. She told me that she and her Mother wanted me to have the horse for Shauna. She said that they knew how very much I loved that horse and knew that we would always see that he was in the best of hands. I was overwhelmed with relief and gratitude and told her that Mrs. Schoonmaker had offered to meet the escalated price. Kristy replied, "No, Mrs. C., mother and I have agreed that we would let you have him at the original price." I am aware that I am getting very personal in this narration, but every once in a while someone will do something so right - so magnanimous, that it is a moment that will be remembered forever by me and by the Schoonmakers. Those people loved that horse so much that they wanted him to be with the people who had conceived the idea of his origin and had felt so deeply about everything that had happened to him. One hears so many stories about the horse business, that I feel everyone should know what can happen when true horse lovers care more for their horse than the almighty dollar. Kristy and her mother will always be very special people and the true story deserves telling.

    I will not chronicle all of Shauna's winnings on Warlock but they, like most of the horse's succeeding owners were almost invincible. Shauna had won the UPHA final in 1977 on The Deputy. I was always proud of my riders, but the combination of Shauna and Warlock changed the whole face of equitation forever. Shauna thought like a horse and Warlock thought like a person and everyone who saw them in their two years of partnership will never forget them. In Shauna's final years with Warlock she showed in the Good Hands in New York. The Schoonmakers and the Crabtrees agreed that Warlock would be in considerable jeopardy in the cramped stabling at the Garden, so accepting the very kind offer of Dr. and Judge Meanor, we shipped the horse to their stable in New Jersey two days prior to the competition and made the trip into New York the morning of the Final. His groom, L.T. Armstrong adored the horse and of all of the good ones he has cared for over many years he considers him the brightest and kindest horse he ever rubbed. He surely was one of the greatest dual purpose horses if not the best - of all times. He was also one of the bravest. It must not have been a pleasant ordeal to have the prosthesis put in every time he showed, but in very short order, with L.T.'s gentle handling, Warlock would let me put the eye in without any restraints. He would see me coming into the stall with all of the sterile bottles, etc., and he knew what was coming. He would hold his head down, squint shut the good eye and let me put the eye in. Then he would take a big breath (I guess he held his breath during the procedure). Then he was almost on tip toes, ready to go and challenge all comers. It was at this time that he developed the habit of whinnying when he halted before a figure eight. That one was beyond us! But it certainly got the judge's immediate attention.

Shauna Schoonmaker and Warlock burst on the equitation scene at Lexington, just three weeks after his "discovery" at the Cincinnati show. Like Lynne Girdler and Storm Cloud in 1958, they were sensational. But where as Storm Cloud was truly more than a decade before his time and was looked on as a sort of "freak" in equitation, Warlock came at a time when all of the equitation horses were of increasing stature and ability and the "young equitators" had been honing their skills on three and five-gaited ponies and juvenile walk-trots; so it was not unrealistic that all instructors began to look to the open and stake classes for horses that would fit into the new dual role as equitation and junior exhibitor horses.

Shauna and Warlock were almost without defeat in 1978 and 1979. Shauna was a very correct rider in the technical sense but the pair truly embodied what the UPHA pioneers had in mind when we envisioned what the impact of the UPHA Challenge Cup would have on rewarding riders for getting superior performances from their horses on the rail and knowing enough about horse psychology and motivation to execute the many intricate individual workouts off the rail. Warlock could raise up and go like a stake horse, then Shauna would collect him to a shorter stride to accommodate the tight turns and maneuvers off the rail and still maintain a controlled balance - the mark of a super rider getting a perfect performance from a horse gifted enough to demonstrate the high ability of the rider. One cannot give a recital on an old tinny piano - and Warlock was the ultimate artistic instrument that the UPHA had in mind.

Warlock and Shauna set a pattern for all who followed to aim for. They were not only a great combination but the catalyst for teachers and riders to find the difference between making a ride and just taking a ride.

In her final class - the AHSA Medal - the contest finally wound down to a change of horse between Shauna and Ashley Tway, a splendid rider coached by Harold Adams. This was during an era when judges seemed bent on devising workouts with incredible numbers of seemingly endless components. These two riders had flawless individual workouts, so a change of horse seemed to be the logical tiebreaker. I noticed with dismay that Ashley's dainty mare which Shauna changed to was a truly spent horse and her shoulder muscles and front legs were shuddering uncontrollably. Shauna was really worried and just walked the mare during the brief warm-up time trying to give her a chance to get control of her exhausted muscles. The valiant mare did her best, but by the reverse canter she faltered and fell to her leading knee. With lightning reflexes Shauna threw her weight back in the saddle and actually hauled the mare to her feet. It certainly was not pretty but every horseman in the stands recognized a difficult feat and knew they had seen extraordinary horsemanship.

To tie Ashley on Warlock was not wrong at all. I, myself, never before or since have been prouder of a rider than I was when Shauna went down to defeat on that gallant mare. Although she had one more year in equitation Shauna gave it up and Warlock passed into the hands of a rapidly improving rider, Suzanne Fischer, and I was able to keep Warlock "home" again.

Suzanne Fischer had two successful years with Warlock. I will tell a story of what happened to her final ride. It was the Medal at Kansas City and Suzy was in a near faint from the tension. Danny Daniels was the judge and for the initial part of the class, the riders were lined up with their backs to the west rail. I had found a gate directly behind Suzy and I told her to listen for the first two numbers of her back number and to reach back and tap Warlock with the whip, as all of the horses were extremely tired. As luck would have it, Suzy's number was called first and she hit Warlock. That might be the first time he was ever hit, because he flinched and out shot his artificial eye! Danny was not even out of the judges' stand yet and I raced into the ring to call time. With that, Danny turns to the announcer who said, "Wait, Helen wants to say something." A message that came loud and clear to the spectators. I have had many close calls and am happy to be alive, but I have never wanted to die as much as I did at that moment. Fortunately Vandy Vanderwall, the ringmaster, had seen the eye fly out and he tried to get the judge's stand calmed down. He walked over, picked up the prosthesis and sneaked it to me. That was one time when I wanted the world to know the situation - and many did, and many did not. Suzy went on out to make her figure eight while I stood helpless with the eye in my pocket - praying for lightning to strike me dead. As he had done times before, Warlock went to the midpoint, paused and let out the loudest whinny I have ever heard! Suddenly I realized that the whole event would be explained to Danny and save my neck from the apparent interruption of the class. We are still friends, thank goodness! Needless to say, Suzy's ride was trashed for her and I always felt sad that the last ride was such a disaster.

Shivelys were waiting in the wings to purchase the horse for one of the great riders of her time - Jama Hedden. The pair were almost unbeatable, thrilling audiences everywhere. Marilyn Macfarlane had a deal with Lillian that if Jama won the medal finals, that Marilyn could buy the horse for Janna Weir. Warlock took one false step on a figure eight and Marilyn almost passed out. However the error was so slight that Jama did win the Medal and Marilyn wound up with Warlock.

By this time Warlock was such a coveted horse that Marilyn was able to keep him up to the last. Janna had him and won in '83 to February of '85 when he went to Isobel Llobet who showed the horse in juvenile classes and equitation after the rule change. Finally, at Warlock's 16th year the "artificial eye" rule was changed - apparently with Warlock seeming to no longer pose a threat in open three-gaited.

Warlock was always a very sound horse, but the years of showing and the severity of equitation scheduling were beginning to tell, and Marilyn watched him and treated him for the bouts of founder that were beginning to appear. He was a lucky horse to be with such a wise trainer who treated him like the king that he was. He had been considered as a donation to Stephens College, and while that name appears on his papers, Marilyn could not bear to see the horse leave and she bought him from the Llobets. Since the "eye rule" had been changed in the spring of 1986 when Warlock was 17 years old, it was a great surprise when Marilyn took him to the Roanoke Horse Show as many people had counted the horse out. But that was premature, because he made a tremendous show for Marilyn who rode him not only with talent but belief in the heart and ability of the gelding. He not only won but he made a spectacular show as if to tell everyone, "Don't count me out yet."

In 1987 when Warlock was 18 years old he still appeared to be a show horse, so Marilyn entered him in the juvenile three-gaited at Louisville. To ride him, she selected Kim Schipke, a very talented horsewoman and they won their division. Once a champion, always a champion seldom applies, but in Warlock's case it was never truer. He had begun his under saddle world's championships with my riding him to win the junior championship and he returned to the hallowed ground to win again, 14 years later at the age of 18. Jules Verne could not have thought up a more fanciful scenario for a story than the true life of Warlock. He ended his show ring career as he began it - a WORLD'S CHAMPION. The term "Great" is so often loosely applied, but those of us who were privileged over the many years to train, show and develop riders on this magnificent animal all knew that he was something special. Grooms even argue bragging rights over who rubbed Warlock and in what year.

Marilyn kept Warlock at Walnut Way for the next three and a half years. He was never formally retired, which I think is a tribute to Marilyn and her sense of class. Warlock left the public eye as he entered it - not just as a world champion, a term so loosely bandied around now - but a true honest to God champion - a champion on the record books for 14 years and a champion in the hearts of everyone who was privileged to know him. His last three years were carefully seen after by Marilyn and she made the horse as comfortable as could be. Warlock was never happy to miss the show scene and he turned into a crochety old gentleman who lived out his life wishing to be in the ring. He died in November of 1990 at age 21, and he's buried at Walnut Way.

I can say no more. My feelings for this magnificent horse run so deep that mere words would be only an anticlimax for a horse that lived, performed and gave the best of himself to his owners, trainers and riders - truly in our business, a horse for ages.

36

Legal Tender - Born to Show
(S & B November, 1991 — June, 1992)

He stood there, a blazing horse lined up under the bank of brilliant lights in the center of Madison Square Garden. He stood there stripped of his saddle - a picture that every trainer has dreamed about, but never expects to see.

The always-willing gelding had just given me the ride of my life, responding to demands that even exceeded my highest expectations.

His mahogany coat was almost black with the sweat of a hard workout, his arching neck tilting that fabulous head to stare at the highest rows of seats in the cavernous old Garden. I stepped back the length of the curb reins in awe of what I was seeing, barely holding the end of the leather. As the judge approached, there was a momentary hush, then a sudden crash of clapping and cheering for the inspired animal. Cheers had followed horses in the workout but this was different. As if to acknowledge the magic of the moment he swung his head first to the right, then to the left, his incredible flashing eyes seeming to catch fire with the intensity of emotion filling the arena. This was a moment that I and many who saw that New York championship will never forget. That was in November of 1962, but my story of Legal Tender begins several years earlier, even before he was foaled.

Charlie returned from World War II on November 11, 1945. He joined me at Missouri Stables in St. Louis where I was teaching and training. Over 500 private academy riders and 20 horses in training had become a terrible burden for me alone and aside from my joy at my husband's return, I was relieved of much of my duties when he came into Missouri Stables as manager and trainer.

The week before Charlie's return, I had bought a grey over-two mare from Bill Cunningham in Mexico, Mo. I had shown horses before Bill many times and I respected and admired him as a judge. We had never bought a horse from him, and the very next day after Charlie's return, I told him that we would have to drive over to

Legal Tender and Randi Stuart Wightman, up.

Legal Tender and Helen Crabtree, up, 1963.

Mexico to give Bill his check for the grey mare and pick up our commission. You will realize how things have changed since the 50's, when I recount Charlie's amazement that a half-finished walk trot mare would sell for the "huge" price of $4000.00! The new ready wealth following the war had escalated the prices of show horses and many people who had never had the finances to own show horses found themselves ready, willing and able to get into business.

I thought that a nice little drive over to Mexico to see some horses would be a great treat for a man who had just endured three years of terrible fighting up the length of Italy. I knew from his letters how much he missed the horses. So, we drove to Mexico to Cunningham's establishment. It was not a large training stable, more the sort of stable a dealer would have. First he showed us one of the most gorgeous geldings I had ever seen — a bright, light chestnut with a George Ford Morris head and neck. We asked him to move him and he said, "He doesn't move" - and we had just seen him negotiate the sill in the stall door (although just barely). Then Bill started to laugh. He was a very engaging man and had the Irish wit to entertain one for hours. He told us that he just kept the gelding to look at. Which truly was all he was good for. Finally, after more joviality, Bill and I exchanged checks. Since it was our first commission check earned after Charlie's return, I opened the envelope and we looked at the check. I turned to Bill and said, "Bill, there has been an error, this check should be for $400 and it is made out for $300." Still the jolly Irishman, Bill insisted that he had told me that he could only pay $300 - not the usual ten percent. Well, I was not in love with mathematics but I knew that the arrangement was not true. Charlie was red in the face and I didn't know whether it was from embarrassment over the eternal wifely errors that so often occur to husbands, or if he realized that Cunningham was pulling a fast one on a couple of young green trainers who were just getting a toehold in the show horse business. We quickly agreed to say nothing more, take the check and leave. I am sure at the time that Bill was very pleased with his sale, secure in the fact that we would not talk about getting taken in by a smiling Irishman. We had hardly gotten off the premises when Charlie wanted to know what had really happened and I assured him that the ten percent had been agreed upon and there was never any effort to "bush" the deal. It was a very upsetting occurrence for us - and Charlie's re-entry into the business. We finally talked the situation out and decided to say nothing more about it at that time. While Bill may have been gloating over his "huge" bonus, what he did not know was that he had done the Crabtrees a huge favor - because before we got back to St. Louis, we had agreed that there was only one way for us to succeed in the horse business and that was to be totally honest, never to cheat anyone and if it came down to brass tacks that we would not only not cheat young trainers, but that we would do all we could to help them get started. We were kind to Bill not to make a scene but I have to say that his "mistake" cost him many thousands of dollars in the succeeding years. We did not ever deal with him again and on appropriate occasions took our revenge in recounting our first "big deal" when we were getting a start in a business that was to become one of the largest training stables in America in a few short years.

In 1961 I received a letter from Bill Cunningham from Harvey's Lake, Pa., where he was the advisor to Sen. T.N. Wood Stables. I remember every word of the short note - it said, "Helen, there is a gelding here that if you had him he would win every ladies class in America. I have heard that you folks would never buy anything from me, but I am really doing you a favor to tell you about this gelding." I promptly crumpled up the note and threw it in the wastebasket. By pure chance, I was to see this horse worked by Billy Hill at the 1962 Tattersalls Summer Sale - his name was "Legal Tender."

Legal Tender was foaled on March 25, 1953, a bay colt with white left hind coronet. He was by LaVeeda's Knight by Gallant Knight, out of Annie Martin by Captain King by Bourbon King. He was bred by Dyas B. Hulse, father of Ron Hulse to whom I am indebted for much of the information concerning the colt's early years. Legal Tender (what an inspired name!) was truly a sport. In biological terminology a sport is an animal that shows unusual or singular deviations from the norm or parent type. LaVeeda's Knight sired one full sister, a bay mare called Our Country Cousin who was in no way whatsoever like her brother. Three other progeny of LaVeeda's Knight out of different mares were not show stock. Ron Hulse gaited this colt when he was a two-year-old and his description of him was that he was a sport, a term used to describe this unusual animal the rest of his life. Ron speaks of his wild expression, his ability to learn five gaits - and right from the start, the gelding excited all who saw him and the terms "light-footed and graceful" were used by everyone who either trained, rode him or saw him show. Ron says that Legal Tender was so gifted that it was a pleasure to train him and I think much of the gelding's success stems from the intelligence of Ron in realizing that he had something really special and was willing to keep calm with the wild youngster and let him retain the very traits and expression that would set him apart from other horses the rest of his life.

Legal Tender was sold in October of 1955 to Sen. T.N. Wood of Harvey's Lake, Penn. Bill Cunningham was the agent and the horse remained at Cunningham's stable until late summer of 1957, where he made his first public appearance at Louisville in the junior five-gaited class. He was shown by Jimmy Little of Memphis, Mo., who apparently had been working the horse for Cunningham after his purchase. Hulse said the horse was electrifying, but so wild and scared that he was unplaced. But this did not dim his introduction to the tanbark, as the wild bay colt was the talk of the trainers and many tried unsuccessfully to buy him. So many people who were associated with Sen. Wood's Brynfyn Tyddn Stable are lost in time or are reluctant to comment on the horse's progress under Eddie Gutteridge, who was trainer for Wood. I called Billy Hill, one of Indiana's greatest trainers and also one of the most modest. Billy is now 87 years old, but his faltering voice took on an amazing tone when I told him who I was and that I wanted to know about Legal Tender. One of the most quiet-spoken trainers I have ever talked with, Hill told me that he "commuted" to Pennsylvania to train the horse before the 1959 and 1960 fall season where he won at Harrisburg, Penn., and Toronto, Canada. I asked if the Senator ever showed the horse and he diplomatically replied that he "rode him around the farm". I asked Billy what kind of a horse Legal Tender was and he said, "Miss Helen, the ground wasn't good enough for him."

Ray Pittman told me that he saw Hill show the horse at Harrisburg. "Helen, it was a sight I will never forget. All of the other horses were already in the ring and here came Billy and Legal Tender right down the center of the ring and the horse was racking wide open. The crowd went wild over the horse." I am fortunate to have an old magazine that described him in this way..."without doubt, one of the greatest five-gaited horses before the public. It is doubtful if there is a living horse that can look him in the eye and beat him doing five gaits with the gifted Billy Hill in the saddle." There was a reference to Sen. Wood's having won with the horse in amateur stakes, but no one can recall seeing him show the horse ... the article continued, "Bill Hill and Legal Tender make an unbeatable combination as Legal Tender is perfection in symmetry, beauty and action. Mr. Hill is a master horseman who operated two pair of reins as a virtuoso does his violin. He put on an exhibition of artistry in showing Legal Tender both at Harrisburg and Toronto that thrilled the expert and added more prestige to his reputation as a man with velvet hands and a showman of superlative ability." I stress the training and limited showing of the horse, not only to give Billy Hill's great talent recognition, but to remark that Hill's influence on Legal Tender is what made him the great horse that he was for everyone who owned him. A "grizzly bear" approach to such a high-strung horse might have "conquered" him but there would have been a robbing of the God-given spirit that made the gelding such a brilliant and totally different show horse.

In the summer of 1962 Charlie and I were showing about 35 head at the Lexington Junior League Horse Show. The Tattersalls Summer Sale was during the show, but I was so busy and so tired that it never entered my mind to read the catalogue, let alone attend the sale. However, I did hear that the Wood's consignment included a walk trot mare that had been very successful and so I drove over to the sales ground to look at the mare in her stall. As I drove in, I noticed a group of trainers and, thinking something was wrong hurried out of my car to see if I could be any help if there truly had been an accident. When I breathlessly asked, "What happened?", I was told by Lloyd Teater that everyone was waiting to see Billy Hill ride Wood's bay gelding. There was such a palpable air of excitement that I stayed and almost immediately Billy Hill came riding the horse out of the stall. Even before he was out from under the shed row, I was startled by the horse's expression - particularly in his eyes. They were electrifying and stopped everyone in their tracks. Billy proceeded to work the gelding on a path behind the stabling area and everyone rushed to get a better look as the horse moved down the path. He turned and came back at a trot and I have never had such a reaction to a show horse. I felt like someone had hit me in the solar plexus and I could hardly breathe! I believe that all who saw that horse had the same reaction. I thought, "That horse will never get to the sale - someone will get him bought beforehand." I had been looking for a top gaited horse for Randi Stuart and I raced back to the hotel to ask Mrs. Stuart to call Mr. Stuart in Tulsa to get permission to try to buy the horse. She asked me if Randi would be able to ride him and I said, "I will make him ready for Randi." Where does intelligence and emotion conjoin to permit an otherwise sensible trainer make such a declaration? God must have had me by the hand because I had no doubt in the world that this was the horse for Randi.

As Mrs. Stuart turned to go to the telephone, she asked, "What is the horse's name?" and I replied, "Legal Tender."

Very shortly Mrs. Stuart returned and reported that Mr. Stuart had said for me to buy the horse. I asked her how much could I spend and she said, "Harold just said go ahead and buy him!"

Well, there I was ... during the year of 1962 after just having been given permission to buy for the Stuarts, what was the most exciting five-gaited gelding I had ever seen. Now the task of going about "getting the job done" was before me. I had finally looked at the sale catalogue and was somewhat startled that I had set out on a course to buy a nine-year-old gelding that was not represented as an amateur horse and the ever popular phrase "ready for a juvenile" was conspicuously missing. But in analyzing what I had just seen - no horse ever existed that had better bones and tendons and the muscular agility to be a great performer with a minimum of effort. He might run off (I thought about that once) but he would never be a quitter and I was buying him for a child of 13 who was not a quitter under any circumstances, so my doubts were fleeting and time would prove we had made the right decision. Sen. Wood's manager was the aforementioned Bill Cunningham who had sent me the letter about a bay gelding, a letter which I promptly threw away.

Finally, I decided on a course of action. I would go directly to Cunningham and offer him $20,000 (which, at that time, was a big price for an aged gelding). This I did, and Bill said that it was a deal but that he would have to get Sen. Wood's permission and work something out with the sales company as they felt that their best consignments were Legal Tender and Indiana Peavine (whose future and ours were also bound together in later years when we bred Sorceress to him to produce Warlock). I told Bill that I wanted to buy the horse before the sale so we arranged a meeting the next morning with Hawthorn Eddy, owner of Tattersalls at that time, J.T. Denton, the auctioneer, and Dick Duncan, manager. To my surprise and relief, they agreed to my buying the horse on the condition that he must go through the sale, and while we already owned the horse, they would be sure to carry him to our purchase price.

The next afternoon the horse sold. I was so nervous I did not sleep that night before the sale and all of the horses that preceded him in that venue were just a blur to me. At last he came into the ring and I moved to stand next to J.T. who was crying the Wood's consignment. The opening bid called for was $10,000 and someone responded with a bid of $7,500. Just as quickly came $10,000 and they were off to the races. In reviewing an old newspaper clipping it was mentioned that the bidding on the gelding was so fast that the horse was never stopped or stripped. In no time at all the bidding had reached my bid of $20,000 and to my great surprise it continued to mount. At the $25,000 bid, J.T. grabbed my elbow and said "Helen, this is real money and you can make a profit." All I remember saying was that he would go to a million and he was still ours. I did not want anything but that horse! $27,500 was bid by Tommy Lavery (Dick's brother). He and his wife were bidding and they had the money to back up their taste. Another bidder back of me raised the bid another thousand and I countered with $30,000 and the horse finally belonged to the Stuarts. I did not know that the bidder of the $28,500 was Marty Mueller who was bidding for Jean McLean Davis. He told me this last summer - and I asked him to tell me if Legal Tender was really a good horse. In his own inimitable way, Marty stepped back a pace, threw his hands in the air, popped his eyes wide open and declared "A good horse? Why, Helen, he was a great horse".

When it became apparent that I was not going to stop bidding and the hammer fell at the $30,000 mark, I found myself looking into Tommy Lavery's eyes and tears were running down his cheeks. Tommy was one of the greatest, eye-catching riders in the country and I know he was sitting there at the auction, not in the seat, but imagining himself in the middle of Legal Tender - and what a picture they would have made!

In reviewing the news accounts of the Lexington show I noticed that Julianne Schmutz had won the juvenile five-gaited stake on the great horse Stonewall Imperial. They were the best anyone had ever seen in juvenile gaited competition up to that point and I know that must have been in the back of my mind when I decided that I had to have Legal Tender for Randi. The then astounding world's record price of $30,000 was headlined in papers everywhere. It was not until 20 years after that I revealed the entire story of his purchase.) I had immediately gone to the magazine writers to ask them not to refer to Legal Tender's price as I felt that he would always be judged against himself and the price tag that so aptly fitted the obvious stable name, "Cash".

We took extra precautions in shipping Legal Tender to Simpsonville. We gave him half of a three-horse van, put I've Decided (who would be his stablemate all of the time that he was at our stable) next to him and had two grooms ride with the horses. It was evident by the time the van arrived at home, that other measures would have to be taken. Here was a nine-year-old gelding that had shipped less than most three-year-olds and he did not care for any part of it.

I believe that the success Randi and I had with the horse depended most of all in the selection of his groom. We did not have a "nervous" horse, we had a horse that thought entirely differently from any horse that any of us had ever known. Yes, he was nervous like many high strung horses are, but it went several steps further. Happily for both horse and people, he would be trained by a woman whose best talent was getting along with high-strung horses, he had a rider who would do as she was told (when necessary, as she was so gifted that she often did the right thing before I could tell her) - but most of all, Cash had a groom named Johnnie Washington. One of the finest humans I have ever known, Johnnie had a voice that would calm a hungry cobra, hands that were like satin and an understanding of a horse's brain that very few people had. He immediately saw that he had the privilege of caring for this weird acting horse, but he felt from the word go that he would get along with him. All he asked was that he be left alone with the horse and that his day off correspond to the day we did not train.

Johnnie Washington was a master of animal psychology even to disagreeing with getting a goat for the horse's companion — "Miss Helen, he'd be jealous of a goat and would kill him. What he needs is a cocky little 'Banty' rooster that he will respect and learn to like." So we immediately went to the Shelby County Fair and bought the champion rooster of the entire chicken department (for the enormous sum of $2.65!) - a beautiful, colorful little Cochin rooster who was immediately dubbed "Carry". And Cash and Carry were inseparable friends over the years. We had the dream horse, we had the student-trainer combination that worked well together and we had Johnnie Washington, without whom the transformation from a stay-at-home horse to a star of the show ring would never have happened. And we had "Carry" the wonder rooster!

Perhaps this is a good time to explain why I am writing about a horse that many people showing today never saw. There have been many great horses and there will be more. I do not imply that Cash was the greatest gelding of all - my interest in writing about him is the fact that he was so very different from any horse I have ever known or have trained. When his name comes up in conversation with those who saw him show 20 or 30 years ago, he is indelibly imprinted on everyone's mind. The feature that all remember is his wonderful intense expression and the way he would always "turn it on" in the show ring. Most of all it was his eyes. They were so wild looking and piercing that it sets him apart from all others. I do not know what it was that made his vision different. He was not a horse that was constantly "peering" like a nearsighted horse - he gave the impression that he knew everything and that he focused intensely on everything. The moment the gate opened at the show ring he was a completely transformed horse. To list his many, many wins would be boring. I am telling his story because he was so different, so completely different from other horses.

After we got our combination of Cash and Carry (the rooster) in Johnny Washington's care and had rigged the large stall in the van with mattresses until it looked like a recovery room, we were ready to test the waters. It is a tribute to Eddie Guttridge, who trained him at the stables for Senator Wood to ride at home that he was perfectly mannered at home. Randi's previous experience with Amber Wave (her "learning gaited horse") and the wonderful Peacock Peavine prepared her for gaited competition at the highest level - and that is where we were headed. This was hard to figure out as the horse was perfectly mannered and at ease during the practice training at home. Even after we got to the Illinois State Fair, which was but a few weeks after Randi got him, the horse was still quiet and mannerly as I jogged and rode him in the practice sessions. I knew that there was something that transformed the gelding into the wild, exciting show horse I had seen at the sale. There were no drug rules at that time, but I was certain that they had never been used with Legal Tender. No, there was something else - but, what was it? There was only one way to find out, so Randi came into the ring in the juvenile class at Springfield. As we were getting the horse ready in the stall he broke out in a sweat and and was so tense you could have struck a match anywhere on his body. He was only 15.3 hands but he seemed to grow before our very eyes and that intense light in his eyes turned on.

Randi made a perfect show the first way of the ring, but when the reverse was called for, the horse suddenly spun to the left to turn. He did not rear up but the whirling against the guiding was real. I instantly asked Randi to take the gate - not that she could not handle the horse or that she would lose that class, but the mystery of what Legal Tender was all about was apparent. The title of these articles tells it all - this horse was truly born to SHOW and he had what I always called a double standard. Nothing mattered to this horse but showing. I had not bought one horse, I had bought two!

Randi understood being asked to leave the ring. It was nothing but the realization that we had finally found out what made Legal Tender click and we had to get his misdemeanor corrected before it became a problem.

The following night I came to the show dressed to ride, but since I had 20 horses by myself at the show, it was a surprise to Stuarts when the gate opened and I came in on Cash. What a thrill he was! I have been so fortunate to have shown many exceptional horses, but here was truly a dream horse. The trick to showing him was to think 40 feet ahead of him and sit up straight, because I had the feeling that if I leaned forward or opened my mouth that I would have had a mouth full of ears. I have never ridden a horse who could raise up and set himself right in the rider's hands and speed around the ring with the grace of a leopard. As Billy Hill said, "The ground wasn't good enough for him." His ease and cadence of movement were very deceptive and many a rider got ready to pass him and found themselves looking at the rider's back number. When the horses were ready to reverse, I watched the judge and when he turned to the ringmaster, I whirled Legal Tender into the rail and he was reversed before he had time to perform his little dipsy-doodle. The rest was easy and he won the class outstandingly.

This summer when I asked Randi what she remembered about showing Cash, she said that the thing she remembered the most was my telling her to keep that right rein bouncing in his mouth during the walk preceding the reverse. She said, "Helen, I was so busy bouncing that right rein that I can hardly remember anything else!" But we did have the horse figured out and he made wonderful and exciting shows for Randi for three years. However, he never forgot his bad habit of whirling to the left and every year he whirled and stepped on Cornelia Serpell's feet during the trophy presentation at Lexington. After the second year she called me to see if Cash was in the juvenile class so she would know what shoes to wear! That first winter we considered letting Legal Tender down and turning him out several hours a day. That was an impossibility - he went bonkers and tried to jump the fence to get back to his stall and his best friend "Carry". It was quite a sight to see the careful way that horse would look after the rooster and Cash would doze for hours in his stall while Carry sat on his back, warmed by the blanket and the horse's body heat. I often wondered, watching the two of them, if they were dreaming. Perhaps not, but the devotion shared by those two could bring tears to one's eyes. What a fabulous pair - "Cash and Carry".

Harold Stuart, Randi's father, had been Asst. Secy. of the Air Force in World War II and maintained a law practice in Washington, D.C. So when the Washington International Horse Show decided to include Saddle Horses in their production, we entered Legal Tender and Randi's good walk-trot mare, I've Decided. School prevented Randi's showing there and I had the two horses for the open and stake classes.

No show was ever more of a disaster than Washington International. Unhappily, it was held during the Cuban Missile Crisis. That clearly affected everyone in the Capitol, especially the large committee of ladies who apparently had never put on a show.

The chairman was a nice, knowledgeable lady, but her committee was out of control. Every member showed up bright and early in the mornings and no one had an answer to any question. Getting stalls, bedding, etc., was like dropping a rattlesnake in a chicken yard! Jimmy Shane was Charlie's assistant and he accompanied me to the show. His motel was near the arena, but I was excited to find that Mr. Stuart had arranged for me to stay on Embassy Row. The Ambassador and his family were out of town and I was sole tenant of the apartment and also had been graciously offered the use of the Ambassador's Cadillac. Now this was 1962 and Cadillacs were quite a novelty in Kentucky. I was feeling my oats because of the anticipated thrill of steaming up to the show in such a luxury vehicle. That Cadillac must have been one of the first built! It was huge, ponderous and did not have power steering. Mix that with the crazy street plan in D.C. and it is a wonder I ever negotiated the trail to the arena which was situated on the opposite side of the city.

President and Mrs. Kennedy were to appear at the show, but the President was in the midst of settling the most frightening moments for our country when he stood nose to nose with Russia and kept us out of our closest moments of possible atomic conflict. Apparently the committee felt that they should try to get many added attractions to replace the Kennedys - and did they ever - 11 "added attractions"! The first night of the show our gaited class entered the ring at 1:30 in the morning. Poor Carry, Cash's rooster companion, was crowing at all the wrong times. Trainers and grooms had horses in the crossties two and three hours waiting to be called. We managed to win the qualifying classes with "Ivy" and "Cash". It is no fun to show horses when you have to wake them up - and try to keep oneself awake and alert.

Finally stake night came. The walk-trot stake was scheduled for approximately 11:30 (our first appearance of the evening!). Having worn a hole in my jodhpurs from sitting on the tack trunks for hours, I decided that I would stay at the apartment to hear Kennedy's great and brave speech that informed the world in no uncertain terms that the Soviet ships carrying nuclear warheads would be turned around on the high seas. I paid dearly for the chance to live a part of our country's terrible travail, because when I arrived at the show around 8:30, I walked into an eerily quiet stabling area - no one in sight, Ivy's stall door ajar and at that moment I looked up to the ramp to see Johnny leading the mare back down to the stall. Unbeknownst to me the show had announced about 7:00 P.M. that the saddle class would be moved up to the beginning event of the evening. When I die, it will be only an anticlimax to the sinking feeling I had at that moment. The managers could not be found. One lone lady appeared and told me I should sue the show and revealed that the managers were not on the grounds - one of them was at his motel taking a bath and his brother was padlocking a stall in the hunter barn. I went up to the boxes and there sat Mr. Stuart and half of the Senate, waiting to see their friend's horse win the three-gaited championship! Needless to say, about four hours later I was on time for the five-gaited stake. The judge, whom most of us thought had died years ago, tied Earl Teater and Primrose Path. I grabbed the reserve ribbon at a wide open rack and got out of the ring post haste because the owners and trainers were pouring through the ingate as the judge was ushered from the ring under police protection. I suppose we were all under terrific tension because of the Missile Crisis and the idiotic timetable (it was after one o'clock and there still was the jumper stake to go). I have told this story to many people over the years and often they would interrupt me to say, "You should hear what happened to me that night!"

Mr. Stuart was a good friend of Fred Korth, Assistant Secretary of the Navy, who had invited Randi (who had flown to the show that night), Mr. Stuart and me to have breakfast the following morning as his guests at the Pentagon. It was not until we were seated, only the four of us in a huge dining room, that it dawned on me that we were in the Pentagon having breakfast with Navy Assistant Secretary Korth at the very hour that our forces were turning back the Russian vessels. Suddenly I realized that the missing of a class was small potatoes compared to the fix we were in at that moment.

What was a dumb horse trainer from Simpsonville doing sitting next to the Assistant Secretary of the Navy in Washington, D.C. in the Pentagon? I had completely forgotten that the Chiefs of Staff made the policies. When a large door swung open and a uniformed gentleman came in and whispered to Assistant Secretary Korth I nearly fainted. It was only a WAITER who wanted to know how he wanted our eggs cooked! I have spent your time in reading about my troubles when you thought you were going to read about a horse, but that is as close to being a part of history as I ever want to be and it did make me put our showing of horses in a more proper perspective. There are things a lot worse than losing a five-gaited stake.

From the Washington International we shipped right to the New York National. Randi could not miss any more school so I was in New York with her horses, showing in the ladies classes to qualify for the stakes.

After the fiasco that was the Washington show, I was ready and willing to go for it all. Management encouraged me to show Legal Tender in the five-gaited stake. When the program was issued it was apparent that the waters were very deep but I believed in Legal Tender - I had gotten to know him and was ready for anything. My My, with the incomparable Frank Bradshaw in the irons, The Tempest with saddle artist Marty Mueller, Primrose Path with the master Earl Teater, and three other very nice horses from the east made up the championship. Although the ladies class was not big, it did have a few quality horses in it and the win was not difficult.

At the time, the National Horse Show was in the original Madison Square Garden - with the horse show traditionally opening the New York Social season. It was, and still is, a top hat and tails affair. Society flocked into the Garden, packing it to the rafters.

I soon discovered that there was absolutely no place to work a gaited horse to train or warm up, so I decided if I wanted to win the stake that there could be no mistakes whatsoever. Therefore I worked the horses only in the jog cart, and on Cash used a very close set of blinkers with a snaffle bit and headstall, and obviously, no overcheck. His most outstanding trait was his incredible wild expression and his response to the roar of the crowd, and I was not about to bore him to death racking and trotting around the ring he was going to show in. Until class time, he never saw anything but the footing in the ring.

Johnny had Cash in high order and Carry, the rooster, was having the time of his life. Johnny had taught him to crow on command. One evening before showtime I saw a most impressive trio daintily coming down the narrow aisle in the stabling area - a top hatted squire with two adoring females hanging on his arms. He was giving the grand tour with his explanation of the saddle horses. The man obviously knew nothing about horses and his dressed-to-the-hilt friends knew even less. Quickly I hustled back to the stall and asked Johnny to make Carry crow when I gave him the signal. I believe that was the only practical joke I ever played at a horse show but the temptation was irresistible! As they came within two stalls I signaled Johnny to get going with Carry. Well, the rooster let loose with the loudest crowing demonstration imaginable. The guests stopped dead in their tracks and got out of there immediately before the gentleman had to decide whether horses really did crow!

Finally the night of the gaited stake arrived. I knew what we were up against - only the best in the country, but it was an opportunity that would probably never come again as Randi would show her horse in 1963.

After working with my "equitators" one morning, I noticed that the lights in the center of the ring were very bright - they were the extra banks of lights that shone on the boxing ring during the year. It was then that I started to plan my strategy. The upcoming duel was getting larger by the minute in my mind and I knew that everything had to be just right if I wanted to win - we had to be the best at everything.

Consequently, I did not warm up Legal Tender in the tiny inadequate make-up ring. Instead all of the grooms came to his stall and five of us gave that horse the most concentrated massage imaginable. His blood was really coursing through his entire body and he was fit and ready to go. We threw the saddle on him as the class was called and I jumped on, trotted up the circling ramp and Cash hit the ring like a bomb and we never looked back. All of the horses were at their very best. The huge crowd (known for their disinterest in saddle horses at that time) surprised us all with their enthusiasm. The more they cheered, the better the horses worked and the faster and higher they sped. The tension was a palpable thing in Madison Square Garden that night. Those spectators who were accustomed to respond only to the International Jumping Teams came alive with the new sensation that Saddle Horses could excite anyone, and all of the riders knew that they were taking part in the transformation that made Saddle Horse classes drawing cards in New York.

When the call came to line up, I dashed for the brightly lit center spot in the head-to-tail line up that has always been the custom at the Garden. Quickly the saddles were removed and the judge began his inspection. Legal Tender posed there, a blazing horse under the bank of brilliant lights. He stood there, stripped of his saddle - a picture that every trainer has dreamed of but never expects to see. The always willing gelding had just given me the ride of my life, responding brilliantly to demands exceeding even my highest expectations. His mahogany coat was almost black with sweat, his arching neck tilting the fabulous head to stare at the top rows of the cavernous old Garden. I stepped back the length of the curb rein in awe of what I was seeing, barely holding the end of the leather. As the judge approached, there was a momentary hush, then an explosion of clapping and cheering for the inspired animal. Cheers had followed the horses during the workout but this was different. As if to acknowledge the magic of the moment, Legal Tender swung his head first to the right, then to the left, his incredible eyes seeming to catch fire with the intensity of emotion filling that huge arena. This was a moment that I and many who saw that gaited championship at the Garden in 1962 will never forget.

Then the announcer called for three numbers to go to the rail for a second workout. They were My My, The Tempest and Legal Tender. As we started, the announcer kept repeating, "Will the following THREE horses work", but there were four on the rail! Earl Teater was there with Primrose Path and he wasn't about to go back to the line up. The ringmaster later told me that he asked the judge if he wanted to make Earl go back but the judge said that he had already tied Primrose Path fourth and to let her stay. For those people who never had the thrill of seeing Earl Teater show the Dodge Stable horses, especially the immortal Wing Commander, I must state that there was never a man who wanted more to win (and generally he had the stock to do it). A red ribbon was a disgrace in Earl's way of thinking. He had a habit of twisting his neck around to watch the horses behind him and no one ever rode faster or harder than Earl Teater. Frank, Marty and I knew our horses's strong suits and we positioned ourselves accordingly. Before we had reversed it became apparent that the duel was between the bold and powerful My My and the elegant and fascinating Legal

Tender. I wanted to stay away from My My because of her speed and Frank wanted to stay away from the gorgeous Legal Tender who was getting bigger and faster with every roar of the crowd. Marty was a cool customer and he stayed away from both of us. Primrose Path did her best, but was an obvious fourth. The noise was thunderous and the riders had to watch the ringmaster for the change of gaits. At last the workout was over. In a moment that seemed like an eternity the announcer called the winner. It was Legal Tender, My My was second and Tempest was third. What I did not know was that we had defeated My My one of the very few times she was beaten and that it would be the last loss of her career as she went on to win the World's Grand Championship for the next incredible six years - 1963-1968, tying Wing Commander's record - records that stand to this day.

The picture shows us trying to receive the trophies. Mr. Devereaux, president of the AHSA, having had Cash knock the "Keepers" trophy out of his hand, finally settled for handing me that trophy and keeping the main Waldorf Astoria sterling in his arms. Cash seemed to know that he had been judged the best and I could hardly control him. He had been great and he knew it! And I still hold that moment, years later, with great emotional gratitude for the unselfish owners and a super horse.

Randi Stuart and Legal Tender began their outstanding dominance of classes on the mighty Southwest Circuit when Randi made her circuit debut in 1963 in her home town, Tulsa, Oklahoma. Randi now had the key to the powerful gelding and won her class and the first of many standing ovations. Oklahoma City and Pin Oak at Houston rounded out the circuit and Randi and Cash won every class entered. They would show in juvenile open and juvenile stakes (if stakes were given), otherwise they would win the ladies or amateur classes.

The entire records of the 1963 shows are almost impossible to find but one of the most memorable classes that I recall that year was the Kentucky State Fair juvenile stake in which Randi and Julianne Schmutz had one of their many duels. Stonewall Imperial had been without defeat for several prior years and was firmly established as the "horse to beat" with Julianne in the saddle. At that time, both three-gaited and five-gaited juvenile-to-ride were the Minton Memorial classes at Lexington and Louisville. Randi and her great three-gaited mare, "I've Decided", won both classes at the two shows and repeated to win and retire the trophies in 1963. There was only the one juvenile gaited class offered then (what a difference from the present!) and the confrontation of the two geldings at Louisville was awaited with much excitement. Each meeting became more and more intense. Randi at 14 years, and Julianne in her last year in juvenile, were sensational. Their horses were extremely impressive and with their tall and beautiful riders made up a foursome that has never been equalled.

The Minton Memorial class at Louisville finally arrived and it was knee deep in good horses and riders. Randi and Julianne were making the rides of their lives - out to win the world's championship - Julianne for her last appearance there, with Randi showing Cash there for the first time. All was equal in the first workout and the judges, after much deliberation (this was during the years of first and second judges and a referee to break ties) all three judges decided that they could not tie the class without working the two entries again. Julianne's horse was brilliant, consistent and always well ridden. Randi had served notice on the Southwest circuit that there was a new kid on the block a gifted rider on a gifted horse that had to be taken seriously.

A second workout was called and the two horses went to the rail. The crowd cheered them every step of the way and it was pandemonium by the time they reversed. Stonewall Imperial was not a high going horse, but he had such a regal presence that his rolling front motion went unnoticed. Legal Tender was a very light footed horse and his motion and animation increased with every gait. On the final rack, Imperial seemed to tire and on the last pass before the two judges, Legal Tender racked past the other horse with brilliance to spare. Whenever those two showed, there was no loser - they were both that great. But Randi's final brilliant pass seemed to me to be the deciding factor and I was honestly surprised when Stonewall Imperial was called out to win the stake and retire the Minton Memorial Trophy. The applause was deafening and it continued when Legal Tender's number followed. The knowledgeable spectators at the World's Championship knew that they had just witnessed what is still considered the duel of the decade. I was crushed, but knew that we had been judged second to a great team.

It was the next week that I received a call one evening from

Welch Greenwell. He had been the referee in the class and had been called in immediately after the workout. He was furious as he explained to me that he had been called in to break a tie for fifth place, not first! Of course it appeared that he had voted for the winner in the class, whose tie had not even been discussed. He felt that he had been very badly used by the other two judges, especially since his vote would have been for Legal Tender. He said "Helen, I had to call you and tell you what happened. I got so much flack for that class I just had to call you as I favored your horse to win it." I recount this story for no other reason than to pay homage to two remarkable pairs. I believe that each horse was only defeated by the other when those two talented juveniles met in the ring. Legal Tender affected people profoundly and Welch had been made to look like his was the final word in a decision that he had nothing to do with.

In 1964, Randi and Legal Tender had an undefeated season, adding to an already envious place in Saddle Horse history. I showed the horse twice that year, winning the stake at Madison Square Garden to retire the Waldorf Astoria Trophy. I believe that the horse was the best yet for me in winning the championship at Pin Oak. But I was in for an unbelievable treat at the Lexington Junior League Show that summer when Randi showed Cash in the Minton Memorial. Crabtree Farms had five horses entered in that same class and Johnnie Washington was too short and slight built to lead his horse into the ring. Our son, Redd, was showing there, so we asked him to get Randi in the ring and Charlie and I would take care of the other four. Redd is very tall and has long arms, but he was barely tall enough to reach the horse's snaffle. Legal Tender was only 15.3 but he could swell up and elevate his front to unbelievable heights and that is the way he entered the ring and that is the way he stayed for the entire class.

I had five to watch in that class but Randi and Legal Tender were hypnotizing. Those people sitting in ringside boxes said that the horse was so spirited and elevated at the rack and the trot that they could not hear his feet hit the ground as he charged around the ring. This is a quote from Elizabeth Culley's book, Who's Who In Horsedom 1963-1969. She wrote "In July of 1962 history was made with Burning Tree Farm's purchase of the dream gelding, Legal Tender. This model Saddle Horse, skillfully shown by Randi, dominated the five-gaited ladies, juvenile and amateur classes winning the world's championships in both of the latter divisions. Many trainers today call the performance that Randi and "Cash" made at the 1964 Lexington Junior League Horse Show as the most thrilling of all amateur triumphs. Legal Tender, undefeated in 1964, was one of the great Saddle Horses of the decade."

I have been privileged over the years to see so many great horses, and the thrills have been legion, but I and all who saw Legal Tender win on that magical July night on the Big Red Mile will never forget it.

The year 1965 began as all others for Randi and Legal Tender with blue ribbons, but with some changes in store. I had bought the elegant Sensational Princess for Randi and between the two horses, Burning Tree Farm had the amateur, ladies and juvenile divisions completely covered. The two horses won the amateur world's championship from 1964 five straight years through 1968. They divided the ladies, amateur and juvenile at Louisville winning all of their qualifying and championship classes. Cash's rooster companion, Carry, was found dead in an adjoining stall early in the spring of 1965 and it was fortunate that Randi did have Sensational Princess to show, as Cash was so disconsolate after Carry's death that he became more and more difficult to keep in top order as the show season wore on. He almost refused to eat and we fed him everything known to man or beast to keep him in flesh. Johnny, his groom, spent many a night at the shows sleeping in front of the gelding's stall. Always sound, Legal Tender was never lame in his entire life, but the chance to ease up and show Princess instead made it possible to keep Cash fat enough to show - Southwest Circuit, Junior League and Louisville where Legal Tender and Randi finished their career together with the world's amateur stallion and gelding and the amateur grand championship. It is only fitting that they ended their wonderful championship with the world titles.

John Shively of Winter Haven, Fla. had been trying to buy Cash all year and it was decided to let him have the horse as he had shown brilliantly for three years and it was a time for a change of scenery. We were unable to retire the horse because he would not stand turning out and we had a full barn and also waiting in the wings were such geldings as The Tempest, Rebel Command, Busy Agent and others. It was with a heavy heart that the decision was made to sell. On the last day of 1965, Legal Tender became the property of Susan Shively. I agreed to keep the horse in training and deliver him at the Winter Haven Horse Show that spring and to help Susan to get acquainted with her new horse. She won both of her classes at that show.

Even now I am filled with despair, remembering walking away from that horse's stall for the last time. Through my tears I could see that gallant head above the top boards of his stall watching me with those wondrous eyes. That was 26 years ago and I can hardly bring myself to write about it.

Susan's trainer in Florida was in very poor health and within a very successful year, Jim B. Robertson took over the talented blonde rider and the striking gelding. Susan was very successful, winning in Florida and in New York in 1967. In that period, the Florida circuit was not covered by the magazines as it is today. I had counted on Jim to fill in the Florida years for me, but his serious illness prevented our anticipated reminiscing. Jim B wanted to help, but I just could not bother him at such a difficult time. I do want to thank Ray Sheffield for permitting me to use the *National Horseman* library nearby to try to track down the Legal Tender years in Florida. I did find that Susan won the juvenile High Point Award for the Florida Circuit in 1966 and I feel sure that she won many many other classes through 1967-1968.

Late in 1968, all of the Shively horses came to Lexington for Jim B to disperse. Legal Tender evidently had been pastured and was very thin and not in show condition, though still bright and sound. In 1969, he was 16 years old when Jimmy Robertson got to show him at the Harrodsburg, Ky. Horse Show. Jimmy said it was his first juvenile ride and he and the horse were both the same age.

I was judging a great deal in those years so it is understandable that I would never see Legal Tender until the 1969 Junior League Show. One of our grooms believes that it was Legal Tender, at the 1969 Lawrenceburg Show, who tried to drink out of a bucket containing an electric water heater and narrowly escaped dying. I did see the horse in the ring at Lexington but he appeared to be not fully recovered and I believe that he was withdrawn from the class.

I could not get the horse out of my mind. I talked once with Jim B about him but nothing came of our trying to work something out. One cannot know the elation I felt upon learning that he had been purchased after Lexington by Dick Durant for Gail Wirtz of Chicago and would be with such a grand trainer and brought back to condition by Dick and Jeanette. Gail was very kind in trying to remember her classes but unless one keeps a personal show record, it is almost impossible to keep the facts in mind.

In 1970 I was judging the Great Midwest Horse Show in Crete, Ill. (a show that was supposed to take the place of the famous Chicago International). It was a far cry from the old show and the ring was scratched out of a pasture. It was barely possible for the horses to negotiate the footing. When the gate opened for the amateur class, I happened to look up and was startled to see a rider and horse come out of the darkness — a horse with flashing eyes and the wild look that could belong to none other than Legal Tender!

None of the horses stood out in the miserable ring so I called for all horses to the rail for a second workout (in the hopes that the footing had been trampled down so that the horse had a chance to truly show.) I was really surprised to find that Legal Tender had won the class. (Jim B. had the very same experience when he judged that show the next year.)

They went to New York that fall and Gail Wirtz rode Cash perfectly to win the amateur stallion and gelding and the juvenile, admitted by Gail to be one of the highlights of her life. She wrote, "It was a thrill to ride such a pro as he lit up the Garden. My grandfather, Arthur Wirtz, had owned Madison Square Garden at one time along with several other arenas and had to sell the Garden because of the anti-trust laws. Some who were watching my grandfather say that he was crying watching the class. The question, is was it Legal Tender's competitive showmanship or the fact that Arthur Wirtz had finally won at the Garden.

Gail and Cash, also were born in the same year— "old enough to show me the ropes.

For four years Gail and Cash won everywhere in the northern shows — Madison, Illinois State Fair, Minnesota State Fair, Milwaukee and others. Legal Tender was 20 years old when they stopped showing him and took him out to their Blackhawk Stables (named after Wirtz's Chicago Blackhawk hockey team). He was pampered and babied for six more years. Durant said that the horse loved to be cared for by a girl, as he had evidently developed a hatred for male caretakers. He threw a 160 pound groom from his stall! They still could not pasture him with other horses but he would graze in the center of their work ring — anything that would keep his showring memories alive. Gail's letters told of her great love for the horse, how he loved to be bathed and petted during his six years at Blackhawk Farm.

In 1979 he died as he lived — on his own terms. He was found dead in his stall one morning of an apparent heart attack and was buried at Blackhawk Farm.

Many people believe that animals have souls, myself included. How could God forget those who have given so much of themselves? I'm sure that Carry, the rooster was there and had told St. Peter that he would have to lead the unforgettable Legal Tender through the Pearly Gates!

37
Carlyn and Glad Tidings
(S & B July, 1992)

Horse trainers can look back to certain owners with pleasure and gratitude for their part in developing a lifelong commitment to the Saddlebred horse. Fond memories linger forever and it is just such memories that will always keep Carlyn Barmeier fresh in our minds.

It was Carlyn's complete devotion to horses and her abiding sense of humor that made her a good sport when her two girls, Amy and Judy were showing and her enthusiasm for horses and horse shows never waned.

Both of the Barmeier girls were very good riders and win or lose, Carlyn always had that same breathless, smiling personality that made horse shows fun for everybody.

One day she approached me with her idea of showing a fine harness horse. At that time we had Mrs. Sinclair and her group of undefeated harness mares. I mentioned that fact but Carlyn said, "Oh, I don't expect to win but I would love to be able to show and own a horse that I could drive and be good enough that we would not embarrass the barn."

Fortunately there appeared to be just such a five-year-old gelding in a stable in Louisville. He drove well in the arena, a very attractive horse with good motion and he wore an overcheck very well and had a good mouth. He would not win at Louisville, but he would not look out of place there. Here seemed to be the horse for the job. He was pretty, sound and very reasonably priced, so I purchased him and when I called to tell Carlyn she almost jumped through the telephone with delight.

I worked the gelding for a couple of weeks and liked him more every day. Finally, Carlyn came down from their home in Youngstown, Ohio, to see her next adventure. Her beautiful grey eyes glittered with excitement and she could hardly get her breath.

The next day we started the lessons. A jog cart was the proper equipment as our arena was 200 by 50 ft. My pupil did fine and

Busy Agent and Judy Barmeier, 1974.

Glad Tidings and Carlyn Barmeier, whip, Rock Creek, 1969.

when I stood as a ringmaster to line up on, Carlyn would miss me by 30 feet. She was so excited to be driving that her mind blanked out on her and as she made the turns, she would yell "Which line and how much?" I told her that driving a horse was like guiding a bicycle but in characteristic style, she laughed and told me that she didn't ride a bicycle!

River Ridge Horse Show in Columbus, Ohio, was always our first show of the season and since the previous year there had been only two entries in the ladies fine harness, I entered Glad Tidings in that class. You may imagine my surprise when we got to the show and saw that there were 12 entered in the class.

The morning before the show I hitched Glad Tidings to the jog cart and drove into the arena. The ring was filled with horses being ridden and driven and I was pleased with my horse's behavior. He was a little lamb until someone asked to reverse the field. When I turned to cut across the ring my gelding took off for the moon, jerking the bike wheels off the ground! I was astounded at the horse's reaction and caught up with Charlie and said, "Did you see what this horse did when we reversed?" And in typical husbandly fashion he replied, "Yes. I saw it. What did you do to him?" "Not a dern thing," I replied through clenched teeth. So it was decided that I would stay in the ring until we reversed again. The results were the same and we knew that we faced a real problem. I told Carlyn that because the class was so crowded that I should drive the horse in the ladies class to be sure that he was O.K. We had to figure out our problem.

The next afternoon the ladies class was scheduled and everyone was breathless - Carlyn with anticipation, and we with apprehension.

I remembered that Dr. Harthill had given us a brand new drug, Ace Promazine, to calm any bad shippers. We had it in the trunk. As this was before the AHSA drug control, our only problem was to figure out the dosage. Always the optimist, I said, "I guess we should give a dose like you would give anything else."

At that time, we always had large strings of horses and it was our habit to get many horses ready to show and then put them back in the stall, crosstied with the halter over the bridles. As my class time approached I made a tour down the aisle checking to see that all the horses were tacked properly. When I reached Glad

Tiding's stall, I nearly dropped dead. There he was all tacked up and sound asleep with his nose snoring in the feed box! What to do?? Upon my discovery I ran to find Charlie and said, "Come here quick - we have a real problem!" He was flabbergasted when he saw Glad Tidings in such a blissful state - truly "asleep in the manger."

We literally pulled the horse out of the stall, frantically fanning him with rub rags; the horse was so relaxed that he was over stepping at a walk and being a male horse he had relaxed all of his muscles including the rear end! "Go ask Frank Bradshaw if we can borrow his buggy whip." It was the biggest whip I had ever seen and I knew that I needed all the help that I could get. I didn't know whether to laugh or cry, but seeing Charlie struggling to keep from laughing, I finally dissolved into tears of laughter. "Go on into the ring, maybe he will wake up with the organ music." Well, the organist must have been playing a funeral march because I could barely get the horse into a trot. Every time I passed Charlie he would say, "Hit him" and hide behind the ring wall. We reversed very carefully. After what seemed to be hours the class was over. Here came Carlyn! Before I could say a word, she said, "Helen, he is beautiful!" All I could say was that she would never see more of her gelding than she had seen that day. We immediately told her the whole story and suggested that I show him in the stake, in the hopes that the dream dose would be out of the horse's system by then. I did show him in the stake and as we reversed "Pegasus" took another flying leap and I asked to be excused from the ring. Before I could get out of the buggy, here came Carlyn laughing so hard she could scarcely talk. "Helen," she choked, "Guess what? Everybody thinks that the horse was too gentle in the ladies class and that you loaded him for the stake!" How many owners would have accepted such a turn of events and managed to smile and laugh about it? Bless her heart. I have never forgotten her incredible sportsmanship and understanding.

After three disastrous and hilarious (can they blend?) attempts to show Glad Tidings, Mrs. Barmeier was undaunted and announced that come what may she was going to show her horse at the Cincinnati show where we went the next weekend.

At that time the show was held in the Cincinnati Gardens. While the ring was fine the impossible-to-imagine route from the concrete aisles of the stabling area into the ring was extremely difficult. One must drive down a sharp slope, over a large metal drain, then an immediate 90 degree turn through a very narrow pathway between the stored jumps and standards, followed immediately by another right angle turn into the ring. Even after walking through the maze on foot Carlyn was still eager and willing to show her horse at last.

Redd was still out on a private job and so there were only Charlie and me to help our drivers. It so happened that Mrs. Sinclair was making her first drive with her world champion mare, Glenview's Radiance. Although Kathryn had shown many great horses before then, Charlie was a little concerned about the entryway to the ring, so I was on my own with my driver of no experience and a horse of doubtful temperament. While Glad Tidings had trained well at the show , I could not forget his spontaneous desire to perform "airs above the ground".

The class was called and I was very proud of my beautiful driver and her handsome horse. As we started into the entryway, the enormity of the situation suddenly overcame Carlyn and she whispered in my ear as Slick, her groom, was leading her into the ring, "Helen, I'm scared". I told her we couldn't turn around then and to go on in the ring, and in desperation, I said, "Follow Kathryn and do everything she does!" Radiance was making a sparkling show and there was Glad Tidings and Carlyn right behind them. I had a sudden horrible flash of seeing Glad Tidings jump right in beside Kathryn at the reverse, but thanks be to God, the horse was a lamb and trotted smartly along in Kathryn's wake.

It so happened that Ed Teater was there with an amateur making his first drive. Ed was quick to get his owner lined up close to the outgate, Radiance pulled in next and of course Carlyn and Glad Tidings pulled in beside them. Carlyn was aglow with pride and excitement. We were the last three entries in the lineup. First, Ed's horse reared up and came down to circle back into position. I could see what was coming so I yelled to Charlie to give me a hand and he told me "I have to take care of my own horse!" And just then Radiance lunged forward and circled around to her place. Without further ado, Glad Tidings took off and made his circle back. The "wave" that sports fans execute had not yet been thought of but those three horses invented it. The sequence was repeated and this time Carlyn's horse stopped at the gate and finally came back for her turn in the "Pas de trois". George Axt, the photographer, came down the line. He loved to shoot the pictures of the drivers only and just as he fired away, Glad Tidings executed another leap. By this time the class was mercifully over and Mrs. Sinclair with her winner Glenview's Radiance were called for first place. Charlie trotted out of the difficult lineup to head the mare for the presentation picture. I can still see his face when he glanced back to find that Carlyn and Glad Tidings were right behind his buggy! I was a poor third in the race but finally got Glad Tidings turned around and headed him for the outgate. Just then, as the horse was outside the gate and the owner and buggy were yet inside, we heard Carlyn's number called for fourth place! She was so thrilled that she tried to back the horse up to go get her prize. By this time Slick had a hold on the horse and I told Carlyn to go on out and I ran back and collected her ribbon.

When we got back to the barn after the congratulations were shared I got Carlyn off to one side and asked her why she had stopped at the gate on one of her extra-curricular tours and she said, "Helen, I was so scared. I tried to cluck and I didn't have any spit and Slick clucked and got him going again!"

It was finally decided that this was not the horse for Carlyn and after trying him as a three-gaited horse with many surprises in store, we finally gave up after he had practically stood on his head in the lineup. Cecil Wheeler was the man we had bought the horse from and I am certain that he did not know of the horse's peculiar habits when we bought him. I called him and I am still indebted to Cecil because he told me that he would take the horse back. So I returned the commission and the horse, and that was the end of the most inappropriately named horse ever - Glad Tidings.

Carlyn did have her fun, however she would ask her non-horsey friends if they would like to go down to the rec room to see a picture of her and her fine harness horse. She told me they would reluctantly go to see their friend's "bragging picture" only to see Mr. Axt's picture that he had taken in the lineup - a wonderful shot of a pair of lines aimed heavenward and poor Carlyn with her mouth wide open very obviously yelling "HELP!"

That was 20 years ago and recently Carlyn called me from her home in California to say that a trainer had let her jog a horse.

She said, "And, Helen, you know that I hadn't forgotten a thing."
And furthermore, she was looking for a fine harness horse.

Flamenco and Kelly Swisher.

38

A Wild and Wonderful Mare – Flamenco
(S & B November, 1992)

Horse trainers are always on the lookout for that extra special horse for their customer. This was certainly the case when I spotted a spectacular brown mare in the junior three-gaited stake at Louisville in 1975. I was in the same class and just happened to observe this wild going mare during the workout. If anyone remembers my mount, a big, impressive and highly unpredictable gelding named Mr. Christopher Columbus (every ride was another discovery!) it accentuates the fact that anyone in that eight horse workout was riding to win - and I was doing my best, but like the song "Just One Look" was enough for me to know that I had seen the horse that I had been seeking for months. *Saddle & Bridle Magazine* wrote of the class, "it was now time for the junior three-gaited stake, which may have been the most remarkable class of the whole week, if not of the entire season. Twenty-one of the best young horses entered the ring and each seemed to be putting on the show of their young lives." I stayed busy with my horse but that magnetic brown mare just seemed to reappear in my eyes and my excited mind.

We had two sisters from Oklahoma City, Ann and Kelly Swisher. Ann was one of the most regal and talented equitation riders I ever had and she won the UPHA Finals in 1976. Kelly was a different sort of rider. She had loads of talent and had been riding Quarter Horses at home and the constraints of equitation did not appeal to her. We always tried to have siblings in different divisions, so my search for a three-gaited mount for Kelly was very difficult because the horse had to have at least as much brilliance and spirit as Kelly. She wasn't afraid of the Devil himself and her infectious humor and exhilaration called for a very special, brilliant kind of horse for the juvenile ranks.

At the Cincinnati show just before Lexington, I had seen a bay mare that might work out. I had almost given up finding just the right horse for Kelly, so I told the family to watch this mare in the junior class at Louisville. Perhaps she was better than what I had seen in her performance in Ohio. The Swishers had the bay mare's number and were instructed to watch her to see if they liked her.

After the workout the class was tied. I got fifth and spent my whole time watching this hot, exciting mare that Bobby Gatlin had in the workout that had gotten my head racing. Of course the brown mare won to thunderous applause and I never took my eye off of her. My assistant, Lisa Rosenberger was on the gate and I hastily told her to rush up to the Swisher's box and tell them that I had given them the wrong number and to watch the winner make the victory pass. I rode up for my fifth ribbon hastily and let my horse do what we had argued about all summer - I let him gallop from the ring and I jumped off in flight, threw the reins to his groom and planted myself at the outgate to see Bobby make the victory pass. He was barely out of the gate when I stopped him and asked if the mare was for sale. He answered that she was and gave me a price - then he added, "Miss Helen, she's low in the back" and I said, "I don't care if she has five legs I want your promise that I have first refusal after my rider has a chance to try her". Bobby answered, "You have my word on it." I told the Swishers what I had done. No trainer should ever lie to a customer, but time was of the essence and it would have taken too much time to say more than one sentence to Lisa. I have to thank my assistant for getting the message to the Swishers so fast. She could be on my track team anytime. We all had a good laugh and the Swishers were enchanted by the brown mare. Only then did I find time to look up the mare's name in the program. It was Contract's Miss Larrymore owned by Tom Beebe, a very good owner at the time. The following night Mr. Swisher was out-of-town and that gave the mare time to rejuvenate after the tremendous class she had won. Twenty-one entries and eight called out for the second work. I was soon to learn that it was just a walk in the park for this gritty little mare. Bobby had accomplished a remarkable training feat as the mare had been pastured all her life and only her extreme motion and magnetism caused Bobby to put her in training and she had but 90 days work before her tremendous win.

On Friday after the show we waited at our tack room for the mare to appear. Minutes seemed like hours and finally I began to worry, so I got on an electric cart and went to their tent. It is obvious that Bobby was just getting along in the big time as he was stabled almost on Interstate Highway 65!

As I drew up at the tent, Bobby came out and had a very worried look. Before he had a chance to speak, I said, "There's a problem, you've been offered more money." Yes, a bigger offer had been made the following day. I told Bobby, "You know, Bobby, you did give me your word that I had the first refusal, but I know how deals can get messed up. I wish you would go back to the stall and decide what you are going to do. We will still be friends if I do not get the mare, but you and Dede have just gotten married and your test has come very early as it did for Charlie and me. You must decide if you mean what you say or are out for the quick buck." A worried young man went back to the tent, but almost immediately returned with a relieved smile on his face and he said, "Our deal is on. You can have her if you want her." Kelly and the mare were great together. Bobby came with me to the hotel and I wrote a check for the mare and then wrote another good sized check and handed it to Bobby. It was made out to Bobby Gatlin. "That's for making the right decision - not just because we got the mare, but you have made the right start in this business with your word as your bond." I have never forgotten that experience and am a great admirer of not only an extremely talented trainer, but a gentleman of his word.

We had the mare I had almost given up hope of ever finding. For several years I had a name in mind for a flamboyant horse and that very night Kelly agreed that it suited her new mare. The name was FLAMENCO.

After discovering and buying the exciting winner of the Junior Walk-Trot Stake at Louisville and naming her Flamenco, I began her training to ready her for her fortunate and excited new Oklahoma City owner, Kelly Swisher. Since school was going to take all of Kelly's time until Christmas, I entered the mare in the junior stake at the American Royal. What a thrill she was to ride. I had never before, nor since, had a horse that could do a true flat footed walk in her fashion - she was flat behind and her front action was as high and sharp at the walk as it was at the trot. And in those days of 1975, the walk was judged as a true flat walk - not the jig we see today in most of the open horses. Here is what *Saddle & Bridle* had to say about the class..."One of the most stylish Junior World's Champions to come along in years, Flamenco ... teamed by

Helen Crabtree to take what veteran observers proclaimed the best Junior Three-Gaited Stake ever held at the American Royal ... we look forward to seeing Kelly in the saddle next year." I, too, was looking forward to seeing the spunky owner show the mare.

In the early spring, a group organized a one afternoon Sunday show in Shelbyville. This was the perfect location to give Kelly her maiden voyage. She had come at the winter holidays and she and the mare were just what I had imagined they would be. In addition to her parents, a favorite aunt who lived in Lexington came over and anxiously awaited the appearance of Kelly's now famous mare.

How humbling fate, and horses can be! The mare had shown only twice in her life, both times at indoor shows. This I was VERY aware of but the two had been collaborating so well that I felt this would be the next step up the ladder. It was a nice balmy March day and I got Kelly on the mare and started up to the warm-up area. There were three straight-of-ways parallel to each other and we chose the middle stretch as there were already horses on the two outside lanes. I asked Kelly to walk the mare down and back before trotting. It was a great idea, but the results were not exactly what I had in mind. Unnoticed by me were two other horses coming back - one each on the inside and outside paths. Just as they happened to bracket Flamenco between, their trainers hit the fire extinguishers in unison. I know this was purely coincidental and I should have seen it coming. I did not but Flamenco did and when the loud noise erupted the mare stopped and reared straight up in the air - she was so straight that her hocks looked like stilts. She did not paw the air but she let out the loudest snort imaginable and topped that off with a shrill whistle. Poor Kelly! She immediately did the right thing and draped herself around the mare's neck. It seemed to me that the pose lasted forever, but dangerous as it was, it was hysterically funny to me. I have been told that I will probably laugh at my own funeral, but I did manage to tell Kelly to "Get off when she comes down!" So much for the long awaited introduction to the senior Swishers and the favorite aunt. Back we went to the barn, two grooms trying to keep the mare on the ground. So it was back to the drawing board and we did everything to erase the frightening experience for the mare and to acquaint her with hazards of outdoor showing.

River Ridge Show, in Columbia, Ohio was our first show. There were two age groups for the juveniles and Flamenco won the section for riders 14 and under while Kate Williams and Barbados Exit won the 15-18 class. It was a relief to all of us that our newest "pair" were truly a pair.

At the Pin Oak show, Kelly and Flamenco were second to Barbados Exit in the juvenile and second in open under-two class. Barbados Exit and Kate Williams, also of Oklahoma City, had the juvenile classes pretty much for their own and Kelly was right behind them throughout the Southwest Circuit, getting reserve in every class she showed in. Our outdoor performances were beginning to show us that a problem was developing. Flamenco was a lady going away from the gate, but coming to the gate she would get revved up. That summer we had the Cincinnati Show at Lebanon, Ohio on the narrowest race track I have ever seen - but it was excellent practice for the track at Lexington. Another second and Flamenco was beginning to hesitate at the outgate. It was evident that she was working up to balking, so I had prepared Kelly to never walk past the outgate, but fate caught us and the mare whirled around. Fearing that this would happen, I was prepared with a bike whip and told Kelly to ask to be excused. I played a tune on that mare's rear end with the whip all the way back to the stall and we did not show her again at that show.

I am going to describe what we did to break the mare of a very bad habit, but I want amateur riders and trainers not to follow this example. It was "put up or shut up" and drastic measures were called for. We had the ideal setup for the experiment in our indoor arena. It was concrete block, 200' x 50'. The entire logic behind our "cure" was to punish the mare severely but in such a fashion that she would not connect her rider with the cure. Should we have done otherwise, we would have been adding fear and excitement for the rider as well as a fight.

In order for the mare not to connect her punishment with her rider, I put a very close set of blinkers on her, a stirrup leather around her neck to grab, because she was bound to take off when the "sky fell in". I had a wide leather strap doubled back so it would make a loud crack when I hit her between the ears; Charlie had a long lash whip for her legs, an assistant had a VERY loud "bird gun", and hiding behind the half open outer door were two grooms with big rubber buckets of water - intended for the horse! After entering the ring, I trotted the mare and then slowed at the open door inviting her to whirl and balk. We were right on target - I headed her down the arena, then grabbed the neck strap to keep from jerking her mouth and simultaneously the gun roared, the whip found her front legs, I whacked her over the head with the strap and the two grooms hit both of us with very cold buckets of water. Well, if the arena had been wooden we would have done a "cookie cutter" at the end, but by this time I had the astounded mare under control. Did the ploy work? Yes it did - the mare never connected the frightening experience with the rider. She never balked again, but I must admit that for a few weeks it was a little tough to make her walk!

We were ready for Louisville and I experienced one of my biggest thrills when Kelly and Flamenco, her wild and wonderful mare, won the amateur under-two and Flamenco was once again a World's Champion. Then on to the New York National. The following *Saddle & Bridle* write up describes the class that Kelly said was her biggest thrill - the open under-two. "History may have been made in the open under-two class. Kelly Swisher and Flamenco took the class decisively over other amateurs and professionals alike, and the win set people to thinking if this wasn't the first time an amateur let alone a (14-year-old) juvenile had won the highly coveted open class." The American Royal was a repeat of New York with a win in the amateur under-two. Still too hot to win the juvenile classes, Flamenco added up seconds in juvenile.

By 1977 the juvenile division was finally a winning spot - Southwest Circuit and back to Louisville to win the juvenile 15-17 and repeat that win at the Royal in a class of 24. They won the juvenile at New York to end that year. Kelly's last show on Flamenco was the juvenile win at Lexington - at last the mare would accept that show and behave herself.

The next owner was Sheila Carpenter, Marsha and Woody Henry having chosen the mare for her. They had much success with the combination and were virtually undefeated in the East. When Sheila moved the mare to Kentucky to show with Frank and Nancy McConnell, she was quite successful - I do not mean to lessen the contributions of trainers as they deserve great recognition, but space is short and by this time the mare was settled at last and very consistent. Always a favorite of the crowd, those at Louisville were shocked and saddened when Flamenco, having won her class the night before, was discovered dead in her stall. Later it was determined her death was the result of an aneurysm. Those of us who loved Flamenco still feel a tug at the heartstrings to remember a little brown mare that flashed across the show scene and left the horse shows a little less exciting with her passing from the scene.

Mrs. Sinclair and La La Success.

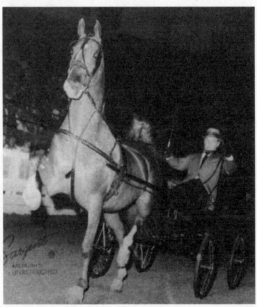

Charlie Crabtree and La La Success.

39
LaLa Success
(S & B January, 1993)

The year was 1975 and the Louisville crowd had barely settled down after the exciting junior three-gaited class when the ring opened to the two-year-old fine harness horses. No one expected anything earthshaking, and many had started to leave their seats to roam and visit friends, when into the ring burst a most astounding sorrel mare and her attractive but unknown driver. Everyone scrambled to return to their seats as it was instantly obvious that they were looking at a once-in-a-lifetime shocker. *Saddle & Bridle* described the class..."and then out of the blue there came a virtual unknown to upstage all the old pros. Suzanne Coulias and LaLa Success were too much for everybody. It looked as if Miss Coulias, herself, hardly knew what was happening. She would take LaLa Success slowly around the turns and then hit the straightaway with her after which the filly herself seemed to take over. The Louisville box holders who seem to have an uncanny way of sniffing out a great new horse before the railbirds or even the judges would notice it, would begin applauding her and LaLa would respond in a way not seen since the great Lemon Drop Kid. Miss Coulias would then come almost to a stop on the turns as if to get her bearings and then send the filly down the rail again to even greater acclaim as she swelled up and seemed to be on the point of bursting with pride in her own super performance. This was the kind of thing that happens only at Louisville and that makes the show worth waiting for from year to year. Needless to say, LaLa won the class...." Offers came thick and fast for the mare and within the week, Ed Jenner had bought her and turned her over to Don Harris where Jenner's son, Danny, was working.

Harris showed the mare four times in her three-year-old year — Cincinnati, Rock Creek, Lexington and Louisville, winning all of her classes except for a second at Lexington.

That winter, the mare moved to Redd Crabtree's when Danny

went to work there. I remember so well our taking Mrs. Sinclair up to Redd's barn for an unannounced visit and he was working LaLa when we walked in. After a few rounds, Redd stopped and asked Katherine if she would like to drive her. She said she would and Charlie assisted her into the jog cart. Sometimes the best things happen by chance and that night at the restaurant Charlie asked Mrs. Sinclair what she thought about the mare (she and Charlie had just finished an undefeated year with her three harness mares, Glenview's Radiance, Supreme Airs and Mandala - a total of 43 blues - a record undoubtedly never to be broken). Katherine replied "I think I will buy myself a present as I haven't gotten myself anything recently." Charlie nearly fell off his chair as the whole episode was so sudden and out of the blue.

I might say it was a marriage made in heaven because Charles Crabtree and Glenview horses had already amassed many years of dominating the fine harness division and here was another potential great winner dropped in his lap. LaLa Success was sired by Stonewall's Main Event and out of a mare by Broadland's Kilarney, a big striking chestnut with perfect white markings.

Mrs. Sinclair's daughter, Mary Lou Gallagher, was a student at SMU, so the next spring we took LaLa, Lad O'Shea, Fancy Stonewall (all Glenview horses) and a few others and made the long trek to San Antonio. Charlie had been reluctant to take LaLa because of her being just a junior and he was afraid the mare would be worn out after the long trip.

Katherine drove the mare in the amateur class. I was working Lad and hearing the wildest commotion in the ring, trotted up to the high entry gate and had to stand in the stirrups to see what was going on. What I saw were the front feet of LaLa Success going the highest I had ever seen any horse go. I could see the bottom of her feet, shoes and all. Jack Nevitt was judging and to this day gets breathless just remembering that lady driving the unbelievable, big chestnut mare. The Walking Horse judge ran back to the stalls to tell Charlie that he had never seen a horse like that, going so high and "putting on" as he described it. Charlie won the junior class with the mare and the big experience began.

The mare would keep you guessing at home and also in the ring. When she felt ready to win she would light up the ring, but when she didn't choose to be a star, she would not only spit up the bit, but the whole bridle! In spite of these tendencies she won several classes for Mrs. Sinclair and then after she pulled too hard for Katherine to show after she had a hand operation, Charlie took over completely. LaLa won the junior stake at Louisville making a grand show, but nothing would ever match her astounding performance as a two-year-old, until she made her final show at Louisville in 1980. (I feel that the reader will be bored by listing placings and shows. I choose the horses to write about because of different characteristics that make them memorable and interesting to those who came to the shows and to those who only got to hear about them.)

Actually, LaLa was a trainer's nightmare. The trainer really had no control over how the mare was going to show - that depended a great deal on the crowd reception. She was truly an eccentric. She is the only horse that I would have been glad to "hop up" but we never used drugs and by that time the drug rules were in effect. I told Charlie that if he ever got to heaven it would be because he put up with that mare who should have been in the buggy driving the trainer. I should not be too tough on LaLa as she did win a great majority of classes during the years and established herself in history.

1980 was the last year LaLa came to Louisville to defend her mare class title and to try to win the big stake. At that time we had a grand young law student, Jim Carpenter, taking care of the mare. I was frantic for Charlie and wracked my brain for some way to get the mare back to her brilliance of her first Louisville appearance. As it happened, Kate Williams had moved from Oklahoma City and had a gaited gelding named Windsor King. He was a nice little horse, but he did something so unusual that it planted a seed in my desperate mind about how to animate a mare who had bowed her neck and rubbed the buggy into the rail in the mare class. Windsor King always went with his ears frozen forward, seeming to stare at the ground. FEAR OF FALLING! Of course! But how to get that idea into the mare's head?

Jim and I got an oat sack and split it lengthwise and tied a string to one end. Our stalls were next to the work ring, the aisle deep in sawdust and it was the perfect set up for the tricky idea. We would bury the sack under the sawdust in the aisle and then jerk the sack away just as the mare was going to step on it. It looked like the earth was caving in. When I broached the idea to Charlie he said

"She'll kill herself and me too!" But I said "You've been dead ever since the mare class" - so we got set up. As the prior class was showing, Jim and I buried our sack in the aisle. Charlie drove the mare out and started her walking in the direction away from the ring. I pulled the string and the mare took off like a jumper in a triple-bar class. Charlie stayed with her and we buried the sack again as the class was being bugled into the ring. He put the excited mare into a trot and again the sawdust erupted under her front foot. Charlie had a good hold of the lines and buggy seat and he never looked back, he just sailed right on into the ring and there she was again - the LaLa of her two-year-old form, and she showed the entire class brilliantly. She won, and someone asked Tom Moore (who had beaten the mare in the qualifying class) "Tom, when did you know you were beat?"; and he laughed and said, "When she hit the makeup ring!" That was the last year that Charlie showed LaLa and she went up to Redd's that winter to retire to the broodmare ranks. Some people remember that Redd showed her a few times before breeding season with good success.

She was up and she was down in her career. She made two shows to win world's championships that will never be forgotten and which established her forever as one of the truly great show horses.

40

The Elusive Mare and the Available Stallion –

Glenview Radiance
(S & B April, 1993)

In the summer of 1966, husband Charlie attended the Dayton, Ohio Horse Show and had his first glimpse of a mare that would bring joy forever and memories to last a lifetime.

Radiance was a two-year-old trained by Tom Butler and owned by Mr. Andreoli of Reata Horse Farm, Sharon Center, Ohio. The filly did not show at Dayton as there was no two-year-old harness class, but Charles saw her on the lines one morning, and as he was always on the lookout for a top harness prospect, he tried to get a price on her. Unfortunately, a fellow who had no connection with our farm, watching Charlie's expression when he first beheld the mare, whizzed down and represented himself as Crabtree's agent, and made it clear that he wanted a "piece of the pie." Charlie was so enraged when this was told to him that he walked away from any deal on the mare. I can report that that fellow died of natural causes - much for the betterment of the horse industry, as he was a leech who earned a living by such underhanded tactics, and gave our sport a bad reputation that was not ever deserved.

In the spring of 1967, Reata Farm had a complete dispersal, and Charlie and I went to Ohio to attend the sale - mainly because the stallion, Oman's Desdemona Denmark, was in the venue. Randi Stuart's many-times world champion mare, Sensational Princess, was by this stud, and we wanted to make sure we found where he would be standing that season, as we had six mares that we planned on breeding to him. Somehow or other, we did not notice that a filly by that stud was also in the sale. Very early in the day there was a breathtaking three-year-old filly driven through the ring. I recall standing next to Garland Bradshaw and he was actually squealing with excitement and admiration for the chestnut beauty. At that same moment, Charlie said, "That's the great two-year-old that I wanted to buy at Dayton last year." The bidding was spirited and I thought surely Bradshaw would own the mare. But Garland

Mrs. F.D. Sinclair and Glenview Radiance.

was a very cautious and close-fisted bidder, and when the mare passed $15,000, both Charlie and I lost all composure, and entered the bidding. It was our own money - no wealthy owner to pay the bill - but there was another probable world's champion for Mrs. Sinclair, or any number of other owners who would want the mare. She was knocked down to us at the price of $17,500. We were exultant - but not for long, because Mr. Andreoli jumped up and announced that he could not take such a "ridiculous bid" for his mare. Everyone was stunned, as the sale was supposed to be a complete dispersal with no exceptions. So when sales manager Dick Lavery rushed down to talk to us, he was terribly embarrassed and said, "Charlie, I can't do a thing about this, but he wants $20,000 for her, and you really deserve to have her." Well, our bid was big for us, and referring to it as a "ridiculous bid" was insulting, and also gave lie to the "complete dispersal" idea which had flown out of the window with the surprising situation. Seated nearby was Ben Sadoff of Ledgeview Farm in Fond du Lac, Wisc., who politely waited until the deal was turned down before saying that he would take the mare at that price. As it turned out, we didn't have long to mourn our loss. Bob Whitney came into the sales ring with Oman's Desdemona Denmark. The bidding was going nowhere, and the auctioneer had gone down to a thousand to get the bidding started. I grabbed Charlie and said, "Charlie we can own this horse for a song", because people were leery of the sales terms after the Radiance fiasco, plus the sale would not dare deny us again. So he whispered to Whitney and asked if he would like to own the stud in partnership and stand him. He agreed, but when the bidding dragged to $4,000, Bob said he wanted out as he already had several studs on his farm. Although we had no plans to start a breeding establishment, we saw our chance to get this great horse for a low, low price. Finally at $6,000 he became our property. Poor Mr. Andreoli could not renege on the Crabtrees again, and we arranged for Whitney to trailer the horse to our farm. The next night a man from California called and offered us $25,000 for the horse, but we wanted him nearby, and turned down the offer. Mrs. Joan Farris was a good owner and had a half-dozen horses in training with us, so she called us and wanted to be partners. We have always felt that the best way to lose a customer is to go into business with them. She added that she had almost called and instructed us to go to $10,000 on the horse for her. In light of the fact that we had turned down the California offer, we sold Oman's Desdemona Denmark to Joan for $20,000. The refusal to let us have Radiance had resulted in our getting a great horse to breed to, and it cost Reata $14,000 to find out that "complete dispersal" meant that exact thing. We did notice that Radiance's dam, Dixie Duchess, was not in the sale, and assumed rightly that she was part of Andreoli's way of paying Whitney for his hard work in getting the sale organized. So Joan and I went to Bardstown the very next day, and she bought the dam of Radiance - a mare destined under her ownership to produce Burning Tree's immortal gaited mare, Summer Melody, Five-Gaited World's Grand Champion Belle Elegant, World Champion Denmark's Grand Duchess, and Carol Smith Shannon's stallion, Valley's Desdemona Denmark. With the aforementioned Glenview Radiance, who earned seven world's championships for Mrs. Sinclair in the ladies and amateur ranks, including the world's championship in the junior fine harness, it is difficult, if not impossible, to recall a stallion-mare combination that exceeds such a record.

Charles had almost "bought" Radiance twice, and there was to be the final try that ended with the wonderful mare gracing our stable and establishing an unparalleled record with Mrs. Sinclair, her gifted and grateful owner.

The summer of 1968 was a very busy time for Crabtree Farms. I found myself taking 24 head of horses to the Illinois State Fair. Because of the extreme heat that year, I requested stabling in the most remote barn in hopes that the public would not pester our horses, and that we could keep them as fresh as possible. To use my father's favorite expression, I was "as busy as a one-armed paper hanger." Just working those horses and overseeing the young equitation and juvenile riders kept me too busy to know anything other than our own problems, as no parents came to that show.

I had a lifelong friend, Ralph Peak, one of the famous Peak family known for their great roadster horses. I had asked "Pistol", as he was called by his friends, if he knew where I could find a top young horse to develop as a three-gaited mount for Kathie Gallagher, Mrs. Sinclair's older daughter. One afternoon he told me that the junior fine harness mare, Ledgeview Radiance, might be available, as Mr. Sadoff had decided to sell her because his granddaughter whom he hoped would show the mare was not really interested in horses. Tom and Donna Moore almost had the mare bought, but something went awry, and they did not get her. That evening, I had four riders in "Happy Hollow" as the make-up ring was called, since it adjoined the amusement park. It was then that I saw Mr. Sadoff and made arrangements to buy the mare contingent on Mrs. Sinclair's wanting her. Immediately I rushed into the office and called Charlie to see if he still wanted the mare for Mrs. Sinclair. Time was of the essence as Mr. Sadoff said the sale would have to be completed by noon the next day since he planned on showing Radiance in the amateur fine harness the next night - he truly loved the mare, and he hated to sell her. As the equitation class went into the ring, the office sent out a message on the loud speaker for me to come in for a phone call! I raced to the phone and Charlie told me that Mrs. Sinclair said to buy the mare, and that she would wire the money early next morning to the Marine State Bank in Springfield. I was walking on air, when I chanced to see Billy Otto, Sadoff's trainer, and told him I had bought the mare. He did not know what I was talking about. In my rushed excitement, I had forgotten to discuss the sale with Mr. Sadoff's trainer. I was mortified, and asked Billy if Mr. Sadoff would pay him his commission. He checked it out and everything was taken care of, still with the condition that the money be in Mr. Sadoff's hand by noon the next day.

I had told Charlie that the mare was as good as ever, and that I was sure that she could win the junior fine harness stake at Louisville to retire the trophy for Mrs. Sinclair, as her horses had won the class the two prior years. The rest of the evening was a blur, and after getting the girls back to their rooms, I tried to go to sleep. NO WAY! The long wait and wild happenings of the three years of our trying to buy the mare raced around my head, and there was no sleep for Helen that night. Bleary eyed and shaking with nervous exhaustion, the next morning I worked horses and waited for the clock to register nine. I immediately inquired if the money had been sent from Tulsa - and the bank reported that it had not been received. I called every 15 minutes as the clock climbed inexorably toward 12 noon. Judy Spreckles was at the show - a very sharp editor and producer of the magazine Horses. She suggested that I go with her to the laundromat just to keep me from exploding with nervous tension. "Laundromat!", I exclaimed, "it is 11:30 and no money received yet." I had called Mrs. Sinclair, and she verified that she had wired the money at nine that morning. Where in the world was that money? Fortunately, there was a telephone at the laundromat, and I called the president of the bank, furious and in tears. Finally, he came back to the phone to announce that the money was there, but not where it should have been recorded. It was now 15 minutes before 12. I asked Judy to dial the hotel as my hands were shaking too much to hit the right numbers. Then I took the phone and asked to be connected to Ben Sadoff's room. As the phone rang, I had almost given up and resigned myself to the idea that it must be God who didn't want us to have that mare after those frustrating years of attempting to buy her. "Hello," a masculine voice said. In a strangled voice I inquired if that was Ben Sadoff, and the sweetest words ever uttered came in my ear, "Yes, this is Ben Sadoff." I told him that the money was at the bank and whom to call to confirm the fact. The agony was over - the mare was Mrs. Sinclair's wonderful property and the long chase was ended. The mare cost a big price, but she was worth every cent of it.

Mr. Sadoff had a real sense of humor, and instead of railing at the bank for being so inefficient, he told me that when he went to the bank to get his money, the idiot at the teller's window asked him how he wanted the money. "In quarters," he replied. And so Ledgeview Radiance became Glenview Radiance, and Charlie drove her to victory in the junior fine harness stake at Louisville - thus accomplishing something unheard of. The mare's win retired that famous old trophy, and gave Katherine Sinclair the extreme joy of owning the velvet-mouthed beauty who could trot on a loose rein while buckling up to look like she was ready to pop right out of the harness. Truly, a one in a million horse, and worth three agonizing years of waiting to become the Queen of Crabtree Farms and Katherine's great winner for the next six years.

Those were the days! We shared such mutual trust with our owners that 90% of them never saw their horses before we got them. Is it any wonder that Charlie and I look back fondly to those wonderful days when our owners let us find and buy their great horses?

41
Saturday Knight - Champion Pony and Horse
(S & B July, 1993)

It was in Nashville, Tenn., in 1952 that we saw our first five-gaited pony. Being Yankees come south we did not know such creatures existed. As managers and trainers for Gregnon Farm which we had built in Collierville, Tenn. for J.W. Wrape that winter, we were looking for stock to his three daughters. The pony, a five-year-old, was a gorgeous blood bay with striking white face and hind ankle markings. He was being groomed by Charles D. Smith and watching was Raymond Shively who worked at another stable on the fairgrounds. Little did we know when we immediately purchased the pony that we had met three beings who would leave an indelible mark on the history of the American Saddlebred industry.

Our new pony was a registered Saddle Horse which we immediately renamed Saturday Knight. Searching for a show that offered pony classes, we made our first show on a Sunday afternoon at a tiny town southeast of Lexington and then moved to the Lexington Jr. League show. We knew that we had something extraordinary when Lila Wrape showed the pony for the first time and he was everything a pony should be. His beauty was extraordinary and his five gaits and manners were impeccable. We knew that we were the "new kids on the block" as he had never been shown before. Redd had joined our family and we were so proud. Here was a brand new star and we had a stunning surprise for the gaited pony division.

Two girls from the deep South had the already established champion ponies and their competition was fierce. We were second to one of the ponies in the preliminary and stake night we were second, defeating the other pony with the new sensation that popped up from nowhere - a complete surprise to everyone. Lila made two perfect rides in her baptism in some very hot fire and evidently upset an already agitated apple cart. It was half light and according to the announcement made during the line up in the five-gaited

Saturday Knight and Lila Wrape.

pony championship all entrants had gathered just outside of the show ring on the race track.

How odd, I thought, but it was our first time with our new pony at a recognized show and I assumed that was a regular part of the procedure.

Each pony was led upon a wooden platform for remeasurement. This was before night racing lights were erected and one could barely see what was going on. When our entry Saturday Knight stepped up on the platform, the vet put his measuring stick on the pony's withers, just as he had done on Monday when all animals were measured, he did not say "OK 14.2", he peered at the stick, maneuvered around and finally said that he could not see well enough to read the measurement. Someone held a cigarette lighter close but then the vet, Dr. Proctor handed the stick to Ted Buehl, secretary of the American Horse Show Association, and he carried it over to the grandstand light, returned and announced that the pony measured an eighth of an inch over legal height! I was astounded and so shocked that I could only say to Mr. Buehl, "How can that be? This is the same pony and the same vet who measured him in on Monday morning." A sense of unreality overcame me when he replied, "Mrs. Crabtree, lots of things can happen between measuring and showing." Not only had our pony been disqualified, but my honesty had been dealt a terrible blow with that remark. Still wondering what had hit us, we returned to the stalls after having given our red ribbon back. Our wonderful pony was not a pony and our reputation was shattered.

We did not reshoe the pony and showed him the next week at a county fair. We were assured that the ponies would not be measured, but we insisted and did so at every show that summer and there was never any question of his height. Did he have clay on his shoes that night at Junior League? Was there a high board on that platform? These were thoughts that whirled around in my mind and I made a decision to present a system for measurement cards to be issued to all ponies. I felt so strongly that human error and bickering should be no part of a horse show - especially where children were concerned. That system was presented by me for two years at the AHSA convention and got absolutely nowhere. Finally the third year I asked a highly regarded hunter-jumper trainer why the rule that everyone said was right never appeared. He said, "Helen, present it this year." I did and it was unanimously accepted and is the rule we lived by for 40 years. Upon asking why it took so long to pass, my friend said that one of the "Big Wheels" in AHSA had been showing an oversize Hackney and the man had died that winter before.

In 1953 we grew out our pony's feet to a height of just under 14.3. During Lexington that year Lila was in France and I let Posey, who was ten that summer, show our new "horse" in the open five-gaited class. I was embarrassed when I saw every top trainer in the country enter the ring on terrific horses. The track was very muddy and our entry looked even smaller sinking into the slop at each stride. I can only say that his small feet went right to the underfooting - something that the big horses could not do. There must be a reciprocal deity that looked over the judge's shoulders, as Saturday Knight and his tiny rider won the class. Lila returned in time for Louisville and won the juvenile gaited classes. She also won the three-gaited juvenile, catch-riding for a Chicago girl and won the equitation stake, age group and the AHSA Medal class to make a clean sweep of it. We not only had had a wonderful five-gaited pony, but we had a World's Champion juvenile horse as well. Look carefully at his picture as a pony and you will see that quality and performance count, no matter what the division.

42

How I Got Home From New York
(S & B August, 1993)

One night a crime program on TV named Fort Lee, N.J., as one of the worst cities for gangsters and crime. "That's the place!" I told Charlie, and it was what prompted me to recount the worst 24 hours of my life.

It was in November of 1979 and time for the Good Hands Final at the National Horse Show in New York City's Madison Square Garden. That year I had only one entrant - but that was enough since the rider was Shauna Schoonmaker and her mount was Warlock. Since Shauna was my only rider, we made arrangements to have the horse vanned to New Jersey where he could lay over at Finisterre Farm in Glen Ridge, N.J., until shipping on into the Garden early Saturday morning. Dr. and Judge Meanor had been extremely kind in suggesting that we stay at their stable. Bud Willamon shipped Warlock and his groom, L.T. Armstrong, and as planned, the horse arrived at the Garden early on Saturday morning. I had flown into New York the night before, staying at the old hotel directly across from the show. By eight o'clock the horse had arrived, Shauna was dressed to ride and she and Warlock went directly into the ring, qualified for the afternoon final and returned to win the Good Hands Final. Our plan was right on schedule - ride, win and head for home.

What I had overlooked was the fact that I could retire the coveted trainer's trophy so generously given by Dr. Henry Chase, a great saddle seat enthusiast. The trophy is a gorgeous sterling silver long-stemmed rose vase which I had won the first three times it was offered. Since my plane was leaving that evening, there was no time to be lost, but waiting for the red carpet and all the ceremony delayed my departure. I had my street clothes in the suitcase and planned to fly home in my riding clothes. I had assumed that my room was paid but upon leaving found that it had not been paid. I hastily settled in cash, leaving myself 15 dollars and change.

Vince Wholey, Mrs. McDonald, Dr. Henry Chase, "The Vase", Helen Crabtree and John Franzreb.

I had been robbed almost every year during the show and knew better than to carry a large amount of cash, particularly since I assumed that all I had to do was to catch a cab and head for LaGuardia and Eastern Airlines. By this time it was rush hour and Mrs. Schoonmaker and I were frantically looking for a cab and finally flagged down a limousine. Barbara thrust a 20 dollar bill in my hand after the driver had agreed to take me to the airport for that amount. We whizzed through traffic and pulled up to the curb check-in. What happened then I am going to relate - every word is the gospel truth - I have added nothing nor left anything out of the entire escapade. Those two dogs and a cat who had the "Incredible Journey" had nothing on me.

Fortunately the limousine had not moved away when the checker said, "Miss, this ticket is not for LaGuardia it is for JFK!" Clutching my ticket, my suitcase and the conspicuous silver vase, I dived back into the limo and asked the driver if he could get me to JFK for 15 dollars. I was so wild eyed that I think he was afraid to deny me, so we took off cross country for the other airport. It did not make sense but the check-in official had been very emphatic and by that time I was really racing the clock - which does not make for responsible thinking.

We arrived at the main concourse at Eastern Airlines and I ran to check in — surely a curious sight with my small suitcase, carrying a large vase in hand and dressed in a riding suit. Whereupon I was told that my plane left from the other side of the airport and that I should go down a grassy knoll to a corner and wait for a small green and yellow bus. This I did, seating myself next to an elderly soul who asked me if I had the same bus as she was going to Icelandic Airways! The prospects of getting home were getting dimmer by the minute and then I discovered that I had left my suitcase at the Eastern counter. I raced back and was relieved to see my suitcase, forlorn and alone - but there. Thankfully, I started back to the old lady and the seat where we had been told to await our green and yellow bus. As I neared the corner I saw the lady standing in the middle of the street where the taxi cabs roared around a high curve - one was heading right for the confused lady. "GO BACK!" I screamed and she hesitated long enough for the cab to skitter around her. And it was all down hill from there!

We boarded our correct bus and to my surprise the first airline we came to was Icelandic Airway. We proceeded slowly with several stops and finally arrived at Eastern. Approaching the desk I noted that the concourse was completely deserted. I pulled out my rumpled ticket and silently handed it to some girl who answered the service bell. She took one look and started to say something when she let out a shriek and raced across the hall and up a flight of steps to a mezzanine. That was enough for me and I sat down on the balance scales - a forlorn weirdo in "men's clothing" holding my tall silver vase like Excaliber. Immediately another girl appeared and apologized, saying that one of the officials in the mezzanine area had had a heart attack and that was where the first girl disappeared.

By this time I had given up completely. Icelandic Airways was beginning to seem more real by the minute. I said "Lady, I'm old, I'm tired and Eastern Airlines had nearly killed me and another lady and I am putting myself in your hands to get me to Louisville, Ky., because I am not only exhausted but I am dead broke." The awful spectacle got to the attendant because she assured me that my flight really did leave from LaGuardia and that Eastern would bus me back to Fort Lee, N.J., where I would be fed, given a motel room and taken to LaGuardia the next morning to get a flight to Louisville. "Now," she said, "just go out in front and wait. I have called a small bus to take you to Fort Lee." "It isn't green and yellow, is it?" I whimpered. She didn't know what color it was, so I insisted that she come to the curb with me and see me seated on the right bus. Finally a green (no yellow) bus arrived and she helped me on, thrusting meal and motel chits into my hand. At last, I thought - I am finally on my way. Had I known then that my adventure was just shifting into high I would not have believed it. Fate had me by the throat and was not letting go.

I sat directly behind the driver, a Puerto Rican youth whose buddy sat across from him and held a Walkman, turned to the highest decibels. We started around the circle and the next thing I knew, we were back at Eastern Airlines. This was a pickup bus that was sweeping up the flotsam at JFK who had lost their way! One grungy, young woman got on the bus with an infant lying in something that looked like a plastic drain board. Our next stop was for an elderly couple. The man sat down beside me and his wife sat behind us. He immediately began telling me that they were returning from Barbados which they had to leave because they were quite ill with the flu. Convincingly, he sneezed right in my face as they got off to catch their flight home.

We were still circling and by this time I had learned where the exit was and nearly fell out of the seat when the driver started once more around the circle. That and the gosh-awful music did it! I know no Spanish, but when we neared the exit again I clutched his shoulder, and brandishing the silver vase above his head shouted "Vamoose!" It worked, and we were off again cross country to what I thought would be a welcome dinner, a hot shower and sleep until early morning. How naive I was. It was only the beginning with worse to come.

I was finally on the right bus, heading back from JFK to stay at a hotel to catch a flight at LaGuardia for Louisville the next morning. I was exhausted and very willing to sit quietly and wait for what seemed a sensible conclusion to my awful experiences of the last few hours.

We drove to an urban area and after winding around the back streets the bus stopped in front of the worst looking motel I have ever seen. First, a swag of plastic pennants spelled out, DANCING NITELY. The entry was directly on the sidewalk, covered with green outdoor carpeting. The single door was guarded by two huge plaster of Paris lions - deadly white except for an inspired addition of painting the eyeballs black.

I entered and walked directly to the check-in counter. No real lobby, no easy couches, nothing but a cashier's desk, the top half of which was constructed of half-inch thick bulletproof "glass". The desk man reached through an open half circle in the middle of the desk for my credentials. He gave me a room key and said that there would be someone to take me to the restaurant and bring me back in an hour. The room was so dingy that I carefully put everything on the bed, washed my hands, hid the vase under the counterpane and started for the lobby. As I neared, I heard hysterical screaming and came upon two young women. One had blood streaming from a scalp wound and was trying to explain that she had been mugged and her purse had been snatched. Two bored policemen were listening with little interest and I ducked out the door to my waiting bus. This driver was a very accommodating young man who explained that Eastern had an arrangement for taking care of their misled passengers at this motel. We drove through very dimly lit streets and turned into an unpaved area at the rear of several buildings. This was my conclusion as the rats were climbing out of the garbage cans at our bumpy approach. "Driver", I said, "I don't really need anything to eat." But he hastily assured me that we were headed to one of the best Italian restaurants in the city. City? Where was I? He assured me that we were in Fort Lee, N.J., and the food was wonderful. "I'll be back in an hour," he called as the little bus pulled away.

I entered what was a temporary back door where the cashier asked if I was sent by Eastern Airlines; and he seated me in a booth. It was a very bare room, having a four foot high partition separating two rows of booths down the middle of the room. As I looked around I observed that a very large portion of the outer wall was missing, being shut off by very heavy plastic. Remodeling? - a bomb? But there I was for better or worse.

The shrimp dish I ordered was the best I had ever tasted and my shaky nerves were further allayed by the fact that I saw two policemen come in to eat. Directly next to me, across the wooden partition were four elderly men in their fedora hats and black overcoats with velvet collars. They spoke in Italian and were deep in discussion. "I can't stay here," I thought. I decided to move forward away from these Mario Puzo characters. Then I looked directly ahead and noticed a very prissy looking young man smiling and giving me the eye. Great Scott! I had attracted someone who thought I was a cross-dresser in my shirt, necktie and riding suit. So I decided to stay where I was. The police were no solace as they obviously hated each other and were completely oblivious to anyone and soon departed. As I looked at the cashier's stand, I noticed a bright red wall phone as well as the ordinary desk type. Shrilly the red phone rang, the cashier answered and immediately dropped the receiver and rushed out of the restaurant. The longer I looked at the red receiver swinging back and forth on the wall, I was determined to get up and demand from someone that they call my bus to take me back to the motel. As I stood indecisively searching for someone to make my call, one of the four "Dons" rose and asked me if I wanted to get back to the hotel and most graciously offered to drive me back in his car. I graciously declined and stood there, rooted to the floor. Within five minutes, my hero arrived with his bus to take me back to that horrible hotel that was beginning to seem nicer by the minute.

Back at my room, I was relieved to see the trophy still there under the covers. I undressed standing on the bed and exchanged my riding habit for my street clothes and was dressed and ready for the morning call to take me to the airport. My flight was on time and I arrived at Louisville without further incident which suited me just fine. Charlie met me and we had very little to say as we started down I-64 to Simpsonville. Finally I asked him if he had heard from L.T. and "How was Warlock making the trip home?" "They looked OK to me," Charlie replied. "What do you mean?" I inquired. "I mean they looked OK when they got off the van just as I was leaving to come to meet you." My horse had gotten home before I did!

Bandito and Kristy Gruenberg in Juvenile Three-Gaited Stake at River Ridge, 1969.

43

The Big Broadcast
(S & B October, 1993)

On my way to judge the Indio, California Show, I stopped over in Los Angeles to see a three-gaited gelding that Frankie Dye had there, as Kristy Grueneberg, one of our young riders with a lot of talent and moxey to spare, needed a new horse. She had quickly outgrown her first equitation horse and was ready for something that would challenge her ambition and ability.

I looked at the gelding. He was plain chestnut, barely 15.0 hands, but he thought he was 16 hands high. With lots of motion and a cocky air about him, he seemed to be just the thing for Kristy's next rung on the learning ladder.

The Cincinnati Horse Show came early in the season, so I decided to enter the horse in the novice three-gaited class to show him in the ring before Kristy's first class. For one year we were moved from the old Cincinnati Garden to the River Downs Raceway, across the river in Kentucky. As is always the case at race tracks, the show ring was located directly in front of the grandstand and the announcer's stand would be the inevitable funeral tent with it's imitation green grass. Since the track was too narrow for the tent to be in the center of the track, it was located outside of the ring, flush with the infield fence, facing the middle of the ring. Hunters and jumpers were an integral part of the Cincinnati show and their events were held in the early morning on the track infield. The Saddle Horses showed at night and the jumps were piled up along the infield fence on either side of the announcer's tent. It was fortunate that I had entered the new horse for me to ride first, as the green tent and the piles of wooden standards and poles presented a very scary side of the ring for anything less than a perfectly mannered and seasoned show horse.

I knew that Bandito (the name should have been adequate warning!) might be difficult to get up to that inside rail. As it so happened, the stabling was in several barns located around the back side of the track and it took a lot of planning to get the horses to the ring at the proper moment. Since I had riders in the prior class, we had the groom bring Bandito down to the show ring with those horses so that he would be there for me to get on. After seeing the scary infield fence, I hoped to get a moment or two in the ring before his class was called. I had the permission of the show officials to ride the horse into the ring before the class to help in acquainting him with the formidable area.

So I mounted and rode into the ring taking the grandstand side first, trying to get the horse moving smartly before he had to deal with the conglomeration of objects on the other rail. It so happened that the announcer for the show was a very large disc jockey for a Cincinnati radio station and he never stopped talking in a very loud voice. He, alone, was enough to scare a novice horse. All went well until we made the turn and started down that infield fence. Bandito wanted no part of that area and I had a tussle on my hands to urge the horse forward. My contretemps just set off the announcer and in the loudest of voices he started giving me advice - "Get after him, Helen - Yippee, ride him cowgirl" and other infuriating remarks. My only recourse was to haul off and slap the horse up on his jaw as I gave him my heels. That was the beginning of one of the roughest rides I ever had. That little horse's head disappeared toward the ground, he humped his back and proceeded to buck his hardest. The harder he bucked, the louder the announcer shouted. Finally I was about one jump from getting thrown. I had tried all the nice voice commands "Whoa, boy" - "Easy fellow" - "Come up here" as I vainly tried to get his head up. By this time he was grunting and bellowing like a bull, directly in front of the announcer. Niceties didn't get it with that little devil and in desperation, I thought I would use language that he might better understand. "Whoa, you dirty little son of a #!%#* @!" I shouted and it did the trick! Up came his head, down went his back and he went right to the rail at a very showy trot.

Just then, the other entrants had reached the ingate and entered the ring to begin this class. I was not so mortified that I didn't know that I was riding the highest trotting, most animated horse in the ring. At that time, the judge walked the lineup and as he approached me, his red, smiling face gave away his heroic effort not to laugh.

To my surprise, Bandito won the class and I rode him back to our barn to get ready for our next entries. Charlie met me as I dismounted and wanted to know what in the world I thought I had been doing. "I just won a class with this outlaw!" I replied. "That's not all you did," he said. "Did you know that the microphone was open to every stable on this track and we heard every - and I do mean EVERY word you and the announcer said?"

I am happy to report that the horse was a good one for Kristy and served his purpose well. But I learned a few good lessons - stay out of the ring unless you are in a class, never trust a disc jockey and be wary of anything named Bandito!

Lucifer Topper the Sire of Jimmy Joe.

44
Jimmy Joe - The Best Of Two Breeds
(S & B December, 1993 — January, 1994)

Since all trainers must be perfectionists, it is no wonder that one may forget many a triumph, but the stupid mistakes we make remain foremost in our minds. Such was my experience concerning a very fabulous animal.

We were at Rock Creek Club in Louisville. It was just after their spring horse show and I was sitting on the top of the bleachers looking down at a rider who was a good horse handler, an equitation open winner, but who was unable to find the intersection of a figure eight with a compass. I had just made a discovery that has stood me in good stead forever after with equitation riders. It was not a matter of control - this rider simply had no natural sense of proportion - a discovery I verified upon asking her to dismount from her exhausted horse and to stand on her own two feet and "trot" a figure eight for me. I dropped a piece of Kleenex on a spot and told her to look for the Kleenex. It worked! At that moment a good friend, Shine Ogan, drove into the entry and stopped. I was so pleased with myself that God immediately took care of my pride in allowing me to make the dumbest remark of my life. Shine was just returning from judging in Iowa and he could hardly wait to tell me that he had seen the greatest walk-trot pony that ever lived. I asked what his name was, and he said "Jimmy Joe" and my completely idiotic reply was, "I wouldn't have anything with a name like that!" That was in 1956, and it took Charlie and me TEN YEARS to finally get Jimmy in our barn.

Dr. Alan Raun had succeeded in doing what had never been done before - he bred a San Pedro saddle mare to his Hackney stud, Lucifer Topper. This had been tried by many breeders with disastrous results - generally a short Hackney neck and a big Saddle Horse head, ungainly body and a trot that had all four feet in a bucket. The difference is obvious from the pictures. Topper was a very fine and elegant Hackney and the mare, Starlet's Delight was a toppy fine mare that had the terrific stud, Noble Kalarama as a second sire.

Jimmy was foaled at Reedannland in March of 1953. He was broken to ride there as a two-year-old and sold the next year to Dr. Ramsey for his daughter to show him in his third and fourth years. He was put in training with Bud Kinney who was a VERY big man and one wonders how that little pony held him. It was then that Shine saw him and gave us the first chance to own him. The pony was only 14 hands tall. (This was back in the days when ponies were ponies, as identified in history as an equine 14.2 hands and under.)

Ray Pittman was located in Pennsylvania at the time and he purchased Jimmy Joe for a little eight-year-old Irish colleen named Kathy O'Rourke. The pair was magnificent and Ray Pittman certainly established himself as a premier trainer to put two terrific novices together to become an immediate success. I know that many hours of patient training of both child and pony created the magic and I wish to compliment Ray on his ability and patience to get the pair together. They were a sensation wherever they appeared, but unknown to the Midwest until they appeared at Louisville in 1959 where they placed third in the pony stake. Raymond Cowden brought him west and Tom and Donna Moore took over the training. A lovely and very beautiful young lady named Karen Ruth Burke was a client and they got her to show Jimmy at Lexington - which was our first look at the pony. I wanted to fall on my sword when I saw that incredible animal - and I know Charlie would have given me a push. Many stories circulated about Jimmy and Tom Moore. I never believed the legend that Jimmy threw Tom a few times. All Tom would have had to do would have been to take one foot out of the stirrup and step off. Tom must be credited for putting the great finishing touch on the pony as he showed perfectly for Karen Ruth.

We immediately tried to buy the pony. We all had agreed on a price but the sale was contingent on the Burke's decision to buy him. When Louisville time arrived, the Burkes had wisely decided to keep Jimmy. Karen Ruth rode Jimmy to the world's championship in 1962, 1963 and 1964. What a beautiful pair they were and I kicked myself with every victory pass. Shortly after that the pony was bought by Roger Dean and went to Florida where his daughter

Janie showed him on the Southern Circuit. We had had Andrea Walton in mind for Jimmy but when we did not get him we bought her a hot shot, wild gaited pony prospect named Right As Rain who was world's champion gaited pony the next year for Andrea.

Jim Ragsdale was Roger Dean's trainer (a position he held until his death just last winter). Jim was a good friend and we told him we had named him "Instant Answers" because he always had the solution to everyone's problems. But it was friendly kidding because most of the time Jim was right! I had looked forward to talking with Jim about Jimmy Joe but his untimely death robbed me of what would have been an amusing account of Jimmy Joe's training. Janie showed the pony only the one year and he did not come to Louisville. Carter Ragsdale was able to recount one of the experiences that was so characteristic of his Dad. He said that one day Jim decided that Carter was old enough to jog the pony, so they hitched him in the yard and Jim handed Carter the lines. Carter proceeded to get one foot in the cart and was airborn with the other one when Jim shouted "Yup" and slapped Jimmy Joe on the rump. Poor Carter! He got both feet in the cart but that was all - his seat was bumping along in the sand, almost smoking and father Ragsdale calmly called to Carter, "Stop him before you get to the highway." That was characteristic of Jim Ragsdale. He would have laughed at the Christians and the lions if he could have gotten a seat.

Much to our surprise, Jimmy was in Art Simmons's sale and taken back by Dean on a final announced bid of $9,000. He was taken back to Florida and that is where the Crabtrees finally got in the picture. It was ten long years that we waited for the pony and the right customer, Donna Schnipp - a beautiful, petite brunette who needed a three-gaited pony, as we had the five-gaited division wrapped up and Donna did not care for the monotony (to her) of equitation. We had the girl - we knew the pony was available - all we had to do was to get Papa Schnipp to buy the pony. Little did I know what I was in for!

Jimmy Joe was a perfect specimen of a three-gaited pony. His conformation was flawless. He was a solid mahogany brown without any white markings on his legs. A small thin star in the middle of his forehead seemed to accentuate the elegance of his head and matched the brilliance of his ever sparkling eyes. I do not believe that he ever put an ear back in the showring. Jimmy's gaits were perfection - both front and hind action always in complete harmony and his slender legs that went as high as any champion, were like steel - an umblemished animal who never wore a bandage in his life.

No wonder that we, after waiting ten years, were excited when Jim Ragsdale told me that his owner, Roger Dean had agreed on a price and would not entertain any other offer until we could consummate the deal. That is when I began to find white hairs in my hair! Donna Schnipp really wanted Jimmy, but her Dad was not yet convinced. I had talked with him several times and he kept putting me off. That is always understandable as finances generally have to be arranged ahead of time. Each time I talked to him he asked me to wait just a little longer. Every time I called Ragsdale he understood, but finally Mr. Dean set a deadline of midnight on a certain day. I had just called to find out that the Schnipp family had gone to Puerto Rico for a two weeks vacation. Puerto Rico! I managed to wheedle the name of the hotel from the secretary the afternoon of the final day that Jimmy could be bought. One must realize that when we moved to the Simpsonville, Kentucky area the total population was 220 people and it stayed that way for several years. The phone service operated with local "centrals" so when I told this lady that I wanted information for a hotel number in San Juan, Puerto Rico her gasp nearly blew the circuit and she said that she did not know how to do that! Finally I convinced her to call a central operator and find out how to do it. I suggested that there might be an overseas operator. By the time she returned my call it was after eight o'clock - four hours from deadline. When I finally got the front desk of the hotel and asked them if John Schnipp was registered there, the man could not make out Mr. Schnipp's name. "No, madame, we do not have a Mr. Swift listed." We practically went through the alphabet until he got the name right. Yes, Mr. Schnipp was a guest but was not in his room. And he promptly hung up. Fortunately, I had written down the hotel number - so again we started from Kentucky to San Juan. This time I asked the manager not to cut the connection and inquired if there was a bar in the hotel. I was desperate and when he agreed to page the party in the lounge, I was ready to faint. I cannot describe my relief when the American voice of John Schnipp answered. After more hemming and hawing, he finally said that I must really want that pony to track him to Puerto Rico. I said that I wanted the pony for his daughter, not our stable and that he would never regret his decision. I could have extracted impacted wisdom teeth easier than selling that gentleman what was and still is in memory the greatest pony that ever lived. (I do not mean to denigrate those beautiful ponies showing now, but to get such complete perfection in an animal only 14 hands high was truly a miracle).

Now I dialed Florida for Mr. Dean and there was no answer. It was almost ten o'clock and I really prayed when I dialed Ragsdale's number that he would answer - and he did. I explained that I was unable to get Dean on the phone but that I was going to send the check immediately that night. The rest of the saga is almost anticlimactic. Schnipp adored the pony and Donna showed him without defeat for the next three years, 1966, 1967 and 1968. In doing so, she showed the pony to his sixth world's grand championship. To date this record still stands along with two immortal horses, My My and Wing Commander. Only once did Donna fail to ride Jimmy and that was in 1967 when she did not appear at the show in time for the preliminary class. By now I was almost accustomed to Jimmy Joe traumas. Fortunately Andrea Walton was dressed to ride in an equitation class, top hat and all, and she hopped up on Jimmy and made a terrific show to win the class. About a half hour later I looked up to see the Schnipps strolling down the aisle — Donna dressed to ride. She was all smiles and wanted to know how Jimmy was. I said "He's fine - he just won the open class." Donna's big brown eyes doubled in size as she said, "But I wasn't even here!" I told her that as great as Jimmy was, he did have to have a rider and that Andy had done a great catch ride to keep the pony eligible for the championship. Suffice to say that Donna never missed another class.

Donna had a younger sister and the family felt that she should have a chance to show Jimmy. She came to Kentucky and got a crash course in riding just prior to Louisville. Donna had continued winning up to that point. The sister did an excellent job of learning to ride in a hurry, but it was just too much for her to be competent and aggressive in the show ring. Jimmy was second in the open and championship, lost in the lack of ring generalship required to win at Louisville. One of the judges came to me later and said he hated to beat Jimmy Joe but that he was not as good as usual. I have thought since that time that perhaps it was fitting that My My and Wing Commander's record should not have been exceeded. Just to share the record with those two horses was a thrill that has stayed with me these many years.

Jimmy was later retired at the State Fair and lived out his long life at our farm, never again to be ridden. He lies buried at the original Crabtree Farm.

Perhaps a fitting ending to this story is to quote the last paragraph of Jimmy Joe's retirement. The audience stood to honor an animal that had thrilled them for six years - "He leaves the ring tonight for the last time, but he does not leave our memories, for in the years to come, a hopeful trainer may dial a number and say, 'You'd better get in your car and come right over - I think I might have another Jimmy Joe.'"

But the call has never been made.

45

Captivation - A Wild and Beautiful Champion
(S & B May, 1994)

During the 60's, showing Saddlebreds in Florida was difficult. The weather has always been a factor, but the stabling was primitive to say the least. Happily, in recent years, everything about the deep south shows has improved. We had a saying that if we take the first string they would get sick, and if we took the second they would get beat! It was in 1967 that I took the horses on the circuit, beginning at Winter Haven. The weather was so cold that orange grove heaters were placed around the ring.

Every show has its particular high spot and for me the high spot was purely a coincidence. We had worked our horses that morning and a group of us were having breakfast at the Club House which happened to serve meals on the screened veranda overlooking the show grounds. Suddenly there was a wild commotion in the ring and I looked up to watch one of the most gorgeous mares I had ever seen in my life. It had to be a mare because she was fine as silk - a bay with an incredibly long, arched neck and dainty head. Her overall conformation would have made Marilyn Monroe jealous. However, she was going wild and trying to throw her rider who was draped around her neck in a desperate attempt to keep in the saddle. Grooms were getting the mare stopped, but it was not until Doss Stanton pulled her rider off that the mare finally stopped her rampage. I was completely overwhelmed by the gorgeous animal and as soon as everyone left, I went to my room and called Doss Stanton. I was surprised when Jim B. Robertson answered the phone. According to Jim, Doss was not in the room and Jim, always alert to what was going to happen, told me that if I wanted to know about the bay mare, that he and Doss owned her. So I arranged to go to the stall to inspect the mare.

Poor Kenny Carson was the man who had just peeled off the mare. His usual florid complexion was absolutely crimson. Kenny was always a very polite and agreeable trainer. He occasionally had a problem with alcohol and I wondered if the big commotion had been due to "Wild Turkey" or a wild mare! Doss was there and putting a shank on her led her out of the stall. In those days we did our own physical exams on horses we bought. The bay beauty was as sound as she was pretty and was an absolute dream when led at a trot. I have never felt more certain that I was looking at a future world champion - but not under saddle. To me she was the epitome of the perfect fine harness mare. Charlie already had won all of the junior classes the year before with the wild-going black mare Supreme Airs. Little did I know that it was the beginning of a history-making string of fine harness wins for Mrs. F.D. Sinclair. I did feel that the bay mare could win all of the harness junior classes that summer. After getting the price I hurried to call Charlie. He and I have the same taste in horses, so he called Mrs. Sinclair in Tulsa and she agreed to buy Folly's Gypsy. When I called Stanton's room, Jim B again answered and I told him I would be down with a check. He was astounded, but I know that a deal is in jeopardy until money passes hands. There were plenty of other trainers who saw what I saw and "bidding wars" have been known to happen.

Before I left that day I had already renamed the mare Captivation. This was the name of Miss Loula Long Combs' favorite Hackney and the title of her wonderful autobiography. In time I was ashamed of myself for naming a client's horse. But being by Night Of Folly could raise questions in judges' minds as his progeny were tough to work. (This was in the time before John Biggins!)

It was apparent that Captivation would never be a ladies horse but Mrs. Sinclair drove Supreme Airs and would soon own Glenview's Radiance to retire the junior fine harness trophies at both Lexington and Louisville.

Charlie did a wonderful job in getting the fractious mare ready by that same spring to win the junior class at Cincinnati, the first show of the year in our locality. Captivation was undefeated that year, winning all of her junior stakes beginning at Cincinnati, then Oklahoma City (also the grand championship), Tulsa, Pin Oak, Lexington Junior League and the junior world's championship at Louisville. In 1968, Captivation added more blues, ending the year winning the fine harness mare stake at Louisville.

That winter I asked Charlie if I could try working the mare under saddle. He reluctantly said, "Go ahead, but be careful!" Everything went perfectly as I trotted the mare up and down the long barn aisle. Hoping that the two years in harness had cured her previous sins, I cantered her on the left lead. So far all was well. I reversed and as gently as I could "suggested" the right lead and she exploded. Stopping her, I tried once again with even worse results. That mare had more motions than an old maid at a wrestling match! And I mentally apologized to Kenny Carson - No "Wild Turkey" - I had simply bought a mare that would never canter on the right lead.

It was obvious that Mrs. Sinclair had an extra fine harness horse, so she decided to sell the mare at the Tattersall's sale. Mrs. Sinclair said that she wanted $25,000 for the mare - a difficult thing to do at that time as sale prices were generally low.

Charlie drove the mare through the sale's ring and she never looked better. I was at the auction stand with my poor mind in a terrible turmoil. The bidding progressed slowly as the starting bid was high and finally there came a bid of $22,500. I did not know what to do. The bid was close, but the owner had said $25,000. At that moment I could not do anything right. Take the bid? Take the mare out of the sale? I would be wrong either way. I was frozen with indecision when I heard the sweetest words in the English language..."Twenty-five thousand" ' I was so relieved that I yelled "sold" along with the auctioneer! Mrs. Franklin Groves had bought the mare for her North Ridge Farm and planned to breed the mare there. That was an amazing price for a broodmare prospect, but Mrs. Groves was just as attracted to the mare as I had been at Winter Haven.

Captivation was a great foundation dam of many superb show horses. Bred to their stud, Kourageous Kalu, she produced a filly, My Captivation, dam of the great fine harness stallion, Captive Spirit, and many other winners.

Captivation was good to four people; the owner, Mrs. F.D. Sinclair, the trainer, Charles Crabtree, his wife, Helen, who took two big chances - and to Mrs. Franklin Groves who made a very wise choice - a choice that added many good champions to the American Saddlebred Horse industry.

46

A Horse Worth Waiting For
(S & B February, 1995)

There are many reasons why trainers will buy a horse. If you are choosing for a specific rider the needs are obvious. However, in rare times one will see a horse that fills every qualification for many riders. I saw such a horse one night at the American Royal Horse Show in 1965. His name was Rebel Command.

He was a big, bold black chestnut with a white blaze - undeniably a son of the great Wing Commander. What attracted me the most was his equine dominance of the amateur gaited stake. Although he had a good rider, there was the feeling that the horse was going to win the class on his own terms in spite of what the rider did or did not do. It was love at first sight, my kind of horse, and I hastened to the outgate to speak with his trainer. It was Ben Segalla who was waiting to greet the victorious pair. I was almost as excited as Ben whom I immediately congratulated and then asked if the horse was for sale. My spirits sank when he said, "Not now". Then he agreed to let me have first refusal, whenever he was available. I wondered at the time if this promise would hold, but all I could hope for was that Ben would remember. So many times a remark made in a victorious glow will be forgotten immediately. I thought about that gelding all winter. I had Wendy Wagner on hold for a good horse.

Late the next spring Ben Segalla called me and honoring his promise gave me a price on the horse. Mrs. Wagner and Wendy were ready to buy a good horse. I flew to their home in Springfield, Ill.

We first went to St. Louis to Louis Greenspohn's farm to look at the wildly exciting mare, Georgie's Miracle. Glen Lanning, her trainer, had created the champion "contender" from an incorrigible outlaw. I had judged the horse at a show in Raleigh, N.C., late in the show season. Most of the horses had been let down for winter so when Glen and this horse entered the ring, I thought I'd been hit by a bolt of lightning. Glen promised me that he would call me if he ever got the horse readied for an amateur, but Gaynor Spotts bought her. I wondered if he had wrought his magic on the black mare, Georgie's Miracle.

I had sat in a box in front of Mr. Greenspohn that winter at the Chicago International. Georgie's Miracle, obviously having won the class, was lined up and the remainder of the entrants were being worked. Mr. Greenspohn became hysterical and loudly shouted repeatedly at Glen to leave the ring. Red-faced, Glen rode to the farthest corner of the ring. Greenspohn screamed abuses at Glen and the judges, shutting his mouth only when the mare was declared the winner. Glen was a stony faced and furious figure when he made his victory pass, with Greenspohn running after him asking his suit size, promising to buy Glen a new riding habit!

We went to Greenspohns to watch Glen ride the mare. She had not taken three trot strides when she threw her right front shoe, tearing off much of her hoof. So it was back on the plane to Chicago where Segalla met us to drive us to his stable in Half Day, Ill.

It was still quite cold in northern Illinois and both Segalla and Rebel Command were wearing their winter coats. Being a typical Wing Commander horse, Rebel was rather bony and gaunt looking. I couldn't wait for Ben to get aboard when the horse transformed from an ugly duckling into an exciting show horse. After Ben rode, Wendy got in the saddle and it was the picture I dreamed of for many months.

After working the gelding, we waited in the quonset arena while Ben called the owner to see if he would take Mrs. Wagner's offer. Mrs. Wagner stared and then turned to me - "What is that?!" And I replied, "That is the horse you just bought." He was a bony sight, long hair matted with sweat and his body draped in an old torn wool cooler. Poor Ben was as mortified as we were surprised. We were to find in the years ahead that he always hung his head like a dog when being cooled out.

Wendy enjoyed great success, winning at all of the shows including world champion amateur stallion and gelding stakes at Louisville in 1966 and 1967. They were a very popular team and the more the crowd cheered the bigger Rebel pumped his legs and the harder Wendy rode.

The record books contain his wonderful record, but I feel that recitations are boring. I will write only about the hilarious things that abound in every champion's history.

One of Wendy's first shows with Rebel Command was at the Oldham County, Kentucky Horse Show. In fact, we had taken the pair to an even smaller show for their first class where we entered the horse's name as Rebel in case the pair made a bad show. But that never happened. I had seen the sterling silver service trophy at Oldham County and Rebel won it for two years. He and Wendy were established world champions and only my greed for him to retire the expensive trophy convinced me to show there again. The ring was enormous but the judges were kind the first two years and judged quickly. But this was not to be on the attempt to "walk away" with that elegant silver.

An elderly judge (who shall remain mercifully anonymous, and who died the next year) officiated. We took two gaited horses to show. Julie Fawcett, one of the most ebullient and loveable girls was a raw recruit and she had a "beginning" gaited gelding, but I felt she could be second to Wendy and get in a good ride.

Show time came and went and we had no judge. Everyone knew that this judge was not well, a bit senile, and no one wanted to go to his motel to see if he was all right. Finally he arrived and the show started. It was very hot and humid that night and it seemed like an eternity before the class came in to the line-up. Wendy and Rebel had easily won the class, or so we thought. As the judge approached an excited and exhausted Julie at the end of the line-up the poor, red faced girl looked down at the judge and said, "My goodness, aren't you terribly hot?" The judge smiled at her and filled out his card. I nearly dropped dead when the announcer called Julie Fawcett out for first place and Wendy for second. It was so ludicrous that everyone laughed, especially Julie and Wendy who took the surprise with hilarity. It was Julie's only blue ribbon and Rebel's only defeat that year.

Wagners were living in Illinois but by the second season with Rebel, Mrs. Wagner decided to move to Kentucky. Fortunately for all of us and the entire horse industry, the acreage that is known nationwide as Copper Coin Farm was purchased and Mrs. Wagner and I spent many an hour riding the farm marking trees and fences. It was immediately evident that these were prime acres and the beautiful Copper Coin Farm would have a prominent role for many continuing years in Saddlebred history.

When we all realized the importance of the Wing Commander -

Carol Trigg family, we hastily made arrangements to buy Lady Trigg, the daughter of Carol Trigg, who was a full sister to World Champions Chief Of Greystone, Delightful Society and the dam of Imperator. This wonderful mare, at 30 years of age, still lives at the farm and is the pride and joy of Mrs. Wagner and Wendy and her husband who raise and start the great young horses at Copper Coin.

Rebel was sent to Don Harris in the winter of 1970 and continued to carry Wendy to major wins the next season. The following year, Copper Coin Farm was completed and Don came to Kentucky as trainer. It was decided that the gallant horse would be retired at Louisville. Wendy and Rebel never looked better than at his retirement in 1972, and a lavish champagne party was held at his stall. I am very allergic to alcohol in any form, not only drinking but just being exposed to the breath of anyone who had been drinking champagne - my nemesis.

But nothing could keep me from attending a party in honor of one of my all-time favorite horses. Finally the "champagne fumes" were too much for me and I retreated to sit on a tack trunk in front of Rebel's stall. Rebel had been enjoying every drop of champagne that guests had offered him. As I sat there remembering the many thrills that wonderful five-gaited Saddle Horse had given me, I felt my wig ring being pulled from my head! Grabbing it back from Rebel I yelled and he ran back to the corner of the stall. Feeling ashamed, I opened the stall door and coaxed my friend forward to give him the fond farewell that he deserved. As I leaned down to kiss his muzzle for the last time, he let fly with the biggest belch in horsedom. The champagne breath nearly finished me. Rebel, as usual, had had the last laugh.

John Hinkle and Helen Crabtree.

47
Seeds of Compassion

The American Saddlebred Show Horse works hard to achieve the trainer's goal. To those who do not know what goes on behind the show ring, it may seem that too much is asked of the Saddlebreds. Far from it! No other breed is so carefully cared for by dedicated grooms, caring trainers and grateful owners.

One has only to have seen the heartfelt tribute to The Phoenix by the Chancellor family and to know that Katherine Sinclair maintains a farm to retire her show horses and those owned by her friends, to understand the depth of the feeling we all have for our wonderful Saddlebreds. This is not uncommon as the show horses are loved and cared for nationwide. This love and concern is just as real in the Morgan, Arabian and National Show Horses.

Several years ago, Ed Teater and I represented our breed at a gathering of owners and trainers of many light horse breeds in Walla Walla, Wash. I will always remember Penny Tweedy the charming owner of the greatest race horse of all time, Secretariat. She told the assemblage, "I envy Helen, she gets to ride her horses while all I can do is watch."

Perhaps our concern for our horses and our well cared-for dogs and cats leaves us with the delusion that our moral responsibility ends there. Nothing could be farther from the facts.

The dreadful plight of the lost and stray animals who face death in "humane" shelters was brought out on national TV this winter. Heart-rending videos of dogs being dragged to a horrifying death, or animals used for gun target practice as a form of euthanasia were sickening.

Yes our prized friends are well cared for, but what about the untold number of abandoned and unwanted animals, horses included.

Our immediate response was to give a sizable donation to our local Humane Society. That was to effect temporary relief. But we need something in addition to financing to save these doomed animals.

Since I have spent many years working with young riders, I know that morality begins at an early age and love of all God's creatures must be nurtured early so that we have compassionate adults.

With this in mind, I offered a $100 U.S. Savings Bond to our county elementary school pupil who wrote the best essay showing love and concern for animals. The results were astounding. Students age seven to 12 represented every elementary school in Shelby County. Each school was limited to five contenders, but many had as high as 15.

In this age of TV and Nintendo, someone must plant the seeds of compassion in the youngsters. Perhaps many readers can back similar efforts.

Here is the winning essay by John Hinkle, age nine from Heritage Elementary School, Shelby County, Ky.

MY NEW PET

Once I had a baseball signed by my favorite baseball player, Nolan Ryan, but I made the best trade for it that anyone could ever make. I traded it for a best friend.

It was the saddest morning of my life. Yesterday the dog I had ever since it was a puppy got hit by a car. My mom said I could have another pet, but I thought no other pet could replace my dog. As I was walking to school on a hot summer morning, I saw a chestnut pony tied to a post in the middle of a grassy field with a black wooden fence around it. He didn't look too happy. He was pulling on the rope and tossing its head up and down. It was skinny and pawing the ground as if it wanted to get away. I felt sorry for the pony but it was getting late, and I had to get to school.

When I got home I remembered the horse. The pony had looked mistreated, so the owner must want to get rid of it. So I started out toward the pasture where I had seen the pony. When I got to the pasture the pony was still tied to the post in the middle of the field. I took a glance at the pony and started toward the house, where the person who owned it lived.

I stepped onto the doormat and knocked. I heard some footsteps and then the door opened. A man with curly brown hair and a beard stood in the doorway, he had a yellow shirt and red suspenders with patched jeans. I was scared to talk at first but I finally got the words out, "Would you like to get rid of the pony outside in the field?" "Sure," said the man in a gruff voice, "How much do you have?" "What do you mean how much to you have?" "I mean how much money do you have. I expect at least 95 to 100 dollars." "Ninety-five to 100 dollars! Wow! "I um ... sort of don't have that much to spend." How could I get 95 to 100 dollars? I thought. Then I remembered what my mom had said, she would get me another pet to replace my dog. I ran all the way home. I burst through the door, ran upstairs to my mom's bedroom and stopped in front of her. "Mom, you know what you said about getting a pet to replace my dog? Well I found one," I said out of breath. "Slow down, now how much money does it cost, or is it free?" she said. "It is not free, and the owner says he expects 95 to 100 dollars." There was a pause of silence then mom said, "95 to 100 dollars" absentmindedly. I could tell by the way she spoke that there wasn't a chance I could get the pony. I walked out of the room with my mom still standing in the middle of the room with curlers in her hair and her blue bathrobe on. As I walked down the stairs the thought struck me that I could earn the money by mowing lawns, but as I thought about it, I would have to mow 98 lawns at least. Even if I charged two dollars I would still have to mow 49 lawns! There weren't even that many lawns on the next three blocks put together! That idea would not work. Then I thought about how other people get money when they needed it, of course I could sell some stuff to get the money.

After some thinking of good ideas but finding something wrong with it, I decided to sell my baseball signed by Nolan Ryan. As I walked upstairs a lump formed in my throat and my hands got sweaty. I picked up the baseball and started to take the slowest steps I had ever taken down the hall, downstairs, out the door and onto the sidewalk that went toward the houses on my block.

I went straight to the old man that lived in the big house at the corner. I went there first because when he had first found out about the ball, he had offered me the most money $200. As he put the money onto my hands I got real excited, I was going to have a pony of my own!

I ran down the street and paid the owner of the pony. When he handed me the rope to lead it I got more excited with every step I took. After we were a little ways down the street the pony kept nuzzling me in a playful way. It seemed that he knew he would be taken care of. Every day after school he sticks his head out of the door of the shed we keep him in and waits for me to come out and tack him up so we can go ride in the vacant lot behind my house.

Now that I think about how much fun I have had with my pony, even though I would love to have that baseball, I think this horse means more to me than any baseball ever will.

Wild Party and Melinda Moore.

48

Wild Party
(S & B May, 1996)

The telephone rang one winter morning and Billy Otto, a good friend and horse trainer told Charlie that he had discovered a small chestnut stallion in a field in Missouri. Billy was very impressed by the extreme action of the little fellow, along with his beautiful head crowned by a pair of keen hooked ears. He was bright chestnut with just the right white markings.

"Charlie," Billy enthused, "all this little stud needs is time and groceries. I believe that he could be a champion three-gaited pony."

Billy was 100% honest and a smart horseman, so without hesitation Charlie asked the price. "Fifteen hundred dollars and I have his papers to send with him. He is four years old and sound."

Being assured that Billy's commission was included in the price, Charlie said, "Find a way to get him to Simpsonville and the check will be mailed today."

Thus began the career of a pony who was going to share history with the start of the show ring career of one of our greatest trainers, Melinda Moore. He was also the start of younger sister, Melissa's teaming to ride five-gaited. Did any animal ever teach two more talented trainers?

When the little horse arrived, he was thin as a rail, slight bodied and too full in the neck to be three-gaited. His fore-arm muscles were very slender and his pasterns unusually long. This fact accounted for the spring in his five gaits and made him not only a delight to watch but to ride.

His papers revealed his name as Spee's Chief. Only the third generation on his sire's side was recognizable. The bottom side of the papers might as well have been written in Sanskrit, so unknown were all of the animals. I mentioned this only to point out that one can never predict where greatness lies.

We were enchanted by the little stud. Charlie immediately called the vet to alter what was to be a pony.

Charlie was saving his lastest name for the next likely show prospect, so that is how "Spee's Chief" became "Wild Party."

Although Wild Party was four years old, Charlie went very slowly with him. He had obviously been nearly starved and willing as the pony was, Charlie felt that the training should be slow and deliberate. Five gaits was the way to go as the conformation dictated.

Charlie trained Wild Party carefully. It took two years to ready him for the show ring. Charlie recalls with affection and humor that the pony was a slow learner. "I had to gait him all over again every morning. " But the pony tried so hard to please that we all knew that he would be a good pony in time.

Randi Stuart showed Wild Party in his debut at the Shelby County Fair. Poor Randi, she had been showing Legal Tender. The contrast was almost laughable as Randi tried to shrink to a height complimentary to a 14.1 hand pony.

We next took the pony to Illinois State Fair where petite Debbie Basham introduced a gaited pony to the unknowing Illinois shows.

Shortly thereafter, a delicate and fragile looking girl from Akron, Oh., was ready to progress to a second mount. Janie Fawcett was not aggressive enough for the horsemanship competition and she was just the pretty young girl to pair up with Wild Party. Their show season climaxed at Louisville.

I had noticed that one of the judges appeared very nervous and hesitant in picking his winners. Janie and Wild Party were just the pair to help him out. I instructed Janie to watch me if any pony threw a shoe. I would be standing at the gate and would point to the judge. Janie had been told to ride Wild Party back and forth in front of the judge. Do not stop, just keep slow gaiting all the time it takes to replace the shoe. Wild Party was pure gaited, all five gaits were perfect, but his slow gait was sensational.

My prayers for a thrown shoe were answered! Dutifully, Janie looked at me and I pointed at the insecure judge. Bless her heart! Janie slow gaited back and forth. Then the class was over and a very deserving pony and a grand little rider had won their first class — a World's Championship.

Joan Farris then bought the pony for her youngest daughter Barbe, but Barbe was overshadowed by her super sisters, Allison and Andrea Walton.

It was time for Wild Party to be the professor of two young girls who now hold the highest positions as trainers in our industry Melinda and Melissa Moore.

Donna Moore told me that she would be forever grateful to Mrs. Farris, who put a very low price on Wild Party, to enable a recently divorced mother to afford a show animal for her two daughters.

Both girls learned to ride five gaits on the pony, but it was the older Melinda in whom the consuming flame of show competition burned the brightest at that time. Melinda and Wild Party won at Rock Creek, Lexington and Louisville where the World's Championship can be viewed as a portent of further greatness stamped the first family of the American Saddlebred, Donna, Tom, Melinda and Melissa Moore.

Wild Party was small, but his impact on our breed is enormous by way of two little golden haired girls named Melinda and Melissa Moore.

49
Fancy Stonewall - A Very Bright Horse
(S & B September, 1994)

In the spring of 1966, Reata Horse Farm held a dispersal sale. Located in Sharon Center, Oh., and now well known as the Richlon Stables, home of the famous Lavery family. I have written previously of our buying Oman's Desdemona Denmark and of attempting to buy the lovely mare, Reata's Radiance, who later made fine harness history for Mrs. F.D. Sinclair as Glenview's Radiance. There was a three-gaited bay gelding who caught my eye, but in the confusion attendant upon the other transactions, the horse went to Paul St. Charles' bid.

All of the show season I could not get that bay gelding out of my mind. When we went to the Ohio State Fair, the horse was there. His name was Fancy Stonewall (originally registered as On The Way Up), and was trained by Paul for his new owner, Dr. Haggerty, to be ridden by his daughters. I cannot be sure how long that family showed the horse, but I watched him every chance I got. As time wore on, one could see that the horse was not behaving well and had developed the bad habit of going to the center of the ring. I began asking friends in Ohio to let me know if there was ever any mention of selling the horse. Despite his bad manners in the ring, I still wanted the horse as he had always impressed me as a very smart horse. Local gossip had it that while Paul was a good trainer, he was doing a lot of traveling, buying and selling horses and he did not have a good assistant trainer to keep such a gifted horse working steadily, right or wrong. I surmised that the gelding was not being challenged temperamentally - in other words, he was bored.

Sonny Long, with whom we had become good friends when we were at Gregnon Farm, was training nearby in Germantown, Tenn., at the famous Wildwood Stables. Sonny got a price on the horse and met me at the airport where we were having breakfast, satisfied that no one suspected that Crabtree Farms was interested in

Mary Lou Gallagher and Fancy Stonewall — NHS Finals, 1978.

Fancy Stonewall. Had my mouth not been full of waffle, it would have gaped wide open when I saw Dr. Haggerty approaching our table. Expressing surprise - he explained that he just happened to be in the neighborhood and was stopping by to get a cup of coffee. I have always felt that the Saddle Horse grapevine could have taught Mata Hari a few tricks!

Since I already had a price on the horse, I was not too concerned. After riding Fancy and checking him for soundness, I gave the assistant a check. He would be the property of Nancy Lipshultz of Chicago. She was a beautiful girl, horse wise and a good student. Perhaps an over-two mount would be better, but I have always felt that horse size was more temperament than measurement.

I had about two months before the Christmas holidays to train the horse for his new role. I have never enjoyed a horse more. Not just smart, Fancy was brilliant and loved the challenge of equitation discipline. His way of going improved and he was a sport on the rail as well. That horse could count! If he stopped after six strides on a line change, he would stop at the next six strides.

When we took Fancy to Florida that winter, trainers assumed that I was going to show him in open classes. Looks of disbelief followed when I said that he was an equitation horse. Nancy and Fancy swept that show and she continued to be at the top. At Lexington, the equitation championship was held during a terrible downpour with a lightning bolt hitting the eagle atop the ringside flagpole. After the class, I inquired of Nancy why she rode in a slumped position. She said, "Mrs. Crabtree, when that lightning struck I looked around and saw that I was the tallest rider in the ring!"

Kristy Grueneberg was Fancy's new owner and the pair were invincible in the tri-state shows for three years and right at the top in all shows. Kristy became the owner of the truly once-in-a-lifetime Glenview Warlock at the River Ridge show. She had that summer with both grand mounts and the following winter, in 1973, when Fancy was 11 years old, he was purchased by Mary Lou Gallagher who was winning everything in sight with her world's champion juvenile gaited gelding Lad O'Shea.

I was unable to attend the Finals at Madison Square Garden in 1974. Redd took Mary Lou who had qualified on the Southwest Circuit for the Good Hands. The wily Mary Lou got her mother, Mrs. F.D. Sinclair to say she would buy her a BMW if she won.

Never dreaming that Mary Lou would win, mother agreed, but she was at the gate after the big win and said, "O.K. Mary Lou - what color."

50

The Happy Hour
(S & B July, 1996)

It is difficult enough to find one exceptional show prospect but to find two such animals for sisters has to be looked upon as more then coincidence. In the case of the horse who became known as The Happy Hour, I first saw him at the Boone County Fair and Horse Show, a show that I had chosen out of a busy schedule because I heard that the fair had an exhibition for jumping mules, this was absolutely irresistible, so off I went to Columbia, Mo. To my disappointment, the mules were exhibited at a time that conflicted with the horse show and I never saw the mules who jumped the barriers while their owner ran about ten feet at their side, directing them with a long lead rope.

The rains came down and by the time for the five-gaited stallion and gelding class, the footing was a mess. Just one big mud puddle after another. We were all mud spattered, horses, riders and judge.

I was feeling regret that I had ever left Kentucky, when a black chestnut gelding with a brilliant white stripe and three white legs burst into the ring. In his middle sat the proud rider, R.S. Palmer, red-faced and grinning with excitement. There was no way the unruly horse could win the class as every time he came to a puddle, he jumped it! I have no recollection of the other horses at the show, but I returned home singing the praises of one of the most electrifying geldings I had ever seen. Surely, I thought the horse must have Stonewall King blood in his veins, a possibility that made him even more enticing to me.

We had two sisters from Tulsa, Okla., the older sister, Linda Lowary, had made a name for herself in equitation, winning the NHSSE Final in 1974 after many other wins, at the big shows. It was time to move on into the open classes and Linda obviously was anticipating the five-gaited division.

That same year of 1974 we had many horses and riders at the American Royal in Kansas City. The old Royal arena was small, so

The Happy Hour.

we would return to our hotel for a change of clothes and return to work our horses when the traffic in the ring had thinned out.

Charlie and I were sitting in the stands when the gelding stake was bugled. It was an electric shock when R.S. Palmer rode into the ring on that exciting horse I had seen in July of that same year. Because of the conflicting work schedules we had not seen the gelding at the Royal. Charlie was as beguiled as I and we followed R.S. back to the stall. I felt then that a horse showing such progress from July to November was not yet a finished product. Sure enough! R.S. had bred a mare to his stallion, Heart Of Stonewall, in 1966 and owned the wild gelding a year. In this, his first show season, Stonewall Statement was seven years old!

We were very close friends of Ruth and R.S. They wanted to sell but only to someone who would give their wonderful show horse a chance to complete his education and strive for the world championship.

Palmer's aisleway was crowded with interested buyers but our quoted price was never in danger. The Palmer's word was their bond, and still is.

One trainer, in particular, was trying everything to change the Palmer's minds, but they held fast to our agreement.

Mr. and Mrs. Lowary had not seen the gelding stake and were going to see the horse when Linda tried him. But the horse still had a temperature on the last night of the show and was unable to show in the championship. Mr. and Mrs. Lowary had to return to Tulsa, but they left a check authorizing me to complete the purchase if I still liked the horse. What a predicament! I wanted the horse, Linda wanted him and so did a dozen other buyers.

So I asked R.S. if he would bridle the sick horse, put Linda's saddle on him and just let me see them together at a walk. This we did and the horse that was to thrill thousands of horse show fans under the name The Happy Hour, became the prized five-gaited entry of Linda Lowary.

The Palmers insisted on taking the gelding home until he was completely recovered from his serious illness, refusing to cash the check while the horse still had fever. The Palmers called in 30 days to report that the vet had pronounced the horse completely well. Only then was the purchase check cashed and the horse came to Simpsonville.

Happy Hour and Linda made their debut at the famed Pin Oak show where they won and became an instant sensation. However it was at the Lexington Junior League Show that Linda and her horse put on two spectacular shows that are remembered to this day. I knew that this horse was something extraordinary when Owen Hailey, who had trained World's Grand Champion Plainview's Julia and a quiet man of few words ran out on the race track one morning when I was working the horse to say, "Helen, who is that horse? You could win the big stake with him!" I was really convinced by such high praise from a very taciturn man that indeed Linda owned an exceptional horse.

The narrow Red Mile at Lexington is a notoriously difficult ring to show a powerful moving horse. With this in mind I instructed Linda to wait every time she made the turn prior to the stretch in front of the grandstand. "Linda," I said, "I want every trip to be a single exhibition of you and this horse, I don't care if you have to wait 10 minutes at every turn to be by yourself down that straight away." Bless her heart, Linda followed instructions to the letter and the stands went wild. This was the plan that we followed when Linda showed Happy Hour to his many, many victories and thrilled many including the knowledgeable audiences at Lexington and Louisville, and crowds at the Garden who recognized a special horse and rider when they saw it.

Riders progressed to Redd's stable when they were older than the majority of our riders. Linda and Happy Hour were successful under Redd's tutelage and the horse's final show was at the Lexington Junior League where Happy Hour, according to Owen Hailey's prediction won the five-gaited championship with Redd.

Only last year at the brave old age of 29 did Happy Hour die leaving a void in many hearts.

51
Rick Rack
(S & B August, 1996)

The fact that we had found a very gifted five-gaited gelding named The Happy Hour for Linda Lowary made the task of finding an equally wonderful mount for younger sister, Kerry, appear to be an impossible search.

Linda and Happy Hour had the ladies gaited division practically nailed down, including a world's championship.

We had a powerful group of both three and five-gaited horses as well as the world champion three-gaited pony. What to do?

It just had to be providence calling when I answered the telephone one morning and it was Donna Moore telling me of an exceptional five-gaited pony. She said, "Helen, you sold us Wild Party and I think this pony will do for one of your riders what Wild Party did for my girls."

This was certainly "Quid Pro Quo" (a term I can only use in retrospect because it was many years before the politicians found the confusing and politically correct substitute for "tit for tat"!)

We did not wait, immediately after dinner we drove to Versailles to Donna's barn and pulled to a stop in front of the open stable door.

Standing there was a brown and white gelding, fully tacked without a groom in sight. His neck was high, head turned to stare imperiously at us as we got out of the car. I have looked at hundreds of prospects over the years, but no presentation was ever so dramatic.

My first thought was, this is no pony. Those were the days when saddle ponies were truly 14.2 hands and under.

Returning to the car for my measuring standard I walked into the lighted hallway. Donna quietly smiled and said, "He looks big to you doesn't he?" I said a little prayer that this magnificent animal was really a pony. As a groom quietly covered his left eye I eased the stick into position at the height of the withers. "Thank the Lord", I breathed as the cross bar settled at exactly 14.2. It was

Rick Rack and Michele Macfarlane.

Rick Rack and Kerry Lowary.

Rick Rack in September of '96.

love at first sight and the fact that his five gaits were exceptional and ambitious was almost beside the point.

Our search was over and Kerry had a pony as electrifying as her sister's horse, Happy Hour. Now it was only a matter of teaching Kerry and her new pony, Rick Rack, to become a team.

Rick Rack was foaled in May 1966. His breeder, Scott Higgins of Lamar, Mo., registered him in 1967, choosing that wonderful name that was almost a description of every facet of the spotted colt's appearance and attitude. Mr. Higgins valiantly tried to avoid describing the bay and white as spotted on the application for registration. He wrote out a description of "markings" describing every white spot or hair all in a paper denial that the colt was, indeed, spotted.

Rick Rack was gaited in California where Ellen Scripps Davis had brought him at the age of seven.

Donna Moore, judging the California Futurity show two years later, was very impressed by the bay and white animal and realizing that he needed to be in five-gaited pony country, purchased him and brought him to Kentucky.

Rick Rack was 10 years old when we bought him that night for Kerry Lowary. He was as tough and sound as any animal who ever lived, and as the saying goes he "had very low mileage". In fact, as this story unfolds, 10 years was only a childhood for the pony.

Mrs. Davis and her daughter Michele Macfarlane had gone to see a spotted stallion, running with a band of broodmares at Scott Higgins Farm in Lamar, Mo. Michele recalls that the progeny of Rick Rack were not high caliber. One mare was in the stable and Michele asked if the horse had been trained. Without pause, Higgins went into the stall and leaped upon the mare's back. She was terrified, unable to move.

So Rick Rack went to California to Scripps Miramar Ranch. Because of his small size at the age of seven, and the ordinary colts he had sired, Rick Rack was gelded. Michele, barely out of her teens, had already gaited her first horse, so she took on the task of teaching the wild and aggressive seven-year-old to perform five gaits. He was tough, but so gifted that his response to the advanced training was history being made, not only regarding a sensation in the five-gaited pony ranks but in the training efforts of a young woman who would startle the Saddle Horse world by showing her powerful stallion, Sky Watch, to his third world's grand championship in 1988, the only woman to accomplish this tremendous feat. Could her early years with Rick Rack have prepared Michele for this? I like to think so, as no animal was ever more gifted and wild moving than both of these wonderful mounts, Rick Rack and Sky Watch.

We had bought a ten-year-old novice gelding for Kerry Lowary to show in five-gaited pony classes, his name was Rick Rack.

We had only a few weeks before Kerry came for spring break to meet her new pony. It became obvious from the start that Rick Rack had five true gaits and speed to burn. He also had ambition to burn and while one could control him at his gaits, he leaned into the bits and we wondered if we had bought too much pony for a young girl. The solution to this problem was to equalize the contest between pony and rider. Severity of bits was not the answer as he was too high strung to accept any harsh treatment. The answer was a curb bit with an extremely long shank and a soft covered curb chain.

When Kerry arrived three weeks later we had the problem solved and the little girl and the pony were truly a sight to see. Rick Rack was not a lugger, nor was he difficult to control but he had so much ambition and seemed to know what the term horse show meant, that one could always count on a dramatic performance.

The knowledgeable audiences at the Rock Creek show got their first look at Kerry and Rick Rack that spring and they were an immediate sensation winning the open five-gaited pony and championship victories that were to be repeated many times.

Lexington was a real challenge for a young rider and a pony tempted to excessive speed on the big Red Mile. Shades of Linda and Happy Hour! It was obvious that the same game plan was in order for Kerry and Rick Rack. Like Linda, Kerry did exactly as I advised, her elegant slow gait, wide open trot and rack on the straightaways. Then they would wait at the turns until they could make an individual pass in front of the stands. The crowds exploded in thunderous applause. The little girl and her wild-going pony changed the five-gaited pony class.

Although the brown and white pony had to accept some red ribbons in the open and the championships, the spectators had taken the new combination into their hearts. A pattern that was to endure Rick Rack's long show ring career. Unfortunately there was a certain prejudice against spotted horses and ponies at the horse shows, and at times Rick Rack would exit the ring in second place to the wild applause of his fans, but he won the great majority of his classes at Louisville, Lexington and other shows, and fulfilled the dreams we had for Kerry Lowary.

When Kerry's riding career in Kentucky came to a close, Rick Rack was bought for Annie Schoonmaker, younger sister of the national equitation champion Shauna Schoonmaker. Annie had but a very brief time with Rick Rack before Shauna retired from equitation and Annie and Rick Rack moved home to Colorado, where there were no pony classes.

Following is a letter in part from Mia Blevins Morris the final lucky owner of Rick Rack.

Dear Mrs. Crabtree,

My family had been long time fans of Rick Rack. My father began trying to locate him in 1982. We discovered that he was in Colorado and purchased him that year, putting him in training with Pat McConnell. After a winter of hard work, determination, and many wild, fast rides we became a team. We had two unforgettable show seasons. At the age of 17, CH Rick Rack won at the World's Championship Horse Show in Louisville. We retired him at the age of 19.

My nephew, Josh Hanes, showed him in lead line for two years after his retirement. I don't think that class will ever be the same! People would run up and watch the lead line class just to see him again. He was still the same showy, leg-waving Rick Rack, even in lead line!

He is now out to pasture. He has an old Hackney gelding, former world champion James Street, who takes care of him. Of course Rick Rack has some aches and pains and stiffness from time to time, but CH Rick Rack's spirit is still there, being obvious when you try to catch him!

When we bought him we promised him a home for life, and he has one. He is very much a part of our family. He had his 30th birthday May 2 of this year.

Enclosed is a picture of CH Rick Rack on his 30th birthday, 1996.

Sincerely,

Mia Blevins Morris

As I write this story, Kentucky is experiencing another wild thunderstorm. The weather stations have announced that the band of storms are most severe near Bowling Green, Ky. I immediately wondered about Rick Rack, but I did not worry, knowing Rick Rack as we all do, I can imagine him in the pasture, head flung high, eyes wild and mane whipping in the wind while he snorts and whistles his defiance seeming to say come and get me if you can!

52

My Last Show

In 1987 I trained my last horse, a really cute little gelding I named Santana's Best Man. I had a lovely horse called Best Man back in the St. Louis days and Charlie remembered and said, "I think if you just put Santana, the sire of this colt in front, you can get that name because you think so much of him. I said I want him for myself and I want to do all of the training. I am going to put the theories we have been expounding over the years in a true test and train this colt exactly the way we talk. The use of the voice, little use of the hands and increasing use of the leg pressure to control the movement of the horse were a rather unusual way to start a colt especially a two-year-old. But that is what I did.

It is a reality that sometimes we teach and do not know it, whether for people or for horses. I had a habit of when I turned around in the training arena to throw the end of the reins from the right side where they would normally lie over to the left side, so that when the horse would reverse it would be a cleaner picture with out those reins hanging down. One day before I had given the clue to turn, (the leg aid and the guiding hand) I threw the reins over in preparation to turn. The little horse turned around. And I thought at that point one never stops learning. I had been teaching this horse all the time more than I realized. I had been concentrating on the leg aids and he had taken the habit of moving the reins from one side of his shoulder to the other as part of the signal to turn.

He proved to be a Phi Beta Kappa as far as his learning all of his aids. I could perform anything that anybody could dream up in a one minute work out for this horse to do. He loved doing it. I really believe that horse could count. If I wanted to take six strides on one canter lead, halt and change to the opposite canter lead, that little horse could do it. If I wanted to canter on the next time to eight steps, I would have to cluck to him the last two strides be-

Helen's last show ride was on Santana's Best Man.

cause he knew when six was six. It was an absolute delight to train him.

I began to notice that it was becoming increasingly hard to see the horse's ears. Ears indicate a lot. The expression, like the expression on a person's face, that warns you that something is going on, that any reaction they have is about to reveal itself. The horses ears within sight indicate pretty much what is going to happen which is necessary to keep accidents from occurring. It is not enough to know why something happened, one must know what is going to happen. I struggled to see this horse's ears even to the point of stooping a little closer to them to get a good view of them. Then I began to notice a little crack in the arena doors and I suspected what was true that Charlie was really worrying about me and he was looking through that crack to see how I was getting along. He was just afraid the vision problem was getting too great but I would not give up, so the summer of 1989, when that horse was four years old, I said I want to show him in the junior class, a class for horses four years old and under at the Lawrenceburg Horse Show. At first Charlie was horrified, but I said "Oh, please. If I get in the warm up ring and find out I can't do this I will come out, but just one more time. Our grandson Casey was so sweet to come along, he and Charlie took me to the Lawrenceburg Horse Show.

The ring at Lawrenceburg was scary. This was a county fair and so close to the midway that the noise from the various attractions there, plus the sight of this big lighted ferris wheel whirling around, just the general disorganization of what was going on behind the stands was enough to scare any horse.

The thing about Best Man is that we did not have an outside ring at our stable. We had this wonderful arena which is where I trained the horse. Charlie said to me, "Helen, do you realize this horse since you brought him up as a two-year-old has never been outside this arena for two years? He has been inside, he has not seen anything going on outside. I said, "That ought to make him use his ears real well watching where he is going." Charlie said,"You will be lucky if you can get him in the ring."

When we went into the make up ring it was a little tough because there was no organization to which direction people were going or when they were going to pass. All of a sudden I found I was being passed by someone going in the opposite direction and I thought, "Ooh, I do not know about this." At the same time the bugle sounded for us to come in the ring.

Knowing that the Ferris wheel with its bright lights was going to be the main attraction, not only for the little kids but for this little kid of a horse I was riding, I wisely waited until the bulk of the class had entered the ring since there were 14 horses in the class. I waited until about the last horse had gone in and followed him in. The entrance into the ring slanted up somewhat then sloped down as you got in the gate. When I got to the downward slope this little horse looked up and saw the Ferris wheel. I do not know what else he saw, but he did a very strange thing. He started to crouch. He was still trotting but he was crouching towards the ground and as tall as I am, I thought my feet were going to be on the ground any minute. The trainers at that show all had boxes along the rail by the entrance of the ring and they all started laughing and I did too. I knew what a ridiculous sight this was. Finally when he made another trip around the ring he got a little braver and got up to his full height as he was making a tremendous show for me and I looked around enough to think that maybe this horse was going to be second in the class. He was not good enough to win it, but he looked like a good second. The very last minute when the last canter was called for he threw some dirt up the back side of that metal show ring and it hit with a big bang and he jumped away from it.

I had always talked to this horse so spontaneously so, I said,"Hey you know better than this," as the mistake was corrected. We happened to be in front of the row of trainers and we all had to laugh.

Best Man was fourth in the class. When we rode out of the ring, the horse started to stretch his neck and raise up as high as he could. He had crept in as a timid novice and exited a proud performer.

I will be forever grateful to John Alexander, the horse show photographer who surprised me the next day with a large beautifully framed picture of my last time in the show ring.

53

Friendly Advice
(S & B January, 1996)

One may think that being a horse trainer is the hardest job in the world. No doubt about it, it is tough, but not being a horse trainer is even more difficult. That lonely Maytag repairman with his sad-eyed Basset Hound has nothing on a horseless retired trainer.

Retiring is for the birds. Horse trainers work hard all of their productive lives in a profession that they love. The rewards are in the doing, but there is the ever-present concern for what happens when one can no longer ride. Like many others who plan for the future we did just that - we are secure in our retirement, but we are far from fulfilled with the present. Time hangs heavy on the hands and minds that operated at top speed for 50 years.

I always thought that I would pursue my long-delayed interest in art and music, and keep a colt or two to bring on. Now here we are, out of the horse business because of physical problems never anticipated. "Dem Bones" do wear out. But the interest and desire will not leave.

Thank goodness for our dogs. How many times a day do we say, "Are you talking to me?" and the reply is generally, "No, I was talking to the dog." After 53 years, what's new?

The bug anecdote that follows illustrates the importance of inconsequential moments in the retiree's life. But maybe that is what taking time to smell the roses really means.

Little things, and I do mean little, take on incredible importance and bring out the worst in everyone. So when I spied a very black something on the narrow ledge that tops the wood dado in our TV room, I asked Charlie if he could see if it was a bug. "Wait until the commercial," said the president of the Procrastinator's Club. Now do not get me wrong, I am not criticizing, as I am vice-president of this powerful organization, but my discovery called for immediate action.

Going to the kitchen for a fly swatter, I planned my attack. The bug, if that is what it was would squash all over the wall paper if I made a direct hit. No it was better to knock him to the floor and hope that my Welsh Corgi dog would catch and eat him. Alas, I had deliberated too long and the big black something was gone.

That night I was on the prowl. No dumb bug was going to outsmart me! A friend told me that I should wait until the prey was on the kitchen floor and then swat the sucker. Swatting a big black bug is more luck than planning. Although, I cannot outmaneuver a big bug I can wait until he gets near a corner and corral him. You cannot swat a bug where he is, because if you do it becomes where he was. Trying another plan, I waited until night time and took my flashlight into the kitchen. The friend had suggested that I was on the trail of a water bug that comes into the sink cupboard when cold weather sets in.

I was going to do it right this time and quietly stretched out on the floor. When I managed to open the cupboard door, I found myself nose-to-nose with the bug. He did a one-eighty and was gone. My stomach lurched but my poor body, frozen to the floor refused to move.

Then I saw feet and realized that Charlie had come into the room. "Helen, what in the world are you doing on the floor?" I think Flip Wilson had it right when he would say, "The devil made me do it," desperate to appear in charge of the occasion, I replied (lied is more to the point) "I am putting sugar on the S.O.S. pad so the big black bug will eat the pad and commit suicide."

When I was able to get up off the floor Charlie said, "That is probably a waterbug that has come into get warm and crawls up the drain pipe. All you have to do is spray some Raid around all the pipes under the sink and you will be rid of him."

And I did, and I was.

Recently, I received a letter from a good friend whose husband, a successful Saddle Horse trainer, was retiring. She wrote, "I will be living with a retired horse trainer. Can you tell me what to do?"

No, Betty, I cannot tell you what to do, but here is a list of what not to do:
1.) Never sit on the John before turning on the lights in the bathroom. The consequences are obvious.
2.) Never share a pet. He will win this one every time.

3.) Never take a cruise that lasts over three days. The term "man overboard" really means "spouse overboard."
4.) Never fail to remove the obituary notices from all horse publications.
5.) Never suggest that he should visit other training stables. This is a toughie and he will let you know when he is ready.
6.) Never tie an ice cube next to the thermostat. You may get the heat you desire but sooner or later you will be caught. Pouting can last as long as four days.
7.) Never permit anyone to store fly spray and gasoline in identical cans. Your riding mower will actually run on fly spray, but the mileage will kill you if your husband doesn't.
8.) Never purchase an anti-snoring device and leave it on his pillow. Some things are just too obvious.
9.) Never make a request that is too simple (refer to the Big Black Bug).
10.) Never forget to tell him that you love him.

World's Grand Champion Five-Gaited Memories' Citation and Michele Macfarlane, Louisville, 1996.

In Closing...

When I turned in the manuscript of this book, perhaps I was feeling a little sorry for myself because it seemed like my active involvement with horses had come to an end. Imagine my surprise when one of my dear friends, an excellent teacher and trainer invited me to give her young daughter a lesson. I had no idea that I had sufficient sight to do this, but I believe God let me see that little girl. It was one of the most inspiring times of my latter life! I realize that I had uncharacteristically given in to self-pity and self doubt. Another lesson to a timid adult added to my joy of teaching once more.

It was then that I realized that I could really instruct again by keeping the riders within my scope of sight. I began to live again. And I suppose this is the place to recall the many former students who are presently either as professionals or amateurs, contributing to our great sport.

At the terrible risk of omitting someone (and if I do, I beg for understanding), I would like to list those riders who bring me so much joy and are still giving me very proud moments:

Brent Jacobs
Mike Felty
Debbie Foley
Mary Angel
Debbie Wathen
Wendy Johnson
Marilyn Macfarlane
Lisa Rosenberger Erres
Jennifer Joiner
Linda Lowary Price
Anne Judd
Ruth Palmer
Kristy Grueneberg Hammond
Ruth Ann Anderson
Randi Wightman

Mary Gaylord
Linda Fischer
Karen Fischer
Kathy Lyda Berger
Amy Dru
Carlyn Barmeier
Judy Ferguson
Morgan Wolin
Melissa Shirkey
Lindsey Shirkey
Mary Anne Cronan
Andrea DeVogel
Mary Lou Doudican
Jannie Giles
Shauna Schoonmaker Edwards
Liz McBride Jones

It has been many years since a young tomboy in Illinois rode anything she could get in the Morgan County Fair. I did not know when I began this book that this would be a history of women's ascendance in the American Saddlebred world. What brought this home to me was that the great majority of exhibitors and riders were women at the 1996 World's Championship Horse Show.

Just when I thought that my participation in our beloved sport had come to an end, I found myself flying to England to give a clinic. Marlyn Macfarlane joined me and we shared in teaching the British riders whose enthusiasm for the American Saddlebred is growing day by day.

In January 1997, I traveled west to receive a wonderful honor from the American Horse Shows Association, the designation as judge emeritus. While this is very exciting and rewarding for me, I believe that the five-gaited world's championship at the Kentucky State Fair brought women's participation to an all-time high.

Michele Macfarlane made two astounding rides on Memories Citation, former World Grand Champion Three-Gaited horse in 1993 which she had gaited last winter. Her horsemanship enthralled the screaming spectators who saw the supreme communication of horse and rider.

To me, the place for women riders and trainers had come full circle, climaxing my love of the American Saddlebred and those who ride and train them.